2. The Twilight War

This is the second of twelve books which together make up the first complete paperback edition of Sir Winston Churchill's classic memoirs, The History of the Second World War. *Here, full and unabridged, is the greatest Englishman of our time, describing in unforgettable words the follies which brought about the most terrible war known to mankind, and the sacrifices, determination and matchless courage by which it was brought to an end.*

The Moral of the Work

In War: RESOLUTION
In Defeat: DEFIANCE
In Victory: MAGNANIMITY
In Peace: GOODWILL

Winston S. Churchill

THE SECOND WORLD WAR

2. The Twilight War

CASSELL · LONDON

CASSELL & COMPANY LTD
35 Red Lion Square · London WC1

and at Melbourne, Sydney, Toronto,
Johannesburg, Cape Town, Auckland

The Twilight War
was first published as Book 2 of 'The Gathering Storm',
the first volume of Sir Winston Churchill's
The Second World War.

First published 1948
All rights reserved
First published in this edition 1964

Set in 9 point Intertype Times and
printed in Great Britain by Cox and Wyman Ltd.,
London, Reading and Fakenham.
F.564

Preface

(From the Preface to the original edition)

I must regard these volumes as a continuation of the story of the First World War which I set out in The World Crisis, The Eastern Front *and* The Aftermath. *Together they cover an account of another Thirty Years War.*

I have followed, as in previous volumes, the method of Defoe's Memoirs of a Cavalier, *as far as I am able, in which the author hangs the chronicle and discussion of great military and political events upon the thread of the personal experiences of an individual. I am perhaps the only man who has passed through both the two supreme cataclysms of recorded history in high executive office. Whereas however in the First World War I filled responsible but subordinate posts, I was in this second struggle with Germany for more than five years the head of His Majesty's Government. I write therefore from a different standpoint and with more authority than was possible in my earlier books. I do not describe it as history, for that belongs to another generation. But I claim with confidence that it is a contribution to history which will be of service for the future.*

These thirty years of action and advocacy comprise and express my life-effort, and I am content to be judged upon them. I have adhered to my rule of never criticising any measure of war or policy after the event unless I had before expressed publicly or formally my opinion or warning about it. Indeed in the afterlight I have softened many of the severities of contemporary controversy. It has given me pain to record these disagreements with so many men whom I liked or respected: but it would be wrong not to lay the lessons of the past before the future. Let no one look down on those honourable, well-meaning men whose actions are chronicled in these pages without searching his own heart, reviewing his own discharge of public duty, and applying the lessons of the past to his future conduct.

It must not be supposed that I expect everyone to agree with what I say, still less that I only write what will be popular. I give my testimony according to the lights I follow. Every possible care has been taken to verify the facts; but much is constantly coming to light from the disclosure of captured documents and other revelations which may present a new aspect to the conclusions which I have drawn.

One day President Roosevelt told me that he was asking publicly for suggestions about what the war should be called. I said at once 'The Unnecessary War'. There never was a war more easy to stop

Contents

1. WAR   1
2. THE ADMIRALTY TASK   16
3. THE RUIN OF POLAND   34
4. WAR CABINET PROBLEMS   44
5. THE FRONT IN FRANCE   61
6. THE COMBAT DEEPENS   74
7. THE MAGNETIC MINE   87
8. THE ACTION OFF THE RIVER PLATE   98
9. SCANDINAVIA. FINLAND   117
10. A DARK NEW YEAR   133
11. BEFORE THE STORM   151
12. THE CLASH AT SEA   167
13. NARVIK   184
14. TRONDHEIM   196
15. FRUSTRATION IN NORWAY   210
16. NORWAY: THE FINAL PHASE   224
17. THE FALL OF THE GOVERNMENT   231

Illustrations

Polish Uhlans cross a river in the Polish Corridor

Mechanised units of the Polish Army

Polish partisans taken prisoner

Personnel of the Soviet Embassy in Warsaw reach the German lines

Wreck of the first German bomber forced down over Great Britain

The famous German battleship *Admiral Graf Spee*

Finnish soldiers camouflaged

Husky dogs of the Finnish Army

Part of the Mannerheim Line

Allied munition stores in the Maginot Line

Churchill in conversation with Lord Gort

British troops enter a French casemate

Churchill speaking before the great German offensive

Maps and Diagrams

Scapa Flow	25
The German and Polish Concentrations, September 1, 1939	36
The Inner Pincers Close, September 13	39
The Outer Pincers Close. The Russians Advance, September 17	40
Diagram of Scheldt Line and Meuse-Antwerp Line	72
Scapa Flow. Sinking of H.M.S. *Royal Oak*	80
Diagrams illustrating the Action against the *Graf Spee* off the River Plate	105–109
Hunting Groups in South Atlantic	111
Russian Attack on Finland, December 1939	125
Breaking the Mannerheim Line, March 1940	126
Norway, 1940	223
Narvik	229

Theme of the Book

HOW THE ENGLISH-SPEAKING
PEOPLES THROUGH THEIR
UNWISDOM, CARELESSNESS
AND GOOD NATURE
ALLOWED THE WICKED
TO REARM

CHAPTER 1

War

Mr. Chamberlain's Invitation – The Pause of September 2 – War Declared, September 3 – The First Air Alarm – At the Admiralty Once More – Admiral Sir Dudley Pound – My Knowledge of Naval Matters – Contrast between 1914 and 1939 – The Naval Strategic Situation – The Baltic – The Kiel Canal – The Attitude of Italy – Our Mediterranean Strategy – The Submarine Menace – The Air Menace – The Attitude of Japan – Singapore – The Security of Australia and New Zealand – Composition of the War Cabinet – Mr. Chamberlain's First Selections – An Antediluvian – The Virtues of Siesta.

Poland was attacked by Germany at dawn on September 1. The mobilisation of all our forces was ordered during the morning. The Prime Minister asked me to visit him in the afternoon at Downing Street. He told me that he saw no hope of averting a war with Germany, and that he proposed to form a small War Cabinet of Ministers without departments to conduct it. He mentioned that the Labour Party were not, he understood, willing to share in a national coalition. He still had hopes that the Liberals would join him. He invited me to become a member of the War Cabinet. I agreed to his proposal without comment, and on this basis we had a long talk on men and measures.

After some reflection, I felt that the average age of the Ministers who were to form the supreme executive of war direction would be thought too high, and I wrote to Mr. Chamberlain after midnight accordingly:

2.9.39

Aren't we a very old team? I make out that the six you mentioned to me yesterday aggregate 386 years, or an average of over sixty-four! Only one year short of the Old Age Pension! If however you added Sinclair (49) and Eden (42) the average comes down to 57½

If the *Daily Herald* is right that Labour will not come in, we shall certainly have to face a constant stream of criticism, as well as the many disappointments and surprises of which war largely consists. Therefore it seems to me all the more important to have the Liberal Opposition firmly incorporated in our ranks. Eden's influence with the section of Conservatives who are associated with him, as well as with moderate Liberal elements, also seems to me to be a very necessary reinforcement.

The Poles have now been under heavy attack for thirty hours, and I am much concerned to hear that there is talk in Paris of a further note. I trust you will be able to announce our Joint Declaration of War at *latest* when Parliament meets this afternoon.

The *Bremen* will soon be out of the interception zone unless the Admiralty take special measures and the signal is given to-day. This is only a minor point, but it may well be vexatious.

I remain here at your disposal.*

I was surprised to hear nothing from Mr. Chamberlain during the whole of September 2, which was a day of intense crisis. I thought it probable that a last-minute effort was being made to preserve peace ; and this proved true. However, when Parliament met in the evening a short but very fierce debate occurred, in which the Prime Minister's temporising statement was ill-received by the House. When Mr. Greenwood rose to speak on behalf of the Labour Opposition Mr. Amery from the Conservative benches cried out to him, 'Speak for England.' This was received with loud cheers. There was no doubt that the temper of the House was for war. I even deemed it more resolute and united than in the similar scene on August 3, 1914, in which I had also taken part. In the evening a number of gentlemen of importance in all parties called upon me at my flat opposite the Westminster Cathedral, and all expressed deep anxiety lest we should fail in our obligations to Poland. The House was to meet again at noon the next day. I wrote that night as follows to the Prime Minister :

2.9.39

I have not heard anything from you since our talks on Friday, when I understood that I was to serve as your colleague, and when you told me that this would be announced speedily. I really do not know what has happened during the course of this agitated day ; though it seems to me that entirely different ideas have ruled from those which you expressed to me when you said 'the die was cast'. I quite realise that in contact with this tremendous European situa-

* Printed in Feiling, *op. cit.*, p. 420.

tion changes of method may become necessary, but I feel entitled to ask you to let me know how we stand, both publicly and privately, before the debate opens at noon.

It seems to me that if the Labour Party, and as I gather the Liberal Party, are estranged, it will be difficult to form an effective War Government on the limited basis you mentioned. I consider that a further effort should be made to bring in the Liberals, and in addition that the composition and scope of the War Cabinet you discussed with me requires review. There was a feeling to-night in the House that injury had been done to the spirit of national unity by the apparent weakening of our resolve. I do not underrate the difficulties you have with the French; but I trust that we shall now take our decision independently, and thus give our French friends any lead that may be necessary. In order to do this we shall need the strongest and most integral combination that can be formed. I therefore ask that there should be no announcement of the composition of the War Cabinet until we have had a further talk.

As I wrote to you yesterday morning, I hold myself entirely at your disposal, with every desire to aid you in your task.

I learnt later that a British ultimatum had been given to Germany at 9.30 p.m. on September 1, and that this had been followed by a second and final ultimatum at 9 a.m. on September 3. The early broadcast of the 3rd announced that the Prime Minister would speak on the radio at 11.15 a.m. As it now seemed certain that war would be immediately declared by Great Britain and also by France, I prepared a short speech which I thought would be becoming to the solemn and awful moment in our lives and history.

The Prime Minister's broadcast informed us that we were already at war, and he had scarcely ceased speaking when a strange, prolonged, wailing noise, afterwards to become familiar, broke upon the ear. My wife came into the room braced by the crisis and commented favourably upon the German promptitude and precision, and we went up to the flat top of the house to see what was going on. Around us on every side, in the clear, cool September light, rose the roofs and spires of London. Above them were already slowly rising thirty or forty cylindrical balloons. We gave the Government a good mark for this evident sign of preparation, and as the quarter of an hour's notice which we had been led to expect we should receive was now running out we made our way to the shelter assigned to us, armed with a bottle of brandy and other appropriate medical comforts.

Our shelter was a hundred yards down the street, and consisted merely of an open basement, not even sand-bagged, in which the tenants of half a dozen flats were already assembled. Everyone was cheerful and jocular, as is the English manner when about to encounter the unknown. As I gazed from the doorway along the empty street and at the crowded room below my imagination drew pictures of ruin and carnage and vast explosions shaking the ground; of buildings clattering down in dust and rubble, of fire-brigades and ambulances scurrying through the smoke, beneath the drone of hostile aeroplanes. For had we not all been taught how terrible air raids would be? The Air Ministry had, in natural self-importance, greatly exaggerated their power. The pacifists had sought to play on public fears, and those of us who had so long pressed for preparation and a superior Air Force, while not accepting the most lurid forecasts, had been content that they should act as a spur. I knew that the Government were prepared, in the first few days of the war, with over 250,000 beds for air-raid casualties. Here at least there had been no under-estimation. Now we should see what were the facts.

After about ten minutes had passed the wailing broke out again. I was myself not sure that this was not a reiteration of the previous warning, but a man came running along the street shouting 'All clear', and we dispersed to our dwellings and went about our business. Mine was to go to the House of Commons, which duly met at noon with its unhurried procedure and brief, stately prayers. There I received a note from the Prime Minister asking me to come to his room as soon as the debate died down. As I sat in my place, listening to the speeches, a very strong sense of calm came over me, after the intense passions and excitements of the last few days. I felt a serenity of mind and was conscious of a kind of uplifted detachment from human and personal affairs. The glory of Old England, peace-loving and ill-prepared as she was, but instant and fearless at the call of honour, thrilled my being and seemed to lift our fate to those spheres far removed from earthly facts and physical sensation. I tried to convey some of this mood to the House when I spoke, not without acceptance.

Mr. Chamberlain told me that he had considered my letters, that the Liberals would not join the Government, that he was able to meet my views about the average age to some extent by bringing the three Service Ministers into the War Cabinet in spite of their executive functions, and that this would reduce the average age to less than sixty. This, he said, made it possible for him to offer me the Admiralty as well as a seat in the War Cabinet. I was very glad of this, because, though I had not raised the point, I naturally preferred a definite task to that exalted brooding over the work done by others which may well be the lot of a Minister, however influential, who has no department. It is easier to give directions than advice, and more agreeable to have the right to act, even in a limited sphere, than the privilege to talk at large. Had the Prime Minister in the first instance given me the choice between the War Cabinet and the Admiralty, I should of course have chosen the Admiralty. Now I was to have both.

Nothing had been said about when I should formally receive my office from the King, and in fact I did not kiss hands till the 5th. But the opening hours of war may be vital with navies. I therefore sent word to the Admiralty that I would take charge forthwith and arrive at 6 o'clock. On this the Board were kind enough to signal to the Fleet, 'Winston is back.' So it was that I came again to the room I had quitted in pain and sorrow almost exactly a quarter of a century before, when Lord Fisher's resignation had led to my removal from my post as First Lord and ruined irretrievably, as it proved, the important conception of forcing the Dardanelles. A few feet behind me, as I sat in my old chair, was the wooden map-case I had had fixed in 1911, and inside it still remained the chart of the North Sea on which each day, in order to focus attention on the supreme objective, I had made the Naval Intelligence Branch record the movements and dispositions of the German High Seas Fleet. Since 1911 much more than a quarter of a century had passed, and still mortal peril threatened us at the hands of the same nation. Once again defence of the rights of a weak State, outraged and invaded by unprovoked aggression, forced us to draw the sword. Once again we must fight for life and honour against all the might and fury of the valiant, disciplined, and ruthless German race. Once again! So be it.

* * *

Presently the First Sea Lord came to see me. I had known Dudley Pound slightly in my previous tenure of the Admiralty as one of Lord Fisher's trusted Staff officers. I had strongly condemned in Parliament the dispositions of the Mediterranean Fleet when he commanded it, at the moment of the Italian descent upon Albania. Now we met as colleagues upon whose intimate relations and fundamental agreement the smooth working of the vast Admiralty machine would depend. We eyed each other amicably if doubtfully. But from the earliest days our friendship and mutual confidence grew and ripened. I measured and respected the great professional and personal qualities of Admiral Pound. As the war, with all its shifts and fortunes, beat upon us with clanging blows we became ever truer comrades and friends. And when, four years later, he died at the moment of the general victory over Italy I mourned with a personal pang for all the Navy and the nation had lost.

I spent a good part of the night of the 3rd meeting the Sea Lords and heads of the various departments, and from the morning of the 4th I laid my hands upon the naval affair. As in 1914, precautionary measures against surprise had been taken in advance of general mobilisation. As early as June 15 large numbers of officers and men of the Reserves had been called up. The Reserve fleet, fully manned for exercises, had been inspected by the King on August 9, and on the 22nd various additional classes of reservists had been summoned. On the 24th an Emergency Powers Defence Bill was passed through Parliament, and at the same time the Fleet was ordered to its war stations; in fact, our main forces had been at Scapa Flow for some weeks. After the general mobilisation of the Fleet had been authorised the Admiralty war plan had unfolded smoothly, and in spite of certain serious deficiencies, notably in cruisers and anti-submarine vessels, the challenge, as in 1914, found the Fleet equal to the immense tasks before it.

* * *

I had, as the reader may be aware, a considerable knowledge of the Admiralty and of the Royal Navy. The four years from 1911 to 1915, when I had the duty of preparing the Fleet for war and the task of directing the Admiralty during the first ten critical months, had been the most vivid of my life. I had amassed an immense amount of detailed information and had learned many lessons about the Fleet and war at sea. In the interval I had studied and written much about naval affairs. I had spoken repeatedly upon them in the House of Commons. I had always preserved a close contact with the Admiralty, and, although their foremost critic in these years, I had been made privy to many of their secrets. My four years' work on the Air Defence Research Committee had given me access to all the most modern developments in Radar, which now vitally affected the naval service. I have mentioned how in June 1938 Lord Chatfield, the First Sea Lord, had himself shown me over the Anti-Submarine School at Portland, and how we had gone to sea in destroyers on an exercise in submarine detection by the use of the Asdic apparatus. My intimacy with the late Admiral Henderson, Controller of the Navy till 1938, and the discussions which the First Lord of those days had encouraged me to have with Lord Chatfield upon the design of new battleships and cruisers, gave me a full view over the sphere of new construction. I was of course familiar from the published records with the strength, composition, and structure of the Fleet, actual and prospective, and with those of the German, Italian, and Japanese Navies.

As a critic and a spur, my public speeches had naturally dwelt upon weaknesses and shortcomings, and, taken by themselves, had by no means portrayed either the vast strength of the Royal Navy or my own confidence in it. It would be unjust to the Chamberlain Administration and their Service advisers to suggest that the Navy had not been adequately prepared for a war with Germany, or with Germany and Italy. The effective defence of Australasia and India in the face of a simultaneous attack by Japan raised more serious difficulties; but such an assault—which was at the moment unlikely—might well have involved the United States. I therefore felt, when I entered upon my duties, that I had at my disposal what was undoubtedly the finest-tempered instrument of naval war in the world, and I was sure that the time would be granted to make good the oversights of peace and to cope with the equally certain unpleasant surprises of war.

*　　　*　　　*

The tremendous naval situation of 1914 in no way repeated itself. Then we had entered the war with a ratio of sixteen to ten in capital ships and two to one in cruisers. In those days we had mobilised eight battle squadrons of eight battleships, with a cruiser squadron and a flotilla assigned to each, together with important detached cruiser forces, and I looked forward to a general action with a weaker but still formidable fleet. Now the German Navy had only begun their rebuilding and had no power even to form a line of battle. Their two great battleships, *Bismarck* and *Tirpitz*, both of which, it must be assumed, had transgressed the agreed Treaty limits in tonnage, were at least a year from completion. The light battle-cruisers, *Scharnhorst* and *Gneisenau*, which had been fraudulently increased by the Germans from 10,000 tons to 26,000 tons, had been completed in 1938. Besides this Germany had available the three 'pocket-battleships' of 10,000 tons, *Admiral Graf Spee, Admiral Scheer,* and *Deutschland*, together with two fast 8-inch-gun cruisers of 10,000 tons, six light cruisers, and sixty destroyers and smaller vessels. Thus there was no challenge in surface craft to our command of the seas. There was no doubt that the British Navy was overwhelmingly superior to the German in strength and in numbers, and no reason to assume that its science training or skill was in any way defective. Apart from the shortage of cruisers and destroyers, the Fleet had been maintained at its customary high standard. It had to face enormous and innumerable duties, rather than an antagonist.

*   *   *

My views on the naval strategic situation were already largely formed when I went to the Admiralty. The command of the Baltic was vital to the enemy. Scandinavian supplies, Swedish ore, and above all protection against Russian descents on the long, undefended northern coastline of Germany—in one place little more than a hundred miles from Berlin—made it imperative for the German Navy to dominate the Baltic. I was therefore sure that in this opening phase Germany would not compromise her command of that sea. Thus, while submarines and raiding cruisers, or perhaps one pocket-battleship, might be sent out to disturb our traffic, no ships would be risked which were necessary to the Baltic control. The German Fleet, as at this moment developed, must aim at this as its prime and almost its sole objective. For the main purposes of sea-power and for the enforcement of our principal naval offensive measure, the blockade, we must of course maintain a superior fleet in our northern waters ; but no very large British naval forces were, it seemed, needed to watch the debouches from the Baltic or from the Heligoland Bight.

British security would be markedly increased if an air attack upon the Kiel Canal rendered that side-door from the Baltic useless, even if only at intervals.

A year before I had sent a note upon this special operation to Sir Thomas Inskip.

October 29, 1938

In a war with Germany the severance of the Kiel Canal would be an achievement of the first importance. I do not elaborate this, as I assume it to be admitted. Plans should be made to do this, and, if need be, all the details should be worked out in their variants by a special technical committee. Owing to there being few locks, and no marked difference of sea-level at the two ends of the canal, its interruption by H.E. bombs, even of the heaviest type, could swiftly be repaired. If however many bombs of medium size fitted with time fuses, some set for a day, others for a week, and others for a month, etc., could be dropped in the canal, their explosions at uncertain intervals and in uncertain places would close the canal to the movement of warships or valuable vessels until the whole bottom had been deeply dredged. Alternatively, *special fuses with magnetic actuation* should be considered.

The phrase about magnetic mines is interesting in view of what was soon to come upon us. No special action had however been taken.

* * *

The British merchant fleet on the outbreak of war was about the same size as in 1914. It was over twenty-one million tons. The average size of the ships had increased, and thus there were fewer. This tonnage was not however all available for trade. The Navy required auxiliary warships of various types which must be drawn chiefly from the highest class of liners. All the defence Services needed ships for special purposes: the Army and R.A.F. for the movement of troops and equipment overseas, and the Navy for all the work at fleet bases and elsewhere, and particularly for providing oil fuel at strategic points all over the world. Demands for tonnage for all these objects amounted to nearly three million tons, and to these must be added the shipping requirements of the Empire overseas. At the end of 1939, after balancing gains and losses, the total British tonnage available for commercial use was about fifteen and a half million tons.

* * *

Italy had not declared war, and it was already clear that Mussolini was waiting upon events. In this uncertainty and as a measure of precaution till all our arrangements were complete we thought it best to divert our shipping round the Cape. We had however already on our side, in addition to our own preponderance over Germany and Italy combined, the powerful fleet of France, which by the remarkable capacity and long administration of Admiral Darlan had been brought to the highest strength and degree of efficiency ever attained by the French Navy since the days of the Monarchy. Should Italy become hostile our first battlefield must be the Mediterranean. I was entirely opposed, except as a temporary convenience, to all plans for quitting the centre and merely sealing up the ends of the great inland sea. Our forces alone, even without the aid of the French Navy and its fortified harbours, were sufficient to drive the Italian ships from the sea, and should secure complete naval command of the Mediterranean within two months, and possibly sooner.

The British domination of the Mediterranean would inflict injuries upon an enemy Italy which might be fatal to her power of continuing the war. All her troops in Libya and in Abyssinia would be cut flowers in a vase. The French and our own people in Egypt could be reinforced to any extent desired, while theirs would be overweighted, if not starved. Not to hold the Central Mediterranean would be to expose Egypt and the Canal, as well as the French possessions, to invasion by Italian troops with German leadership. Moreover, a series of swift and striking victories in this theatre, which might be obtainable in the early weeks of a war, would have a most healthy and helpful bearing upon the main struggle with Germany. Nothing should stand between us and these results, both naval and military.

*   *   *

I had accepted too readily when out of office the Admiralty view of the extent to which the submarine had been mastered. Whilst the technical efficiency of the Asdic apparatus was proved in many early encounters with U-boats, our anti-U-boat resources were far too limited to prevent our suffering serious losses. My opinion recorded at the time, 'The submarine should be quite controllable in the outer seas, and certainly in the Mediterranean. There will be losses, but nothing to affect the scale of events,' was not incorrect. Nothing of major importance occurred in the first year of the U-boat warfare. The Battle of the Atlantic was reserved for 1941 and 1942.

In common with prevailing Admiralty belief before the war, I did not sufficiently measure the danger to, or the consequent deterrent upon, British warships from air attack. 'In my opinion,' I had written a few months before the war, 'given with great humility (because these things are very difficult to judge), an air attack upon British warships, armed and protected as they now are, will not prevent full exercise of their superior sea-power.' However, the deterrents, albeit exaggerated, upon our mobility soon become grave. The air almost immediately proved itself a formidable menace, especially in the Mediterranean. Malta, with its almost negligible air defences, presented a problem for which there was no immediate solution. On the other hand, in the first year no British capital ship was sunk by air attack.

*   *   *

There was no sign at this moment of any hostile action or intent upon the part of Japan. The main preoccupation of Japan was naturally America. It did not seem possible to me that the United States could sit passive and watch a general assault by Japan upon all European establishments in the Far East, even if they themselves were not for the moment involved. In this case we should gain far more from the entry of the United States, perhaps only against Japan, if that were possible, than we should suffer from the hostility of Japan, vexatious though that would be. On no account must anything which threatened in the Far East divert us from our prime objectives in Europe. We could not protect our interests and possessions in the Yellow Sea from Japanese attack. The farthest point we could defend if Japan came in would be the fortress of Singapore. Singapore must hold out until the Mediterranean was safe and the Italian Fleet liquidated.

I did not fear at the moment of the outbreak that Japan would send a fleet and army to conquer Singapore, provided that fortress were adequately garrisoned and supplied with food and ammunition for at least six months. Singapore was as far from Japan as Southampton from New York. Over these three thousand miles of salt water Japan would have to send the bulk of her Fleet, escort at least sixty thousand men in transports in order to effect a landing, and begin a siege which would end only in disaster if the Japanese sea-communications were cut at any stage. These views of course ceased to apply once the Japanese had occupied Indo-China and Siam and had built up a powerful army and very heavy air forces only three hundred miles away across the Gulf of Siam. This however did not occur for more than a year and a half.

As long as the British Navy was undefeated, and as long as we held Singapore, no invasion of Australia or New Zealand by Japan was deemed possible. We could give Australasia a good guarantee to protect them from this danger, but we must do it in our own way, and in the proper sequence of operations. It seemed unlikely that a hostile Japan, exulting in the mastery of the Yellow Sea, would send afloat a conquering and colonising expedition to Australia. A large and well-equipped army would be needed for a long time to make any impression upon Australian manhood. Such an undertaking would require the improvident diversion of the Japanese Fleet, and its engagement in a long, desultory struggle in Australia. At any moment a decision in the Mediterranean would liberate very powerful naval forces to cut invaders from their base. It would be easy for the United States to tell Japan that they would regard the sending of Japanese fleets and transports south of the equator as an act of war. They might well be disposed to make such a declaration, and there would be no harm in sounding them upon this very remote contingency.

The actual strength of the British and German Fleets, built and building, on the night of September 3, 1939, and that of the American, French, Italian, and Japanese Fleets on the same basis, make an illuminating comparison. It was my recorded conviction that *in the first year of a world war* Australia and New Zealand would be in no danger whatever in their homeland, and by the end of the first year we might hope to have cleaned up the seas and oceans. As a forecast of *the first year of the naval war* these thoughts proved true. I shall in their proper place recount the tremendous events which occurred in 1941 and 1942 in the Far East.

* * *

Newspaper opinion, headed by the *Times*, favoured the principle of a War Cabinet of not more than five or six Ministers, all of whom should be free from departmental duties. Thus alone, it was argued, could a broad and concerted view be taken upon war policy, especially in its larger aspects. Put shortly, 'Five men with nothing to do but to run the war' was deemed the ideal. There are however many practical objections to such a course. A group of detached statesmen, however high their nominal authority, are at a serious disadvantage in dealing with the Ministers at the head of the great departments vitally concerned. This is especially true of the Service departments. The War Cabinet personages can have no direct responsibility for day-to-day events. They may take major decisions, they may advise in general terms beforehand or criticise afterwards, but they are no match, for instance, for a First Lord of the Admiralty or a Secretary of State for War or Air, who, knowing every detail of the subject and supported by his professional colleagues, bears the burden of action. United, there is little they cannot settle, but usually there are several opinions among them. Words and arguments are interminable, and meanwhile the torrent of war takes its headlong course. The War Cabinet Ministers themselves would naturally be diffident of challenging the responsible Minister, armed with all his facts and figures. They feel a compunction in adding to the strain upon those actually in executive control. They tend therefore to become more and more theoretical supervisors and commentators, reading an immense amount of material every day, but doubtful how to use their knowledge without doing more harm than good. Often they can do little more than arbitrate or find a compromise in inter-departmental disputes. It is therefore necessary that the Ministers in charge of the Foreign Office and the fighting departments should be integral members of the supreme body. Usually some at least of the 'Big Five' are chosen for their political influence, rather than for their knowledge of and aptitude for warlike operations. The numbers therefore begin to grow far beyond the limited circle originally conceived. Of course, where the Prime Minister himself becomes Minister of Defence a strong compression is obtained. Personally, when I was placed in charge I did not like having unharnessed Ministers around me. I preferred to deal with chiefs of organisations rather than counsellors. Everyone should do a good day's work and be accountable for some definite task, and then they do not make trouble for trouble's sake or to cut a figure.

Mr. Chamberlain's original War Cabinet plan was almost immediately expanded, by the force of circumstances, to include

Lord Halifax, Foreign Secretary; Sir Samuel Hoare, Lord
Privy Seal; Sir John Simon, Chancellor of the Exchequer;
Lord Chatfield, Minister for the Co-ordination of Defence; and
Lord Hankey, Minister without Portfolio. To these were added
the Service Ministers, of whom I was now one, with Mr. Hore
Belisha, Secretary of State for War, and Sir Kingsley Wood,
Secretary of State for Air. In addition it was necessary that
the Dominions Secretary, Mr. Eden, and Sir John Anderson as
Home Secretary and Minister of Home Security, though not
actual members of the War Cabinet, should be present on all
occasions. Thus our total was eleven. The decision to bring in
the three Service Ministers profoundly affected Lord Chatfield's
authority as Minister for the Co-ordination of Defence. He
accepted the position with his customary good-nature.

Apart from myself all the other Ministers had directed our
affairs for a good many recent years or were involved in the
situation we now had to face both in diplomacy and war. Mr.
Eden had resigned on foreign policy in February 1938. I had not
held public office for nearly eleven years. I had therefore no
responsibility for the past or for any want of preparation now
apparent. On the contrary, I had for the last six or seven years
been a continual prophet of evils which had now in large measure come to pass. Thus, armed as I now was with the mighty
machine of the Navy, on which fell in this phase the sole burden
of active fighting, I did not feel myself at any disadvantage, and
had I done so it would have been removed by the courtesy and
loyalty of the Prime Minister and his colleagues. All these men
I knew very well. Most of us had served together for five years in
Mr. Baldwin's Cabinet, and we had of course been constantly in
contact, friendly or controversial, through the changing scenes
of Parliamentary life. Sir John Simon and I however represented
an older political generation. I had served, off and on, in British
Governments for fifteen years, and he for almost as long, before
any of the others had gained public office. I had been at the head
of the Admiralty or Ministry of Munitions through the stresses
of the First World War. Although the Prime Minister was my
senior by some years in age, I was almost the only antediluvian.
This might well have been a matter of reproach in a time of
crisis, when it was natural and popular to demand the force of
young men and new ideas. I saw therefore that I should have to
strive my utmost to keep pace with the generation now in power
and with fresh young giants who might at any time appear. In

this I relied upon knowledge as well as upon all possible zeal and mental energy.

For this purpose I had recourse to a method of life which had been forced upon me at the Admiralty in 1914 and 1915, and which I found greatly extended my daily capacity for work. I always went to bed at least for one hour as early as possible in the afternoon, and exploited to the full my happy gift of falling almost immediately into deep sleep. By this means I was able to press a day and a half's work into one. Nature had not intended mankind to work from eight in the morning until midnight without that refreshment of blessed oblivion which, even if it only lasts twenty minutes, is sufficient to renew all the vital forces. I regretted having to send myself to bed like a child every afternoon, but I was rewarded by being able to work through the night until two or even later—sometimes much later—in the morning, and begin the new day between eight and nine o'clock. This routine I observed throughout the war, and I commend it to others if and when they find it necessary for a long spell to get the last scrap out of the human structure. The First Sea Lord, Admiral Pound, as soon as he had realised my technique, adopted it himself, except that he did not actually go to bed, but dozed off in his arm-chair. He even carried the policy so far as often to go to sleep during the Cabinet meetings. One word about the Navy was however sufficient to awaken him to the fullest activity. Nothing slipped past his vigilant ear, or his comprehending mind.

CHAPTER 2

The Admiralty Task

Sea War Alone – The Admiralty War Plan – The U-boat Attack – The Asdic Trawlers – Control of Merchant Shipping – The Convoy System – Blockade – Record of My First Conference – Need of the Southern Irish Ports – The Main Fleet Base – Inadequate precautions – 'Hide-and-Seek' – My Visit to Scapa Flow – Reflections at Loch Ewe – Loss of the 'Courageous' – Cruiser Policy – The First Month of the U-Boat War – A Fruitful September – Wider Naval Operations – Ardour of the Polish Navy – President Roosevelt's Letter.

Astonishment was world-wide when Hitler's crashing onslaught upon Poland and the declarations of war upon Germany by Britain and France were followed only by a prolonged and oppressive pause. Mr. Chamberlain in a private letter published by his biographer described this phase as 'Twilight War';* and I find the expression so just and expressive that I have adopted it as the title for this Book. The French armies made no attack upon Germany. Their mobilisation completed, they remained in contact motionless along the whole front. No air action, except reconnaissance, was taken against Britain; nor was any air attack made upon France by the Germans. The French Government requested us to abstain from air attack on Germany, stating that it would provoke retaliation upon their war factories, which were unprotected. We contented ourselves with dropping pamphlets to rouse the Germans to a higher morality. This strange phase of the war on land and in the air astounded everyone. France and Britain remained impassive while Poland was in a few weeks destroyed or subjugated by the whole might of the German war machine. Hitler had no reason to complain of this.

The war at sea, on the contrary, began from the first hour with full intensity, and the Admiralty therefore became the active centre of events. On September 3 all our ships were sailing about the world on their normal business. Suddenly they were set

* Feiling, *op. cit.*, p. 424.

upon by U-boats carefully posted beforehand, especially in the Western Approaches. At 9 p.m. that very night the outward-bound passenger liner *Athenia*, of 13,500 tons, was torpedoed, and foundered with a loss of 112 lives, including twenty-eight American citizens. This outrage broke upon the world within a few hours. The German Government, to prevent any misunder-standing in the United States, immediately issued a statement that I personally had ordered a bomb to be placed on board this vessel in order by its destruction to prejudice German-American relations. This falsehood received some credence in unfriendly quarters.* On the 5th and 6th the *Bosnia, Royal Sceptre,* and *Rio Claro* were sunk off the coast of Spain. All these were important vessels.

My first Admiralty minute was concerned with the probable scale of the U-boat menace in the immediate future:

Director of Naval Intelligence   4.ix.39
Let me have a statement of the German U-boat forces, actual and prospective, for the next few months. Please distin-guish between ocean-going and small-size U-boats. Give the estimated radius of action in days and miles in each case.

I was at once informed that the enemy had sixty U-boats and that a hundred would be ready early in 1940. A detailed answer was returned on the 5th, which should be studied.† The num-bers of long range endurance vessels were formidable, and

---

* See also *Nuremberg Documents*, Pt. IV, p. 267ff.—the confession of the U-boat captain.

† GERMAN SUBMARINES

Type	Tonnage	Numbers in Service August 1939	Numbers expected to be in Service December 1939	Numbers expected to be in Service by early 1940	Estimated Radius of Action	
					Miles	Days
Coastal	250	30	32	32	4,000	33 at 5 knots
Ocean	500	10	10	23	} 7,200	30 at 10 knots
Ocean	517	9	15	17		
Ocean	712	2	2	..	} 8,400	35 at 10 knots
Ocean	740	8	13	16		
Ocean	1,060	..	2	11	10,000	42 at 10 knots
Ocean	1,028	1 (Built for Turkey, not delivered)			8,000	33 at 10 knots
Grand totals	..	60	74	99	..	..

revealed the intentions of the enemy to work far out in the oceans as soon as possible.

*   *   *

Comprehensive plans existed at the Admiralty for multiplying our anti-submarine craft. In particular preparations had been made to take up eighty-six of the largest and fastest trawlers and to equip them with Asdics ; the conversion of many of these was already well advanced. A war-time building programme of destroyers, both large and small, and of cruisers, with many ancillary vessels, was also ready in every detail, and this came into operation automatically with the declaration of war. The previous war had proved the sovereign merits of convoy. The Admiralty had for some days assumed control of the movements of all merchant shipping, and shipmasters were required to obey orders about their routes or about joining convoy. Our weakness in escort vessels had however forced the Admiralty to devise a policy of evasive routing on the oceans, unless and until the enemy adopted unrestricted U-boat warfare, and to confine convoys in the first instance to the east coast of Britain. But the sinking of the *Athenia* upset these plans, and we adopted convoy in the North Atlantic forthwith.

The organisation of convoy had been fully prepared, and ship-owners had already been brought into regular consultation on matters of defence which affected them. Furthermore instructions had been issued for the guidance of shipmasters in the many unfamiliar tasks which would inevitably fall upon them in war, and special signalling as well as other equipment had been provided to enable them to take their place in convoy. The men of the Merchant Navy faced the unknown future with determination. Not content with a passive *rôle*, they demanded weapons. The use of guns in self-defence by merchant ships has always been recognised as justifiable by international law, and the defensive arming of all seagoing merchant ships, together with the training of the crews, formed an integral part of the Admiralty plans, which were at once put into effect. To force the U-boat to attack submerged and not merely by gun-fire on the surface not only gave a greater chance for a ship to escape, but caused the attacker to expend his precious torpedoes more lavishly and often fruitlessly. Foresight had preserved the guns of the previous war for use against U-boats, but there was a grave shortage of anti-aircraft weapons. It was very many months before adequate self-protection against air attack could be provided for merchant ships, which suffered severe losses meanwhile. We planned from these first days to equip during the first three months of war a thousand ships with at least an anti-submarine gun each. This was in fact achieved.

Besides protecting our own shipping, we had to drive German commerce off the seas and stop all imports into Germany. Blockade was enforced with full rigour. A Ministry of Economic Warfare was formed to guide the policy, whilst the Admiralty controlled its execution. Enemy shipping, as in 1914, virtually vanished almost at once from the high seas. The German ships mostly took refuge in neutral ports, or when intercepted, scuttled themselves. None the less, fifteen ships, totalling 75,000 tons, were captured and put into service by the Allies before the end of 1939. The great German liner *Bremen*, after sheltering in the Soviet port of Murmansk, reached Germany only because she was spared by the British submarine *Salmon,* which observed rightly and punctiliously the conventions of international law.*

* * *

I held my first Admiralty conference on the night of September 4. On account of the importance of the issues, before going to bed in the small hours I recorded its conclusions for circulation and action in my own words:

5.ix.39

1. In this first phase, with Japan placid, and Italy neutral though indeterminate, the prime attack appears to fall on the approaches to Great Britain from the Atlantic.

2. The convoy system is being set up. By convoy system is meant only anti-submarine convoy. All question of dealing with raiding cruisers or heavy ships is excluded from this particular paper.

3. The First Sea Lord is considering a movement to the Western Approaches of Great Britain of whatever destroyers and escort vessels can be scraped from the Eastern and Mediterranean theatres, with the object of adding, if possible, twelve to the escorts for convoys. These should be available during the period of, say, a month, until the flow of Asdic trawlers begins. A statement should be prepared showing the prospective deliveries during October of these vessels. It would seem well, at any rate in the earliest deliveries, not to wait for the arming of them with guns, but to rely upon

* This submarine was commanded by Lieutenant-Commander Bickford, who was specially promoted for his numerous exploits, but was soon afterwards lost with his vessel.

depth-charges. Gun-arming can be reconsidered when the pressure eases.

4. The Director of the Trade Division (D.T.D.) should be able to report daily the inward movement of all British merchant ships approaching the Island. For this purpose, if necessary, a room and additional staff should be provided. A chart of large size should show at each morning all vessels within two, or better still three, days' distance from our shores. The guidance or control of each of these vessels must be foreseen and prescribed so that there is not one whose case has not been individually dealt with, as far as our resources allow. Pray let me have proposals to implement this, which should come into being within twenty-four hours, and work up later. The necessary contacts with the Board of Trade or other departments concerned should be effected and reported upon.

5. The D.T.D. should also prepare to-morrow a scheme under which every captain or master of a merchant ship from the Atlantic (including the Bay) is visited on arrival by a competent naval authority, who in the name of the D.T.D. will examine the record of the course he has steered, including zigzags. All infractions or divergences from Admiralty instructions should be pointed out, and all serious departures should be punished, examples being made by dismissal. The Admiralty assume responsibility, and the merchant skippers must be made to obey. Details of this scheme should be worked out in personnel and regulations, together with appropriate penalties.

6. For the present it would seem wise to maintain the diversion of merchant traffic from the Mediterranean to the Cape route. This would not exclude the passage of convoys for troops, to which of course merchant vessels which were handy might add themselves. But these convoys can only be occasional, i.e., not more than once a month or three weeks, and they must be regarded not as part of the trade protection, but as naval operations.

7. It follows from the above that in this period, i.e., the first six weeks or two months of the war, the Red Sea will also be closed to everything except naval operations, or perhaps coastal traffic to Egypt.

8. This unpleasant situation would be eased by the deliveries of the Asdic trawlers and other reliefs. Secondly, by the determination of the attitude of Italy. We cannot be sure that the Italian uncertainty will be cleared up in the next six weeks, though we should press His Majesty's Government to bring it to a head in a favourable sense as soon as possible. Meanwhile the heavy ships in the Mediterranean will be on the defensive, and can therefore spare some of the destroyer

protection they would need if they were required to approach
Italian waters.

9. The question of a breaking out of any of the five (or
seven) German ships of weight would be a major naval crisis
requiring a special plan. It is impossible for the Admiralty to
provide escorts for convoys of merchant ships against serious
surface attack. These raids, if they occur, could only be dealt
with as a naval operation by the main Fleet, which would
organise the necessary hunting parties to attack the enemy,
the trade being cleared out of the way so far as possible till
results were obtained.

The First Lord submits these notes to his naval colleagues
for consideration, *for criticism and correction*, and hopes to
receive proposals for action in the sense desired.

The organisation of outward-bound convoys was brought
into force almost at once. By September 8 three main routes
had begun to work, namely, from Liverpool and from the
Thames to the western ocean, and a coastal convoy between the
Thames and the Forth. Staffs for the control of convoys at these
ports and many others at home and abroad were included in
the War Plan, and had already been dispatched. Meanwhile all
ships outward bound in the Channel and Irish Sea and not in
convoy were ordered to Plymouth and Milford Haven, and all
independent outward sailings were cancelled. Overseas arrangements for forming homeward-bound convoys were pressed forward. The first of them sailed from Freetown on September 14
and from Halifax, Nova Scotia, on the 16th. Before the end of
the month regular ocean convoys were in operation, outward
from the Thames and Liverpool and homeward from Halifax,
Gibraltar, and Freetown.

Upon all the vital need of feeding the Island and developing
our power to wage war there now at once fell the numbing loss
of the Southern Irish ports. This imposed a grievous restriction
on the radius of action of our already scarce destroyers:

First Sea Lord and others   5.ix.39
    A special report should be drawn up by the heads of depart-
ments concerned and sent to the First Lord through the First
Sea Lord and the Naval Staff upon the questions arising from
the so-called neutrality of the so-called Eire. Various considerations arise: (1) What does Intelligence say about possible succouring of U-boats by Irish malcontents in West of
Ireland inlets? If they throw bombs in London,* why should
    * This referred to a criminal act unconnected with the war.

they not supply fuel to U-boats? Extreme vigilance should be practised.

Secondly, a study is required of the addition to the radius of our destroyers through not having the use of Berehaven or other South Irish anti-submarine bases ; showing also the advantage to be gained by our having these facilities.

The Board must realise that we may not be able to obtain satisfaction, as the question of Eirish neutrality raises political issues which have not yet been faced, and which the First Lord is not certain he can solve. But the full case must be made for consideration.

*　　*　　*

After the institution of the convoy system the next vital naval need was a safe base for the Fleet. At 10 p.m. on September 5 I held a lengthy conference on this. It recalled many old memories. In a war with Germany Scapa Flow is the true strategic point from which the British Navy can control the exits from the North Sea and enforce blockade. It was only in the last two years of the previous war that the Grand Fleet was judged to have sufficient superiority to move south to Rosyth, where it had the advantage of lying at a first-class dockyard. But Scapa, on account of its greater distance from German air bases, was now plainly the best position, and had been definitely chosen in the Admiralty War Plan.

In the autumn of 1914 a wave of uneasiness had swept the Grand Fleet. The idea had got round that 'the German submarines were coming after them into the harbours'. Nobody at the Admiralty then believed that it was possible to take a submarine, submerged, through the intricate and swirling channels by which the great lake of Scapa can alone be entered. The violent tides and currents of the Pentland Firth, often running eight or ten knots, had seemed in those days to be an effective deterrent. But a mood of doubt spread through the mighty array of perhaps a hundred large vessels which in those days composed the Grand Fleet. On two or three occasions, notably on October 17, 1914, the alarm was given that there was a U-boat inside the anchorage. Guns were fired, destroyers thrashed the waters, and the whole gigantic armada put to sea in haste and dudgeon. In the final result the Admiralty were proved right. No German submarine in that war ever overcame the terrors of the passage. It was only in 1918, at the very end of the war, that a U-boat made the attempt, and perished in this final desperate effort. Nevertheless, I retained a most vivid and unpleasant memory of those days and of the extreme exertions we made to block all the entrances and reassure the Fleet.

There were now in 1939 two dangers to be considered: the first, the old one of submarine incursion; the second, the new one of the air. I was surprised to learn at my conference that more precautions had not been taken in both cases to prepare the defences against modern forms of attack. Anti-submarine booms of new design were in position at each of the three main entrances, but these consisted merely of single lines of net. The narrow and tortuous approaches on the east side of the Flow, defended only by remnants of the blockships placed in the former war, and reinforced now by two or three recent additions, remained a source of anxiety. On account of the increased size, speed, and power of modern submarines, the old belief that the strong tidal streams made these passages impassable to a submarine no longer carried conviction in responsible quarters. As a result of the conference on my second evening at the Admiralty many orders were given for additional nets and blockings.

The new danger from the air had been almost entirely ignored. Except for two batteries of anti-aircraft guns to defend the naval oil tanks at Hoy and the destroyer anchorage, there were no air defences at Scapa. One airfield near Kirkwall was available for the use of naval aircraft when the Fleet was present, but no provision had been made for immediate R.A.F. participation in the defence, and the shore Radar station, although operative, was not wholly effective. Plans for basing two R.A.F. fighter squadrons at Wick had been approved, but this measure could not become effective before 1940. I called for an immediate plan of action. Our air defence was so strained, our resources so limited, and our vulnerable points—including all vast London—so numerous that it was no use asking for much. On the other hand, protection from air attack was now needed only for five or six great ships, each carrying a powerful anti-aircraft armament of its own. To keep things going the Admiralty undertook to provide two squadrons of naval fighter aircraft whilst the Fleet was in Scapa.

It seemed most important to have the artillery in position at the shortest interval, and meanwhile there was nothing for it but to adopt the same policy of 'hide-and-seek' to which we had been forced in the autumn days of 1914. The west coast of Scotland had many landlocked anchorages easy to protect from U-boat by indicator nets and ceaseless patrolling. We had found concealment in the previous war a good security; but even in those days the curiosity of a wandering aeroplane, perhaps fuelled by traitor hands, had filled our hearts with fear. Now that the range of aircraft exposed the whole British Islands at any time to photographic reconnaissance machines, there was no sure concealment against large-scale attack either by U-boats or from the air. However, there were so few ships to cover, and they could be moved so often from one place to another, that, having no alternative, we accepted the hazard with as good a grace as possible.

* * *

I felt it my duty to visit Scapa at the earliest moment. I had not met the Commander-in-Chief, Sir Charles Forbes, since Lord Chatfield had taken me to the Anti-Submarine School at Portland in June 1938. I therefore obtained leave from our daily Cabinets, and started for Wick with a small personal staff on the night of September 14. I spent most of the next two days inspecting the harbour and the entrances, with their booms and nets. I was assured that they were as good as in the last war, and that important additions and improvements were being made or were on the way. I stayed with the Commander-in-Chief in his flagship, *Nelson*, and discussed not only Scapa but the whole naval problem with him and his principal officers. The rest of the Fleet was hiding in Loch Ewe, and on the 17th the Admiral took me to them in the *Nelson*. As we came out through the gateway into the open sea I was surprised to see no escort of destroyers for this great ship. 'I thought,' I remarked, 'you never went to sea without at least two, even for a single battleship.' But the Admiral replied, 'Of course, that is what we should like; but we haven't got the destroyers to carry out any such rule. There are a lot of patrolling craft about, and we shall be into the Minches in a few hours.'

It was, like the others, a lovely day. All went well, and in the evening we anchored in Loch Ewe, where the four or five other great ships of the Home Fleet were assembled. The narrow entry into the loch was closed by several lines of indicator nets, and patrolling craft with Asdics and depth-charges, as well as

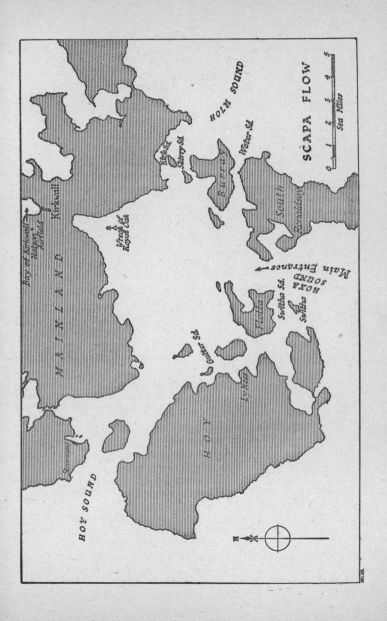

SCAPA FLOW

HOLM SOUND

Weisr Sd.

Kirk Sd.
Skerry Sd.

Burray

South
Ronaldsay

Sea Miles
0 1 2 3 4 5

Wreck of
Royal Oak

Main Entrance
HOXA SOUND

Switha Sd.
Switha

Flotta

Fara

Cava

Switha Sd.

Gutter Sd.

Ly Ness

H O Y

HOY SOUND

MAINLAND

Bay of Kirkwall
Harbour
Airfield
Kirkwall

Stromness

N

24

picket-boats, were numerous and busy. On every side rose the purple hills of Scotland in all their splendour. My thoughts went back a quarter of a century to that other September when I had last visited Sir John Jellicoe and his captains in this very bay, and had found them with their long lines of battleships and cruisers drawn out at anchor, a prey to the same uncertainties as now afflicted us. Most of the captains and admirals of those days were dead, or had long passed into retirement. The responsible senior officers who were now presented to me as I visited the various ships had been young lieutenants or even midshipmen in those far-off days. Before the former war I had had three years' preparation in which to make the acquaintance and approve the appointments of most of the high personnel, but now all these were new figures and new faces. The perfect discipline, style, and bearing, the ceremonial routine—all were unchanged. But an entirely different generation filled the uniforms and the posts. Only the ships had most of them been laid down in my tenure. None of them was new. It was a strange experience, like suddenly resuming a previous incarnation. It seemed that I was all that survived in the same position I had held so long ago. But no ; the dangers had survived too. Danger from beneath the waves, more serious with more powerful U-boats ; danger from the air, not merely of being spotted in your hiding-place, but of heavy and perhaps destructive attack !

Having inspected two more ships on the morning of the 18th, and formed during my visit a strong feeling of confidence in the Commander-in-Chief, I motored from Loch Ewe to Inverness, where our train awaited us. We had a picnic lunch on the way by a stream, sparkling in hot sunshine. I felt oddly oppressed with my memories.

> For God's sake, let us sit upon the ground
> And tell sad stories of the death of kings.

No one had ever been over the same terrible course twice with such an interval between. No one had felt its dangers and responsibilities from the summit as I had, or, to descend to a small point, understood how First Lords of the Admiralty are treated when great ships are sunk and things go wrong. If we were in fact going over the same cycle a second time, should I have once again to endure the pangs of dismissal? Fisher, Wilson, Battenberg, Jellicoe, Beatty, Pakenham, Sturdee, all gone!

> I feel like one
> Who treads alone
> Some banquet-hall deserted,
> Whose lights are fled,
> Whose garlands dead,
> And all but he departed.

And what of the supreme, measureless ordeal in which we were again irrevocably plunged? Poland in its agony ; France but a pale reflection of her former warlike ardour ; the Russian Colossus no longer an ally, not even neutral, possibly to become a foe. Italy no friend. Japan no ally. Would America ever come in again? The British Empire remained intact and gloriously united, but ill-prepared, unready. We still had command of the sea. We were woefully outmatched in numbers in this new mortal weapon of the air. Somehow the light faded out of the landscape.

We joined our train at Inverness and travelled through the afternoon and night to London. As we got out at Euston the next morning I was surprised to see the First Sea Lord on the platform. Admiral Pound's look was grave. 'I have bad news for you, First Lord. The *Courageous* was sunk yesterday evening in the Bristol Channel.' The *Courageous* was one of our oldest aircraft-carriers, but a very necessary ship at this time. I thanked him for coming to break it to me himself, and said, 'We can't expect to carry on a war like this without that sort of thing happening from time to time. I have seen lots of it before.' And so to bath and the toil of another day.

In order to bridge the gap of two or three weeks between the outbreak of war and the completion of our auxiliary anti-U-boat flotillas, we had decided to use the aircraft-carriers with some freedom in helping to bring in the unarmed, unorganised, and unconvoyed traffic which was then approaching our shores in large numbers. This was a risk which it was right to run. The *Courageous*, attended by four destroyers, had been thus employed. Towards evening on the 17th two of these had to go to hunt a U-boat which was attacking a merchant ship. When the *Courageous* turned into the wind at dusk, in order to enable her own aircraft to alight upon her landing-deck, she happened, in her unpredictable course, by what may have been a hundred-to-one chance, to meet a U-boat. Out of the crew of 1,260 over 500 were drowned, including Captain Makeig-Jones, who went down with his ship. Three days before another of our aircraft-carriers, later to become famous, H.M.S. *Ark Royal*, had also been attacked by a submarine while similarly engaged. Mercifully the torpedoes missed, and her assailant was promptly sunk by her escorting destroyers.

* * *

Outstanding among our naval problems was that of dealing effectively with surface raiders, which would inevitably make their appearance in the near future as they had done in 1914.

On September 12 I issued the following minute:

First Lord to First Sea Lord   12.IX.39

CRUISER POLICY

In the past we have sought to protect our trade against sudden attack by [means of] cruisers; having regard to the vast ocean spaces to be controlled, the principle was 'the more the better'. In the search for enemy raiders or cruisers even small cruisers could play their part, and in the case of the *Emden* we were forced to gather over twenty ships before she was rounded up. However, a long view of cruiser policy would seem to suggest that a new Unit of Search is required. Whereas a cruiser squadron of four ships could search on a front of, say, 80 miles, a single cruiser accompanied by an aircraft-carrier could cover at least 300 miles, or, if the movement of the ship is taken into account, 400 miles. On the other hand, we must apprehend that the raiders of the future will be powerful vessels, eager to fight a single-ship action if a chance is presented. The mere multiplication of small, weak cruisers is no means of ridding the seas of powerful raiders. Indeed they are only an easy prey. The raider, cornered at length, will overwhelm one weak vessel and escape from the cordon.

Every Unit of Search must be able to find, to catch, and to kill. For this purpose we require a number of cruisers superior to the 10,000-ton type, or else pairs of our own 10,000-ton type. These must be accompanied by small aircraft-carriers carrying perhaps a dozen or two dozen machines, and of the smallest possible displacement. The ideal Unit of Search would be one killer or two three-quarter killers, plus one aircraft-carrier, plus four ocean-going destroyers, plus two or three specially-constructed tankers of good speed. Such a formation cruising would be protected against submarines, and could search an enormous area and destroy any single raider when detected.

The policy of forming hunting groups as discussed in this minute, comprising balanced forces capable of scouring wide areas and overwhelming any raider within the field of search, was developed so far as our limited resources allowed, and I shall refer to this subject again in a later chapter. The same idea was afterwards more fully expanded by the United States in their Task Force system, which made an important contribution to the art of sea warfare.

* * *

Towards the end of the month I thought it would be well for me to give the House some coherent story of what was happening and why.

First Lord to Prime Minister 24.ix.39

Would it not be well for me to make a statement to the House on the anti-submarine warfare and general naval position, more at length than what you could give in your own speech? I think I could speak for twenty-five or thirty minutes on the subject, and that this would do good. At any rate, when I saw in confidence sixty Press representatives the other day they appeared vastly relieved by the account I was able to give. If this idea commended itself to you, you would perhaps say in your speech that I would give a fuller account later on in the discussion, which I suppose will take place on Thursday, as the Budget is on Wednesday.

Mr. Chamberlain readily assented, and accordingly in his speech on the 26th he told the House that I would make a statement on the sea war as soon as he sat down. This was the first time, apart from answering questions, that I had spoken in Parliament since I had entered the Government. I had a good tale to tell. In the first seven days our losses in tonnage had been half the weekly losses of the month of April 1917, which was the peak year of the U-boat attack in the first war. We had already made progress by setting in motion the convoy system; secondly, by pressing on with the arming of all our merchant ships; and, thirdly, by our counter-attack upon the U-boats. In the first week our losses by U-boat sinkings amounted to 65,000 tons; in the second week they were 46,000 tons; and in the third week they were 21,000 tons. In the last six days we have lost only 9,000 tons.'* I observed throughout that habit of under-statement and of avoiding all optimistic forecasts which had been inculcated upon me by the hard experiences of the past. 'One must not dwell,' I said, 'upon these reassuring figures too much, for war is full of unpleasant surprises. But certainly I am entitled to say that so far as they go these figures need not cause any undue despondency or alarm.'

Meanwhile [I continued] the whole vast business of our world-wide trade continues without interruption or appreci-able diminution. Great convoys of troops are escorted to their various destinations. The enemy's ships and commerce have been swept from the seas. Over 2,000,000 tons of German shipping is now sheltering in German, or interned in neutral, harbours. . . . In the first fortnight of the war we have actually arrested, seized, and converted to our own use 67,000 tons more German merchandise than has been sunk in ships of our own. . . . Again I reiterate my caution against over-sanguine conclusions. We have in fact however got more supplies in this country this afternoon than we should have if no war had been declared and no U-boat had come into action. It is not going beyond the limits of prudent statement if I say that at that rate it will take a long time to starve us out.

From time to time the German U-boat commanders have tried their best to behave with humanity. We have seen them give good warning and also endeavour to help the crews to find their way to port. One German captain signalled to me personally the position of a British ship which he had just sunk, and urged that rescue should be sent. He signed his message 'German Submarine'. I was in some doubt at the time

* The following are the corrected figures:

BRITISH MERCHANT SHIPPING LOSSES BY ENEMY ACTION, SEPTEMBER 1939
(*Number of ships shown in brackets*)

					Submarine (Gross tons)	Other Causes (Gross tons)
1st WEEK (September 3–9)	..	..	..	..	64,595 (11)	—
2nd WEEK (September 10–16)	..	..	..	..	53,561 (11)	11,437 (2) (mine)
3rd WEEK (September 17–23)	..	..	..	..	12,750 (3)	—
4th WEEK (September 24–30)	..	..	..	..	4,646 (1)	5,051 (1) (surface raider)
Total	..	..	..	..	135,552 (26)	16,488 (3)
					152,040 (29)	

In addition there were losses in neutral and Allied shipping amounting to 15 ships, of 33,527 tons.

to what address I should direct a reply. However, he is now in our hands, and is treated with all consideration.

Even taking six or seven U-boats sunk as a safe figure,* that is one-tenth of the total enemy submarine fleet as it existed at the declaration of war, destroyed during the first fortnight of the war, and it is probably one-quarter, or perhaps even one-third, of all the U-boats which are being employed actively. But the British attack upon the U-boats is only just beginning. Our hunting force is getting stronger every day. By the end of October we expect to have three times the hunting force which was operating at the beginning of the war.

This speech, which lasted only twenty-five minutes, was extremely well received by the House, and in fact it recorded the failure of the first German U-boat attack upon our trade. My fears were for the future, but our preparations for 1941 were now proceeding with all possible speed and on the largest scale which our vast resources would allow.

*   *   *

By the end of September we had little cause for dissatisfaction with the results of the first impact of the war at sea. I could feel that I had effectively taken over the great department which I knew so well and loved with a discriminating eye. I now knew what there was in hand and on the way. I knew where everything was. I had visited all the principal naval ports and met all the Commanders-in-Chief. By the Letters Patent constituting the Board, the First Lord is 'responsible to Crown and Parliament for all the business of the Admiralty', and I certainly felt prepared to discharge that duty in fact as well as in form.

On the whole the month of September had been prosperous and fruitful for the Navy. We had made the immense, delicate, and hazardous transition from peace to war. Forfeits had to be paid in the first few weeks by a world-wide commerce suddenly attacked contrary to formal international agreement by indiscriminate U-boat warfare ; but the convoy system was now in full flow, and merchant ships were leaving our ports every day by scores with a gun, sometimes high-angle, mounted aft, and a nucleus of trained gunners. The Asdic-equipped trawlers and other small craft armed with depth-charges, all well prepared by the Admiralty before the outbreak, were now coming daily into commission in a growing stream, with trained

* We now know that only two U-boats were sunk in September 1939.

crews. We all felt sure that the first attack of the U-boat on British trade had been broken, and that the menace was in thorough and hardening control. It was obvious that the Germans would build submarines by hundreds, and no doubt numerous shoals were upon the slips in various stages of completion. In twelve months, certainly in eighteen, we must expect the main U-boat war to begin. But by that time we hoped that our mass of new flotillas and anti-U-boat craft, which was our First Priority, would be ready to meet it with a proportionate and effective predominance. The painful dearth of anti-aircraft guns, especially 3·7-inch and Bofors, could, alas, only be relieved after many months ; but measures had been taken within the limits of our resources to provide for the defence of our naval harbours ; and meanwhile the Fleet, while ruling the oceans, would have to go on playing hide-and-seek.

* * *

In the wider sphere of naval operations no definite challenge had yet been made to our position. After the temporary suspension of traffic in the Mediterranean our shipping soon moved again through this invaluable corridor. Meanwhile the transport of the Expeditionary Force to France was proceeding smoothly. The Home Fleet itself, 'somewhere in the North', was ready to intercept any sortie by the few heavy ships of the enemy. The blockade of Germany was being enforced by similar methods to those employed in the previous war. The Northern Patrol had been established between Scotland and Iceland, and by the end of the first month a total of nearly three hundred thousand tons of goods destined for Germany had been seized in prize, against a loss to ourselves of a hundred and forty thousand tons by enemy action at sea. Overseas our cruisers were hunting down German ships, while at the same time providing cover against attack on our shipping by raiders. German shipping had thus come to a standstill. By the end of September 3, 25 German ships, totalling nearly 750,000 tons, were immobilised in foreign ports. Few therefore fell into our hands.

Our Allies also played their part. The French took an important share in the control of the Mediterranean. In home waters and the Bay of Biscay they also helped in the battle against the U-boats, and in the central Atlantic a powerful force based on Dakar formed part of the Allied plans against surface raiders.

The young Polish Navy distinguished itself. Early in the war three modern destroyers and two submarines, *Wilk* and *Orzel*, escaped from Poland, and, defying the German forces in the Baltic, succeeded in reaching England. The escape of the submarine *Orzel* is an epic. Sailing from Gdynia when the Germans invaded Poland, she first cruised in the Baltic, putting into the neutral port of Tallinn on September 15 to land her sick captain. The Esthonian authorities decided to intern the vessel, placed a guard on board, and removed her charts and the breech-blocks of her guns. Undismayed, her commanding officer put to sea, after overpowering the guard. In the ensuing weeks the submarine was continually hunted by sea and air patrols, but eventually, without even charts, made her escape from the Baltic into the North Sea. Here she was able to transmit a faint wireless signal to a British station giving her supposed position, and on October 14 was met and escorted into safety by a British destroyer.

*　　　*　　　*

In September I was delighted to receive a personal letter from President Roosevelt. I had only met him once in the previous war. It was at a dinner at Gray's Inn, and I had been struck by his magnificent presence in all his youth and strength. There had been no opportunity for anything but salutations.

President Roosevelt to Mr. Churchill　　　　　　　11.ix.39
It is because you and I occupied similar positions in the World War that I want you to know how glad I am that you are back again in the Admiralty. Your problems are, I realise, complicated by new factors, but the essential is not very different. What I want you and the Prime Minister to know is that I shall at all times welcome it if you will keep me in touch personally with anything you want me to know about. You can always send sealed letters through your pouch or my pouch.

I am glad you did the Marlborough volumes before this thing started—and I much enjoyed reading them.

I responded with alacrity, using the signature of 'Naval Person', and thus began that long and memorable correspondence —covering perhaps a thousand communications on each side, and lasting till his death more than five years later.

CHAPTER 3

The Ruin of Poland

The German Plan of Invasion – Unsound Polish Dispositions – Inferiority in Artillery and Tanks – Destruction of the Polish Air Force – The First Week – The Second Week – The Heroic Polish Counter-Attack – Extermination – The Turn of the Soviets – The Warsaw Radio Silent – The Modern Blitzkrieg – My Memorandum of September 21 – Our Immediate Dangers – My Broadcast of October 1.

Meanwhile around the Cabinet table we were witnessing the swift and almost mechanical destruction of a weaker State according to Hitler's method and long design. Poland was open to German invasion on three sides. In all fifty-six divisions, including all his nine armoured and motorised divisions, composed the invading armies. From East Prussia the Third Army (eight divisions) advanced southwards on Warsaw and Bialystok. From Pomerania the Fourth Army (twelve divisions) was ordered to destroy the Polish troops in the Danzig Corridor, and then move south-eastward to Warsaw along both banks of the Vistula. The frontier opposite the Posen bulge was held defensively by German reserve troops, but on their right to the southward lay the Eighth Army (seven divisions), whose task was to cover the left flank of the main thrust. This thrust was assigned to the Tenth Army (seventeen divisions), directed straight upon Warsaw. Further south again the Fourteenth Army (fourteen divisions) had a dual task, first to capture the important industrial area west of Cracow, and then, if the main front prospered, to make direct for Lemberg (Lwow), in South-east Poland.

Thus the Polish forces on the frontiers were first to be penetrated, and then overwhelmed and surrounded by two pincer movements, the first from the north and south-west on Warsaw, the second and more far-reaching, 'outer' pincers, formed by the Third Army advancing by Brest-Litovsk, to be joined by the Fourteenth Army after Lemberg was gained. Those who escaped the closing of the Warsaw pincers would thus be cut off from retreat into Roumania. Over fifteen hundred modern aircraft were hurled on Poland. Their first duty was to overwhelm the Polish Air Force, and thereafter to support the Army on the battlefield, and beyond it to attack military installations and all communications by road and rail. They were also to spread terror far and wide.

In numbers and equipment the Polish Army was no match for their assailants, nor were their dispositions wise. They spread all their forces along the frontiers of their native land. They had no central reserve. While taking a proud and haughty line against German ambitions, they had nevertheless feared to be accused of provocation by mobilising in good time against the masses gathering around them. Thirty divisions, representing only two-thirds of their active army, were ready or nearly ready to meet the first shock. The speed of events and the violent intervention of the German Air Force prevented the rest from reaching the forward positions till all was broken, and they were only involved in the final disasters. Thus the thirty Polish divisions faced nearly double their numbers around a long perimeter with nothing behind them. Nor was it in numbers alone that they were inferior. They were heavily outclassed in artillery, and had but a single armoured brigade to meet the nine German Panzers, as they were already called. Their horse cavalry, of which they had twelve brigades, charged valiantly against the swarming tanks and armoured cars, but could not harm them with their swords and lances. Their nine hundred first-line aircraft, of which perhaps half were modern types, were taken by surprise, and many were destroyed before they even got into the air.

According to Hitler's plan the German armies were unleashed on September 1, and ahead of them his Air Force struck the Polish squadrons on their airfields. In two days the Polish air power was virtually annihilated. Within a week the German armies had bitten deep into Poland. Resistance everywhere was brave but vain. All the Polish armies on the frontiers, except the Posen group, whose flanks were deeply turned, were driven backwards. The Lodz group was split in twain by the main thrust of the German Tenth Army ; one half withdrew eastwards to Radom, the other was forced north-westward ; and through this gap darted two Panzer divisions, making straight for Warsaw. Farther north the German Fourth Army reached and crossed the Vistula, and turned along it in their march on Warsaw. Only the Polish northern group was able to inflict a check upon the German Third Army. They were soon outflanked and fell back to the river Narew, where alone a fairly strong defensive system had been prepared in advance. Such were the results of the first week of the Blitzkrieg.

The second week was marked by bitter fighting, and by its end the Polish Army, nominally of about two million men,

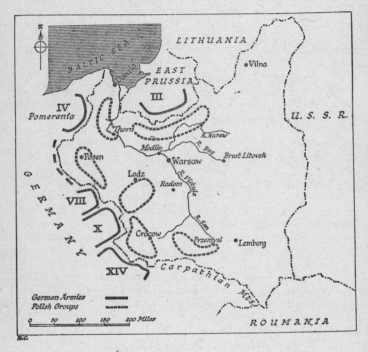

The German and Polish Concentrations, September 1, 1939

ceased to exist as an organised force. In the south the Four-teenth German Army drove on to reach the river San. North of them the four Polish divisions which had retreated to Radom were there encircled and destroyed. The two armoured divi-sions of the Tenth Army reached the outskirts of Warsaw, but having no infantry with them could not make headway against the desperate resistance organised by the townsfolk. North-east of Warsaw the Third Army encircled the capital from the east, and its left column reached Brest-Litovsk, a hundred miles behind the battle-front.

It was within the claws of the Warsaw pincers that the Polish Army fought and died. Their Posen group had been joined by divisions from the Thorn and Lodz groups, forced towards them by the German onslaught. It now numbered twelve divisions, and across its southern flank the German Tenth Army was streaming towards Warsaw, protected only by the relatively weak Eighth Army. Although already virtually surrounded, the Polish commander of the Posen group, General Kutrzea, resolved to strike south against the flank of the main German drive. This audacious Polish counter-attack, called the Battle of the River Bzura, created a crisis which drew in not only the German Eighth Army but a part of the Tenth, deflected from their Warsaw objective, and even a corps of the Fourth Army from the north. Under the assault of all these powerful bodies, and overwhelmed by unresisted air bombardment, the Posen group maintained its ever-glorious struggle for ten days. It was blotted out on September 19.

In the meantime the outer pincers had met and closed. The Fourteenth Army reached the outskirts of Lemberg on September 12, and, striking north, joined hands on the 17th with the troops of the Third Army, which has passed through Brest-Litovsk. There was now no loophole of escape save for straggling and daring individuals. On the 20th the Germans announced that the Battle of the Vistula was 'one of the greatest battles of extermination of all time'.

It was now the turn of the Soviets. What they now call 'Democracy' came into action. On September 17 the Russian armies swarmed across the almost undefended Polish eastern frontier and rolled westward on a broad front. On the 18th they occupied Vilna, and met their German collaborators at Brest-Litovsk. Here in the previous war the Bolsheviks, in breach of their solemn agreements with the Western Allies, had made their separate peace with the Kaiser's Germany and had bowed to its harsh terms. Now in Brest-Litovsk it was with Hitler's Germany that the Russian Communists grinned and shook hands. The ruin of Poland and its entire subjugation proceeded apace. Warsaw and Modlin still remained unconquered. The resistance of Warsaw, largely arising from the surge of its citizens, was magnificent and forlorn. After many days of violent bombardment from the air and by heavy artillery, much of which was rapidly transported across the great lateral highways from the idle Western Front, the Warsaw radio ceased to play the Polish National Anthem, and Hitler entered the ruins of the city. Modlin, a fortress twenty miles down the Vistula, had taken in the remnants of the Thorn group, and fought on until the 28th. Thus in one month all was over, and a nation of thirty-five millions fell into the merciless grip of those who sought not only conquest, but enslavement and indeed extinction for vast numbers.

We had seen a perfect specimen of the modern Blitzkrieg; the close interaction on the battlefield of Army and Air Force; the violent bombardment of all communications and of any town that seemed an attractive target; the arming of an active Fifth Column; the free use of spies and parachutists; and above all the irresistible forward thrusts of great masses of armour. The Poles were not to be the last to endure this ordeal.

*　　　*　　　*

The Soviet armies continued to advance up to the line they had settled with Hitler, and on the 29th the Russo-German treaty partitioning Poland was formally signed. I was still convinced of the profound, and, as I believed, quenchless antagonism between Russia and Germany, and I clung to the hope that the Soviets would be drawn to our side by the force of events. I did not therefore give way to the indignation which I felt and which surged around me in our Cabinet at their callous, brutal policy. I had never had any illusions about them. I knew that they accepted no moral code, and studied their own interests alone. But at least they owed us nothing. Besides, in mortal war anger must be subordinated to defeating the main immediate enemy. I was determined to put the best construction on their odious conduct. Therefore in a paper which I wrote for the War Cabinet on September 25 I struck a cool note.

Although the Russians were guilty of the grossest bad faith in the recent negotiations, their demand made by Marshal Voroshilov that Russian armies should occupy Vilna and Lemberg if they were to be allies of Poland was a perfectly valid military request. It was rejected by Poland on grounds which, though natural, can now be seen to have been insufficient. In the result Russia has occupied the same line and positions as the enemy of Poland which possibly she might have occupied as a very doubtful and suspected friend. The difference in fact is not so great as it might seem. The Russians have mobilised very large forces and have shown themselves able

The Inner Pincers Close, September 13

to advance fast and far from their pre-war positions. They are now limitrophe with Germany, and it is quite impossible for Germany to denude the Eastern front. A large German army must be left to watch it. I see General Gamelin puts it at at least twenty divisions. It may well be twenty-five or more. An Eastern front is therefore potentially in existence.

But it is possible that a South-eastern front may also be built up in which Russia, Britain, and France will have a common interest. The left paw of the Bear has already closed the pathway from Poland to Roumania. Russian interest in the Slavonic peoples of the Balkans is traditional. The arrival of the Germans on the Black Sea would be a deadly threat to Russia. And also to Turkey. That these two countries should make common cause to prevent this is a direct fulfilment of our wishes. It in no way conflicts with our policy

The Outer Pincers Close. The Russians Advance, September 17

towards Turkey. It may well be that Russia will deprive Roumania of Bessarabia ; but this does not necessarily conflict with our major interest, which is to arrest the German movement towards the east and south-east of Europe. Roumania, which gained enormously from the late war, in which she was rescued from utter defeat by the Allied victory, will be lucky if she gets out of this war with no greater losses than Bessarabia and the southern part of the Dobrudja, which latter she ought willingly to cede to Bulgaria in the interests of a Balkan *bloc*. The reactions of the Russian movement, so far as it can at present be judged, should be favourable throughout the Balkans, and particularly in Yugoslavia. Thus, besides the potential Eastern front a potential South-eastern front may be coming into existence, reaching in a crescent from the Gulf of Riga to the head of the Adriatic (and thence perhaps on across the Brenner to the Alps).

Of course we should much prefer that all these countries should fall at once upon the sole and common foe, Nazi Germany ; and this possibility should not be excluded as time goes on. It would come very near if Germany struck through Hungary at Roumania, and to a lesser degree if she struck at Yugoslavia. The policy we are pursuing of fostering this front, of strengthening it and endeavouring to throw it into simultaneous action should any part of it be attacked, seems absolutely right. This policy implies a renewal of relations with Russia, as the Foreign Secretary has swiftly foreseen. It also compels our adherence to the policy declared by the Prime Minister of not committing ourselves to particular territorial solutions and concentrating the whole effort of Britain and France upon smashing Hitlerism, and also of making sure that the German Terror is not renewed upon the Western democracies for a long time to come. This last point, which appeals so much to the French, is exactly expressed by the Prime Minister's words 'Our general purpose . . . is to redeem Europe from the perpetual and recurring fear of German aggression, and enable the peoples of Europe to preserve their liberties and their independence.' This cannot be repeated too often or too widely.

Upon this general appreciation our handling of the Turkish negotiations can more easily be considered. I cannot feel that there is the same urgency about them as there was when Hitler was reported to be about to invade Roumania with twenty-eight divisions, etc. It now seems possible that that man may be warned off his Eastern career ; but of course he may renew his threat at any time, and we besides have a main interest in bringing all the Balkans and Eastern front into hostile action against Germany. It therefore seems most important to make the Turkish treaty.

If it should turn out that Hitler is barred in the East, which, of course, is not yet certain, three courses are open to him :

(1) a major attack on the Western front, probably through Belgium, collecting Holland on the way.
(2) An intensive attack by air upon British factories, naval ports, etc., or perhaps on the French air factories.

(3) What the Prime Minister calls 'the peace offensive'.

Personally, I shall believe that (1) is imminent only when at least thirty divisions have been concentrated opposite Belgium and Luxemburg. As to (2), it seems a very likely thing for that man to do ; but he may not do it, or he may not be allowed to do it by his generals, who now are presumably more powerful, for fear of making a mortal blood-feud with Great Britain, and perhaps drawing in the United States by the air massacres which would be inevitable. As for (3), if he has not tried (2) it would seem our duty and policy to agree to nothing that will help him out of his troubles, and to leave him to stew in his own juice during the winter while speeding forward our armaments and weaving up our alliances. The general outlook, therefore, seems far more favourable than it did in the autumn of 1914, when a large part of France was occupied and Russia had been shattered at Tannenberg.

But there always remains No. 2. That is the immediate pinch.

In a broadcast on October 1 I said:

Poland has again been overrun by two of the great Powers which held her in bondage for a hundred and fifty years but were unable to quench the spirit of the Polish nation. The heroic defence of Warsaw shows that the soul of Poland is indestructible, and that she will rise again like a rock, which may for a time be submerged by a tidal wave, but which remains a rock.

Russia has pursued a cold policy of self-interest. We could have wished that the Russian armies should be standing on their present line as the friends and allies of Poland instead of as invaders. But that the Russian armies should stand on this line was clearly necessary for the safety of Russia against the Nazi menace. At any rate, the line is there, and an Eastern front has been created which Nazi Germany does not dare assail. . . .

I cannot forecast to you the action of Russia. It is a riddle wrapped in a mystery inside an enigma. But perhaps there is a key. That key is Russian national interest. It cannot be in accordance with the interest or the safety of Russia that Germany should plant herself upon the shores of the Black Sea, or that she should overrun the Balkan States and subjugate the Slavonic peoples of South-eastern Europe. That would be contrary to the historic life-interests of Russia.

The Prime Minister was in full agreement. 'I take the same view as Winston,' he said, in a letter to his sister, 'to whose excellent broadcast we have just been listening. I believe Russia will always act as she thinks her own interests demand, and I cannot believe she would think her interests served by a German victory followed by a German domination of Europe.'*

* Feiling, *op. cit.*, p. 425.

CHAPTER 4

War Cabinet Problems

Our Daily Meetings – A Fifty-Five Division Army for Britain – Our Heavy Artillery – My Letter to the Prime Minister, September 10 – To the Minister of Supply, September 10, and His Answer – Need for a Ministry of Shipping – My Letter to the Prime Minister, September 15 – His Reply, September 16 – Further Correspondence about Munitions and Man-power – My Letter to the Chancellor of the Exchequer, September 24 – An Economy Campaign – The Search for a Naval Offensive – The Baltic – 'Catherine the Great' – Plans for Forcing Entry – Technical and Tactical Aspects – The Prize – Views of the First Sea Lord – Lord Cork's Appointment – Progress of the Plan – The Veto of the Air – The New Construction Programme – Cruisers – Destroyers – Numbers Versus Size – Long- and Short-Term Policies – Speeding the Programme – Need of an Air-Proof Battle Squadron – The Waste of the 'Royal Sovereigns' – I Established My Own Statistical Department.

The War Cabinet and its additional members, with the Chiefs of Staff for the three Services and a number of secretaries, had met together for the first time on September 4. Thereafter we met daily, and often twice a day. I do not recall any period when the weather was so hot—I had a black alpaca jacket made to wear over only a linen shirt. It was indeed just the weather that Hitler wanted for his invasion of Poland. The great rivers on which the Poles had counted in their defensive plan were nearly everywhere fordable, and the ground was hard and firm for the movement of tanks and vehicles of all kinds. Each morning the C.I.G.S., General Ironside, standing before the map, gave long reports and appreciations which very soon left no doubt in our minds that the resistance of Poland would speedily be crushed. Each day I reported to the Cabinet the Admiralty tale, which usually consisted of a list of British merchant ships sunk by the U-boats. The British Expeditionary Force of four divisions began its movement to France, and the Air Ministry deplored the fact that they were not allowed to bombard military objectives in Germany. For the rest a great deal of business was transacted on the Home Front, and there were of course lengthy discussions about foreign affairs, particularly concerning the attitude of Soviet Russia and Italy and the policy to be pursued in the Balkans.

The most important step was the setting up of the Land Forces Committee, under Sir Samuel Hoare, at this time Lord Privy Seal, in order to advise the War Cabinet upon the scale and organisation of the Army we should form. I was a member of this small body, which met at the Home Office, and in one single sweltering afternoon agreed, after hearing the generals, that we should forthwith begin the creation of a fifty-five division Army, together with all the munition factories, plants, and supply services of every kind necessary to sustain it in action. It was hoped that by the eighteenth month two-thirds of this, a considerable force, would either already have been sent to France or be fit to take the field. Sir Samuel Hoare was clear-sighted and active in all this, and I gave him my constant support. The Air Ministry, on the other hand, feared that so large an Army and its supplies would be an undue drain upon our skilled labour and man-power, and would hamper them in the vast plans they had formed on paper for the creation of an all-powerful overwhelming Air Force in two or three years. The Prime Minister was impressed by Sir Kingsley Wood's arguments, and hesitated to commit himself to an Army of this size and all that it entailed. The War Cabinet was divided upon the issue, and it was a week or more before a decision was reached to adopt the advice of the Land Forces Committee for a fifty-five-division Army, or rather target.

I felt that as a member of the War Cabinet I was bound to take a general view, and I did not fail to subordinate my own departmental requirements for the Admiralty to the main design. I was anxious to establish a broad basis of common ground with the Prime Minister, and also to place him in possession of my knowledge in this field, which I had trodden before ; and being encouraged by his courtesy, I wrote him a series of letters on the various problems as they arose. I did not wish to be drawn into arguments with him at Cabinets, and always preferred putting things down on paper. In nearly all cases we found ourselves in agreement, and although at first he gave me the impression of being very much on his guard, yet I am glad to say that month by month his confidence and goodwill seemed to grow. His biographer has borne testimony to this. I also wrote to other members of the War Cabinet and to various Ministers with whom I had departmental or other business. The War Cabinet was hampered somewhat by the fact that they seldom sat together alone without secretaries or military experts. It was an earnest and workmanlike body, and the advantages of free discussion among men bound so closely together in a common task, without any formality and without any record being kept, are very great. Such meetings are an essential counterpart to the formal meetings where business is transacted and decisions are recorded for guidance and action. Both processes are indispensable to the handling of the most difficult affairs.

I was deeply interested in the fate of the great mass of heavy artillery which as Minister of Munitions I had made in the previous war. Such weapons take a year and a half to manufacture, but it is of great value to an army, whether in defence or offence, to have at its disposal a mass of heavy batteries. I remembered the struggles which Mr. Lloyd George had had with the War Office in 1915 and all the political disturbance which had arisen on this subject of the creation of a dominating Very Heavy Artillery, and how he had been vindicated by events. The character of the war on land, when it eventually manifested itself eight months later in 1940, proved utterly different from that of 1914–18. As will be seen, however, a vital need in Home Defence was met by these great cannon. At this time I conceived we had a buried treasure which it would be folly to neglect.

I wrote to the Prime Minister on this and other matters:

First Lord to Prime Minister   10.ix.39

I hope you will not mind my sending you a few points privately.

1. I am still inclined to think that we should not take the initiative in bombing, except in the immediate zone in which the French armies are operating, where we must of course help. It is to our interest that the war should be conducted in accordance with the more humane conceptions of war, and that we should follow and not precede the Germans in the process, no doubt inevitable, of deepening severity and violence. Every day that passes gives more shelter to the population of London and the big cities, and in a fortnight or so there will be far more comparatively safe refuges than now.

2. You ought to know what we were told about the condition of our small Expeditionary Force and their deficiencies in tanks, in trained trench-mortar detachments, and above all in heavy artillery. There will be a just criticism if it is found

that the heavy batteries are lacking. ... In 1919, after the
war, when I was S. of S. for War, I ordered a mass of heavy
cannon to be stored, oiled, and carefully kept; and I also
remember making in 1918 two 12-inch hows. at the request
of G.H.Q. to support their advance into Germany in 1919.
These were never used, but they were the last word at the
time. They are not easy things to lose. ... It seems to me most
vitally urgent, first, to see what there is in the cupboard,
secondly, to recondition it at once and make the ammunition of a modern character. Where this heavy stuff is concerned I may be able to help at the Admiralty, because of
course we are very comfortable in respect of everything
big. ...

3. You may like to know the principles I am following
in recasting the Naval programme of new construction. I propose to suspend work upon all except the first three or perhaps
four of the new battleships, and not to worry at the present
time about vessels that cannot come into action until 1942.
This decision must be reviewed in six months. It is by this
change that I get the spare capacity to help the Army. On the
other hand, I must make a great effort to bring forward the
smaller anti-U-boat fleet. Numbers are vital in this sphere. A
good many are coming forward in 1940, but not nearly enough
considering that we may have to face an attack by 200 or
300 U-boats in the summer of 1940. ...

4. With regard to the supply of the Army and its relation
to the Air Force, pardon me if I put my experience and
knowledge, which were bought, not taught, at your disposal.
The making by the Minister of Supply of a lay-out on the
basis of fifty-five divisions at the present time would not prejudice Air or Admiralty, because (a) the preliminary work of
securing the sites and building the factories will not for
many months require skilled labour; there are months of digging foundations, laying concrete, bricks and mortar, drain-
age, etc., for which the ordinary building-trade labourers
suffice; and (b) even if you could not realise a fifty-five-
division front by the twenty-fourth month because of other
claims, you could alter the time to the thirty-sixth month or
even later without affecting the scale. On the other hand, if he
does not make a big lay-out at the beginning there will be
vexatious delays when existing factories have to be enlarged.
Let him make his lay-out on the large scale, and protect the
needs of the Air Force and Army by varying the time factor.
A factory once set up need not be used until it is necessary,
but if it is not in existence you may be helpless if you need a
further effort. It is only when these big plants get into work
that you can achieve adequate results.

5. Up to the present (noon) no further losses by U-boats are reported—*i.e.*, thirty-six hours blank. Perhaps they have all gone away for the week-end! But I pass my time waiting to be hit. Nevertheless I am sure all will be well.

I also wrote to Dr. Burgin:

First Lord to Minister of Supply   10.ix.39
   In 1919, when I was at the War Office, I gave careful instructions to store and oil a mass of heavy artillery. Now it appears that this has been discovered. It seems to me the first thing you should do would be to get hold of this store and recondition them with the highest priority, as well as make the heavy ammunition. The Admiralty might be able to help with the heavy shells. Do not hesitate to ask.

The reply was most satisfactory:

Minister of Supply to First Lord   11.ix.39
   The preparation for use of the super-heavy artillery of which you write has been the lively concern of the War Office since the September crisis of 1938, and work actually started on the reconditioning of guns and mountings, both of the 9.2-inch guns and the 12-inch howitzers, last January.
   These equipments were put away in 1919 with considerable care, and as a result they are proving to be, on the whole, not in bad condition. Certain parts of them have however deteriorated and require renewal, and this work has been going on steadily throughout this year. We shall undoubtedly have some equipments ready during this month, and of course I am giving the work a high priority. . . .
   I am most grateful for your letter. You will be glad to see how much has already been done on the lines you recommend.

*   *   *

First Lord to Prime Minister   11.ix.39
   Everyone says there ought to be a Ministry of Shipping. The President of the Chamber of Shipping to-day pressed me strongly for it at our meeting with the shipowners. The President of the Board of Trade asked me to associate him with this request, which of course entails a curtailment of his own functions. I am sure there will be a strong Parliamentary demand. Moreover, the measure seems to me good on the merits. The functions are threefold:
(*a*) To secure the maximum fertility and economy of freights in accordance with the war policy of the Cabinet and the pressure of events.
(*b*) To provide and organise the very large shipbuilding pro-

gramme necessary as a safeguard against the heavy losses of tonnage we may expect from a U-boat attack apprehended in the summer of 1940. This should certainly include the study of concrete ships, thus relieving the strain on our steel during a period of steel stringency.

(c) The care, comfort, and encouragement of the merchant seamen who will have to go to sea repeatedly after having been torpedoed and saved. These merchant seamen are a most important and potentially formidable factor in this kind of war.

The President of the Board of Trade has already told you that two or three weeks would be required to disentangle the branches of his department which would go to make up the Ministry of Shipping from the parent office. It seems to me very wise to allow this period of transition. If a Minister were appointed and announced, he would gather to himself the necessary personal staff and take over gradually the branches of the Board of Trade which are concerned. It also seems important that the step of creating a Ministry of Shipping should be taken by the Government before pressure is applied in Parliament and from shipping circles, and before we are told that there is valid complaint against the existing system.

* * *

This Ministry was formed after a month's discussion and announced on October 13. Mr. Chamberlain selected Sir John Gilmour as its first head. The choice was criticised as being inadequate. Gilmour was a most agreeable Scotsman and a well-known Member of Parliament. He had held Cabinet office under Mr. Baldwin and Mr. Chamberlain. His health was declining, and he died within a few months of his appointment, and was succeeded by Mr. Ronald Cross.

First Lord to Prime Minister 15.ix.39

As I shall be away till Monday I give you my present thought on the main situation.

It seems to me most unlikely that the Germans will attempt an offensive in the West at this late season. ... Surely his obvious plan should be to press on through Poland, Hungary, and Roumania to the Black Sea, and it may be that he has some understanding with Russia by which she will take part of Poland and recover Bessarabia. ...

It would seem wise for Hitler to make good his Eastern connections and feeding-grounds during these winter months, and thus give his people the spectacle of repeated successes,

and the assurance of weakening our blockade. I do not therefore apprehend that he will attack in the West until he has
collected the easy spoils which await him in the East. None
the less, I am strongly of opinion that we should make every
preparation to defend ourselves in the West. Every effort
should be made to make Belgium take the necessary precautions in conjunction with the French and British Armies.
Meanwhile the French frontier behind Belgium should be
fortified night and day by every conceivable resource. In
particular the obstacles to tank attack, planting railway rails
upright, digging deep ditches, erecting concrete dolls, land-
mines in some parts and inundations all ready to let out in
others, etc., should be combined in a deep system of defence.
The attack of three or four German armoured divisions,
which has been so effective in Poland, can only be stopped by
physical obstacles defended by resolute troops and a powerful artillery. ... Without physical obstacles the attack of
armoured vehicles cannot be effectively resisted.

I am very glad to find that the mass of war-time artillery
which I stored in 1919 is all available. It comprises 32
12-inch, 145 9-inch, a large number of 8-inch, nearly 200
6-inch howitzers, together with very large quantities of ammunition ; in fact, it is the heavy artillery, not of our small
Expeditionary Force, but of a great army. No time should
be lost in bringing some of these guns into the field, so that
whatever else our troops will lack they will not suffer from
want of heavy artillery. ...

I hope you will consider carefully what I write to you. I
do so only in my desire to aid you in your responsibilities
and discharge my own.

The Prime Minister wrote back on the 16th, saying:

All your letters are carefully read and considered by me,
and if I have not replied to them it is only because I am
seeing you every day, and moreover because, as far as I have
been able to observe, your views and mine have very closely
coincided. ... To my mind the lesson of the Polish campaign
is the power of the Air Force, when it has obtained complete mastery in the air, to paralyse the operations of land
forces. ... Accordingly, as it seems to me, although I shall of
course await the report of the Land Forces Committee
before making up my mind, absolute priority ought to be
given to our plans for rapidly accelerating the strength of our
Air Force, and the extent of our effort on land should be
determined by our resources *after* we have provided for Air
Force extension.

First Lord to Prime Minister   18.ix.39

I am entirely with you in believing that Air Power stands foremost in our requirements, and indeed I sometimes think that it may be the ultimate path by which victory will be gained. On the other hand, the Air Ministry paper, which I have just been studying, seems to peg out vast and vague claims which are not at present substantiated, and which, if accorded absolute priority, would overlay other indispensable forms of war effort. I am preparing a note upon this paper, and will only quote one figure which struck me in it.

If the aircraft industry with its present 360,000 men can produce nearly 1,000 machines a month, it seemes extraordinary that 1,050,000 men should be required for a monthly output of 2,000. One would expect a very large 'reduction on taking a quantity', especially if mass-production is used. I cannot believe the Germans will be using anything like 1,000,000 men to produce 2,000 machines a month. While, broadly speaking, I should accept an output of 2,000 machines a month as the objective, I am not at present convinced that it would make anything like so large a demand upon our war-making capacity as is implied in this paper.

The reason why I am anxious that the Army should be planned upon a fifty- or fifty-five-division scale is that I doubt whether the French would acquiesce in a division of effort which gave us the sea and air and left them to pay almost the whole blood-tax on land. Such an arrangement would certainly be agreeable to us; but I do not like the idea of our having to continue the war single-handed.

There are great dangers in giving absolute priority to any department. In the late war the Admiralty used their priority arbitrarily and selfishly, especially in the last year, when they were overwhelmingly strong, and had the American Navy added to them. I am every day restraining such tendencies in the common interest.

As I mentioned in my first letter to you, the lay-out of the shell, gun, and filling factories, and the provision for explosives and steel, does not compete directly while the plants are being made with the quite different class of labour required for aeroplane production. It is a question of clever dovetailing. The provision of mechanical vehicles, on the other hand, is directly competitive, and must be carefully adjusted. It would be wise to bring the Army munitions plants into existence on a large scale, and then to let them begin to eat only as our resources allow and the character of the war requires. The time factor is the regulator which you would

T—s.w.w. –2—c

apply according to circumstances. If however the plants are not begun now, you will no longer have the option.

I thought it would be a wise thing to state to the French our intention to work up to an army of fifty or fifty-five divisions. But whether this could be reached at the twenty-fourth month or at the thirtieth or fortieth month should certainly be kept fluid.

At the end of the late war we had about ninety divisions in all theatres, and we were producing aircraft at the rate of 2,000 a month, as well as maintaining a Navy very much larger than was needed, and far larger than our present plans contemplate. I do not therefore feel that fifty or fifty-five divisions and 2,000 aircraft per month are incompatible aims, although of course the modern divisions and modern aircraft represent a much higher industrial effort—everything having become so much more complicated.

First Lord to Prime Minister   21.IX.39

I wonder if you would consider having an occasional meeting of the War Cabinet Ministers to talk among themselves without either secretaries or military experts. I am not satisfied that the large issues are being effectively discussed in our formal sessions. We have been constituted the responsible Ministers for the conduct of the war, and I am sure it would be in the public interest if we met as a body from time to time. Much is being thrown upon the Chiefs of Staff which falls outside the professional sphere. We have had the advantage of many valuable and illuminating reports from them. But I venture to represent to you that we ought sometimes to discuss the general position alone. I do not feel that we are getting to the root of the matter on many points.

I have not spoken to any colleague about this, and have no idea what their opinions are. I give you my own, as in duty bound.

*   *   *

On September 24 I wrote to the Chancellor of the Exchequer:

I am thinking a great deal about you and your problem, as one who has been through the Exchequer mill. I look forward to a severe Budget based upon the broad masses of the well-to-do. But I think you ought to couple with this a strong anti-waste campaign. Judging by the small results achieved for our present gigantic expenditure, I think there never was so little '*value for money*' as what is going on now. In 1918 we had a lot of unpleasant regulations in force for the prevention of waste, which after all was part of the winning of victory. Surely you ought to make a strong feature of this in your Wednesday's statement. An effort should be made to tell people the things they ought to try to avoid doing. This is by no means a doctrine of abstention from expenditure. Everything should be eaten up prudently, even luxuries, *so long as no more are created.* Take stationery, for example— this should be regulated at once in all departments. Envelopes should be pasted up and re-directed again and again. Although this seems a small thing, it teaches every official— and we now have millions of them—to think of saving.

An active 'saving campaign' was inculcated at the Front in 1918, and people began to take a pride in it, and look upon it as part of the show. Why not inculcate these ideas in the B.E.F. from the outset in all zones not actually under fire?

I am trying to prune the Admiralty of large schemes of naval improvement which cannot operate till after 1941, or even in some cases (when they cannot operate) till after the end of 1940. Beware lest these fortifications people and other departmentals do not consume our strength upon long-scale developments which cannot mature till after the climax which settles our fate.

I see the departments full of loose fat, following on undue starvation. It would be much better from your point of view to come along with your alguazils *as critics* upon wasteful exhibitions, rather than delaying action. Don't hamper departments acting in a time of crisis ; give them the responsibility ; but call them swiftly to account for any failure in thrift.

I hope you will not mind me writing to you upon this subject, because I feel just as strongly about the husbanding of the money-powers as I do about the war effort, of which it is indeed an integral part. In all these matters you can count on my support, and also, as the head of a spending department, upon my submission to searching superintendence.

*   *   *

In every war in which the Royal Navy has claimed the command of the seas it has had to pay the price of exposing immense targets to the enemy. The privateer, the raiding cruiser, and above all the U-boat, have in all the varying forms of war exacted a heavy toll upon the life-lines of our commerce and food-supply. A prime function of defence has therefore always been imposed upon us. From this fact the danger arises of our being driven or subsiding into a defensive naval strategy and habit of mind. Modern developments have aggravated this tendency. In the two Great Wars, during parts of which I was responsible for the control of the Admiralty, I always sought to rupture this defensive obsession by searching for forms of counter-offensive. To make the enemy wonder where he is going to be hit next may bring immeasurable relief to the process of shepherding hundreds of convoys and thousands of merchant-men safely into port. In the First World War I hoped to find in the Dardanelles, and later in an attack upon Borkum and other Frisian islands, the means of regaining the initiative and forcing the weaker naval Power to study his own problems rather than ours. Called to the Admiralty again in 1939, and as soon as im-mediate needs were dealt with and perils warded off, I could not rest content with the policy of 'Convoy and blockade'. I sought earnestly for a way of attacking Germany by naval means.

First and foremost gleamed the Baltic. The command of the Baltic by a British fleet carried with it possibly decisive gains. Scandinavia, freed from the menace of German invasion, would thereby naturally be drawn into our system of war trade, if not indeed into actual co-belligerency. A British fleet in mastery of the Baltic would hold out a hand to Russia in a manner likely to be decisive upon the whole Soviet policy and strategy. These facts were not disputed among responsible and well-informed men. The command of the Baltic was the obvious supreme prize, not only for the Royal Navy but for Britain. Could it be won? In this new war the German Navy was no obstacle. Our superiority in heavy ships made us eager to engage them wher-ever and whenever there was opportunity. Minefields could be swept by the stronger naval Power. The U-boats imposed no veto upon a fleet guarded by efficient flotillas. But now, instead of the powerful German Navy of 1914 and 1915, there was the Air Arm, formidable, unmeasured, and certainly increasing in im-portance with every month that passed.

If two or three years earlier it had been possible to make an alliance with Soviet Russia, this might have been implemented by a British battle squadron joined to the Russian Fleet and based on Cronstadt. I commended this to my circle of friends at the time. Whether such an arrangement was ever within the bounds of action cannot be known. It was certainly one way of restraining Germany ; but there were also easier methods which were not taken. Now in the autumn of 1939 Russia was an adverse neutral, balancing between antagonism and actual war. Sweden had several suitable harbours on which a British fleet could be based. But Sweden could not be expected to expose herself to invasion by Germany. Without the command of the Baltic we could not ask for a Swedish harbour. Without a Swedish harbour we could not have the command of the Baltic. Here was a deadlock in strategic thought. Was it possible to break it? It is always right to probe. During the war, as will be seen, I forced long Staff studies of various operations, as the result of which I was usually convinced that they were better left alone, or else that they could not be fitted in with the general conduct of the struggle. Of these the first was the Baltic domination.

*　　　*　　　*

On the fourth day after I reached the Admiralty I asked that a plan for forcing a passage into the Baltic should be prepared by the Naval Staff. The Plans Division replied quickly that Italy and Japan must be neutral; that the threat of air attack appeared prohibitive; but that apart from this the operation justified detailed planning, and should, if judged practicable, be carried out in March 1940, or earlier. Meanwhile I had long talks with the Director of Naval Construction, Sir Stanley Goodall, one of my friends from 1911–12, who was immediately captivated by the idea. I named the plan 'Catherine', after Catherine the Great, because Russia lay in the background of my thought. On September 12 I was able to write a detailed minute to the authorities concerned.

Admiral Pound replied on the 20th that success would depend on Russia not joining Germany and on the assurance of co-operation by Norway and Sweden; and that we must be able to win the war against any probable combination of Powers without counting upon whatever force was sent into the Baltic. He was all for the exploration. On September 21 he agreed that Admiral of the Fleet the Earl of Cork and Orrery, an officer of the highest attainments and distinction, should come to work at the Admiralty, with quarters and a nucleus staff, and all information necessary for exploring and planning the Baltic offensive project. There was an apt precedent for this in the previous war, when I had brought back the famous Admiral 'Tug' Wilson to the Admiralty for special duties of this kind with the full agreement of Lord Fisher; and there are several instances in this war where, in an easy and friendly manner, large issues of this kind were tested without any resentment being felt by the Chiefs of Staff concerned.

Both Lord Cork's ideas and mine rested upon the construction of capital ships specially adapted to withstand air and torpedo attack. As is seen from the minute of September 12, I wished to convert two or three ships of the *Royal Sovereign* class for action inshore or in narrow waters by giving them super-bulges against torpedoes and strong armour-plated decks against air-bombs. For this I was prepared to sacrifice one or even two turrets and seven or eight knots speed. Quite apart from the Baltic, this would give us facilities for offensive action both off the enemy's North Sea coast and even more in the Mediterranean. Nothing could be ready before the late spring of 1940, even if the earliest estimates of the naval construction and the dockyards were realised. On this basis therefore we proceeded.

On the 26th Lord Cork presented his preliminary appreciation, based of course on a purely military study of the problem. He considered the operation, which he would of course have commanded, perfectly feasible but hazardous. He asked for a margin of at least 30 per cent. over the German Fleet on account of expected losses in the passage. If we were to act in 1940 the assembly of the fleet and all necessary training must be complete by the middle of February. Time did not therefore permit the deck-armouring and side-blistering of the *Royal Sovereigns* on which I counted. Here was another deadlock. Still, if this kind of thing goes working on one may get into position—maybe a year later—to act. But in war, as in life, all other things are moving too. If one can plan calmly with a year or two in hand better solutions are open.

I had strong support in all this from the Deputy Chief of Staff, Admiral Tom Phillips (who perished in the *Prince of Wales* at the end of 1941 near Singapore), and from Admiral Fraser, the Controller and Third Sea Lord. He advised the addition to the assault fleet of the four fast merchant ships of the Glen Line, which were to play their part in other events.

* * *

One of my first duties at the Admiralty was to examine the existing programmes of new construction and war expansion which had come into force on the outbreak.

At any given moment there are at least four successive annual programmes running at the Admiralty. In 1936 and 1937 five new battleships had been laid down which would come into service in 1940 and 1941. Four more battleships had been authorised by Parliament in 1938 and 1939, which could not be finished for five or six years from the date of order. Nineteen cruisers were in various stages of construction. The constructive genius and commanding reputation of the Royal Navy in design had been distorted and hampered by the treaty restrictions for twenty years. All our cruisers were the result of trying to conform to treaty limitations and 'gentleman's agreements'. In peace-time vessels had thus been built to keep up the strength of the Navy from year to year amid political difficulties. In war-time a definite tactical object must inspire all construction. I greatly desired to build a few 14,000-ton cruisers carrying 9·2-inch guns, with good armour against 8-inch projectiles, wide radius of action, and superior speed to any existing *Deutschland* or other German cruiser. Hitherto the treaty restrictions had prevented such a policy. Now that we were free from them, the hard priorities of war interposed an equally decisive veto on such long-term plans.

Destroyers were our most urgent need, and also our worst feature. None had been included in the 1938 programme, but sixteen had been ordered in 1939. In all, thirty-two of these indispensable craft were in the yards, and only nine could be delivered before the end of 1940. The irresistible tendency to make each successive flotilla an improvement upon the last had lengthened the time of building to nearer three than two years. Naturally the Navy liked to have vessels capable of riding out the Atlantic swell and large enough to carry all the modern improvements in gunnery, and especially anti-aircraft defence. It is evident that along this line of solid argument a point is soon reached where one is no longer building a destroyer but a small cruiser. The displacement approaches or even exceeds 2,000 tons, and a crew of more than two hundred sail the seas in these unarmoured ships, themselves an easy prey to any regular cruiser. The destroyer is the chief weapon against the U-boat, but as it grows ever larger it becomes itself a worthwhile target. The line is passed where the hunter becomes the hunted. We could not have too many destroyers, but their perpetual improvements and growth imposed severe limitation on the numbers the yards could build, and deadly delay in completion.

On the other hand, there are seldom less than two thousand British merchant ships at sea, and the sailings in and out of our home ports amounted each week to several hundreds of ocean-going vessels and several thousands of coastwise traders. To bring the convoy system into play, to patrol the Narrow Seas, to guard the hundreds of ports of the British Isles, to serve our bases all over the world, to protect the minesweepers in their ceaseless task, all required an immense multiplication of small armed vessels. Numbers and speed of construction were the dominating conditions.

It was my duty to readjust our programmes to the need of the hour and to enforce the largest possible expansion of anti-U-boat vessels. For this purpose two principles were laid down. Firstly, the long-term programme should be either stopped or severely delayed, thus concentrating labour and materials upon what we could get in the first year or year and a half. Secondly, new types of anti-submarine craft must be devised which were good enough for work on the approaches to the Island, thus setting free our larger destroyers for more distant duties.

On all these questions I addressed a series of minutes to my naval colleagues:

> *Having regard to the U-boat menace, which must be ex-pected to renew itself on a much larger scale towards the end of 1940, the type of destroyer to be constructed must aim at numbers and celerity of construction rather than size and power. It ought to be possible to design destroyers which can be completed in under a year, in which case fifty at least should be begun forthwith. I am well aware of the need of a proportion of flotilla leaders and large destroyers capable of ocean service, but the arrival in our fleets of fifty destroyers of the medium emergency type I am contemplating would liberate all larger vessels for ocean work and for combat.*

The usual conflict between long-term and short-term policy rises to intensity in war. I prescribed that all work likely to compete with essential construction should be stopped on large vessels which could not come into service before the end of 1940, and that the multiplication of our anti-submarine fleets must be effected by types capable of being built within twelve months, or, if possible, eight. For the first type we revived the name corvette. Orders for fifty-eight of these had been placed shortly before the outbreak of war, but none were yet laid down. Later and improved vessels of a similar type, ordered in 1940, were called frigates. Besides this, a great number of small craft of many kinds, particularly trawlers, had to be converted with the utmost dispatch and fitted with guns, depth-charges, and Asdics ; motor launches of new Admiralty design were also required in large numbers for coastal work. Orders were placed to the limit of our shipbuilding resources, including those of Canada. Even so we did not achieve all that we hoped, and delays arose which were inevitable under the prevailing conditions and which caused the deliveries from the shipyards to fall considerably short of our expectations.

*　　*　　*

Eventually my view about Baltic strategy and battleship reconstruction prevailed in the protracted discussions. The designs were made and the orders were given. However, one reason after another was advanced, some of them well-founded, for not putting the work in hand. The *Royal Sovereigns*, it was said, might be needed for convoy in case the German pocket-battleships or 8-inch-gun cruisers broke loose. It was represented that the scheme involved unacceptable interference with other vital work, and a plausible case could be shown for alternative priorities for our labour and armour. I deeply regretted that I was never able to achieve my conception of a squadron of very heavily deck-armoured ships of no more than fifteen knots, bristling with anti-aircraft guns and capable of withstanding to a degree not enjoyed by any other vessel afloat both air and under-water attack. When in 1941 and 1942 the defence and succouring of Malta became so vital, when we had every need to bombard Italian ports, and above all Tripoli, others felt the need as much as I. It was then too late.

Throughout the war the *Royal Sovereigns* remained an expense and an anxiety. They had none of them been rebuilt like their sisters the *Queen Elizabeths*, and when, as will be seen in due course, the possibility of bringing them into action against the Japanese fleet which entered the Indian Ocean in April 1942 presented itself the only thought of the Admiral on the spot, of Admiral Pound, and the Minister of Defence, was to put as many thousands of miles as possible between them and the enemy in the shortest possible time.

*　　*　　*

One of the first steps I took on taking charge of the Admiralty and becoming a member of the War Cabinet was to form a statistical department of my own. For this purpose I relied on Professor Lindemann, my friend and confidant of so many years. Together we had formed our views and estimates about the whole story. I now installed him at the Admiralty with half a dozen statisticians and economists whom we could trust to pay no attention to anything but realities. This group of capable men, with access to all official information, was able, under Lindemann's guidance, to present me continually with tables and diagrams, illustrating the whole war so far as it came within our knowledge. They examined and analysed with relentless pertinacity all the departmental papers which were circulated to the War Cabinet, and also pursued all the inquiries which I wished to make myself.

At this time there was no general Government statistical organisation. Each department presented its tale on its own figures and data. The Air Ministry counted one way, the War Office another. The Ministry of Supply and the Board of Trade, though meaning the same thing, talked different dialects. This led sometimes to misunderstandings and waste of time when some point or other came to a crunch in the Cabinet. I had however from the beginning my own sure, steady source of information, every part of which was integrally related to all the rest. Although at first this covered only a portion of the field, it was most helpful to me in forming a just and comprehensible view of the innumerable facts and figures which flowed out upon us.

CHAPTER 5

The Front in France

Movement of the B.E.F. to France – Fortification of the Belgian Frontier – Advantages of Aggression – Belgian Neutrality – France and the Offensive – The Maginot Line – Accepted Power of the Defensive – Unattractive French Alternatives – Estimates of the British Chiefs of Staff – Hitler's Error – Relative Strength in the West – Possible German Lines of Attack – Opinion of the British Chiefs of Staff; their Paper of September 18, 1939 – Gamelin Develops Plan D – Instruction No. 8 – Meeting of Allied Supreme Council in Paris on November 17 – Plan D Adopted – Extension of Plan D to Holland.

Immediately upon the outbreak our Expeditionary Army began to move to France. Whereas before the previous war at least three years had been spent in making the preparations, it was not till the spring of 1938 that the War Office set up a special section for this purpose. Two serious new factors were now present. First, the equipment and organisation of a modern army was far less simple than in 1914. Every division had mechanical transport, was more numerous, and had a much higher proportion of non-fighting elements. Secondly, the extravagant fear of air attack on the troopships and landing-ports led the War Office to use only the southern French harbours and St. Nazaire, which became the principal base. This lengthened the communications of the Army, and in consequence retarded the arrival, deployment, and maintenance of the British troops, and consumed profuse additional numbers along the route.*

Oddly enough, it had not been decided before war on which sector of the front our troops should be deployed, but the strong presumption was that it would be south of Lille; and this was confirmed on September 22. By mid-October four British divisions, formed into two Army Corps of professional quality, were

---

* Advance parties of the British Expeditionary Force began to land in France on September 4. The 1st Corps were ashore by September 19, and the 2nd Corps by October 3. General Headquarters (G.H.Q.) was set up initially at Le Mans on September 15. The principal movement of troops was made through Cherbourg, with vehicles and stores through **Brest** and Nantes, and assembly-points at Le Mans and Laval.

in their stations along the Franco-Belgian frontier. This involved a road-and-rail movement of 250 miles from the remote ports which had been chosen for landing. Three infantry brigades which arrived separately during October and November were formed into the 5th Division in December 1939. The 48th Division went out in January 1940, followed by the 50th and 51st Divisions in February, and the 42nd and 44th in March, making a total of ten. As our numbers grew we took over more line. We were not of course at any point in contact with the enemy.

When the B.E.F. reached their prescribed positions they found ready-prepared a fairly complete artificial anti-tank ditch along the front line, and every thousand yards or so was a large and very visible pillbox giving enfilade fire along the ditch for machine and anti-tank guns. There was also a continuous belt of wire. Much of the work of our troops during this strange autumn and winter was directed to improving the French-made defences and organising a kind of Siegfried Line. In spite of frost progress was rapid. Air photographs showed the rate at which the Germans were extending their own Siegfried Line northwards from the Moselle. Despite the many advantages they enjoyed in home resources and forced labour, we seemed to be keeping pace with them. By the time of the May offensive, 1940, our troops had completed 400 new pillboxes. Forty miles of revetted anti-tank ditch had been dug and great quantities of wire spread. Immense demands were made by the long line of communications stretching back to Nantes. Large base installations were created, roads improved, a hundred miles of broad-gauge railway-line laid, an extensive system of buried cable dug in, and several tunnelled headquarters for the corps and Army commands almost completed. Nearly fifty new airfields and satellites were developed or improved with runways, involving over 50,000 tons of concrete.

On all these tasks the Army laboured industriously, and to vary their experiences moved brigades by rotation to a sector of the French front in contact with the enemy near Metz, where there was at least some patrol activity. All the rest of the time was spent by our troops in training. This was indeed necessary. A far lower scale of preparation had been reached when war broke out than that attained by Sir John French's Army a quarter of a century before. For several years no considerable exercise with troops had been held at home. The Regular Army was

20,000 short of establishment, including 5,000 officers, and under the Cardwell system, which had to provide for the defence of India, the greater part of this fell upon the home units, which in consequence became hardly more than cadres. The little-considered, though well-meant, doubling of the Territorial Army in March 1939, and the creation of the Militia in May of that year, both involved drawing heavily upon the Regular Army for instructors. The winter months in France were turned to good account, and every kind of training programme was woven into the prime work of fortification. It is certain that our Army advanced markedly in efficiency during the breathing-space which was granted it, and in spite of exacting toils and the absence of any kind of action its morale and spirit grew.

Behind our front immense masses of stores and ammunition were accumulated in the depots all along the communications. Ten days' supply was gathered between the Seine and the Somme, *and seven days' additional north of the Somme*. This latter provision saved the Army after the German break-through. Gradually, in view of the prevailing tranquillity, other ports north of Havre were brought into use in succession. Dieppe became a hospital base, Fécamp was concerned with ammunition ; and in the end we were making use in all of thirteen French harbours.

* * *

The advantage which a Government bound by no law or treaty has over countries which derive their war-impulse only after the criminal has struck, and have to plan accordingly, cannot be measured. It is enormous. On the other hand, unless the victory of the aggressors is absolute and final there may be some day a reckoning. Hitler, unhampered by any restraint except that of superior force, could strike when and where he chose ; but the two Western democracies could not violate Belgium's neutrality. The most they could do was to be ready to come to the rescue when called upon by the Belgians, and it was probable that this would never happen until it was too late. Of course, if British and French policy during the five years preceding the war had been of a manly and resolute character, within the sanctity of treaties and the approval of the League of Nations, Belgium might have adhered to her old allies and allowed a common front to be formed. This would have brought immense security, and might perhaps have averted the disasters which were to come.

Such an alliance properly organised would have erected a shield along the Belgian frontier to the sea against that terrible turning movement which had nearly compassed our destruction in 1914 and was to play its part in the ruin of France in 1940. It would also have opened the possibility of a rapid advance from Belgium into the heart-centre of German industry in the Ruhr, and thus added a powerful deterrent upon German aggression. At the worst Belgium could have suffered no harder fate than actually befell her. When we recall the aloofness of the United States ; Mr. Ramsay MacDonald's campaign for the disarmament of France ; the repeated rebuffs and humiliations which we had accepted in the various German breaches of the Disarmament Clauses of the Treaty ; our submission to the German violation of the Rhineland ; our acquiescence in the absorption of Austria ; our pact at Munich and acceptance of the German occupation of Prague—when we recall all this, no man in Britain or France who in those years was responsible for public action has a right to blame Belgium. In a period of vacillation and appeasement the Belgians clung to neutrality, and vainly comforted themselves with the belief that they could hold the German invader on their fortified frontiers until the British and French Armies could come to their aid.

* * *

In 1914 the spirit of the French Army and nation, burning from sire to son since 1870, was vehemently offensive. Their doctrine was that the numerically weaker Power could only meet invasion by the counter-offensive, not only strategic but tactical at every point. At the beginning the French, with their blue tunics and red trousers, marched forward while their bands played the Marseillaise. Wherever this happened the Germans, although invading, sat down and fired upon them with devastating effect. The apostle of the offensive creed, Colonel Grandmaison, had perished in the forefront of the battle for his country and his theme. I have explained in *The World Crisis* why the power of the defensive was predominant from 1914 to 1916 or 1917. The magazine rifle, which we ourselves had seen used with great effect by handfuls of Boers in the South African War, could take a heavy if not decisive toll from troops advancing across the open. Besides this there were the ever-multiplying machine-guns.

Then had come the great battles of the artillery. An area was pulverised by hundreds and presently by thousands of guns. But if after heroic sacrifices the French and British advanced together against the strongly-entrenched Germans, successive lines of fortifications confronted them ; and the crater-fields which their bombardment had created to quell the first lines of the enemy became a decisive obstacle to their further progress, even when they were successful. The only conclusion to be drawn from these hard experiences was that the defensive was master. Moreover, in the quarter of a century that had passed the fire-power of weapons had enormously increased. But this cut both ways ; as will later be apparent.

It was now a very different France from that which had hurled itself upon its ancient foe in August 1914. The spirit of *revanche* had exhausted its mission and itself in victory. The chiefs who had nursed it were long dead. The French people had undergone the frightful slaughter of a million and a half of their manhood. Offensive action was associated in the great majority of French minds with the initial failures of the French onslaught of 1914, with General Nivelle's repulse in 1917, with the long agonies of the Somme and Passchendaele, and above all with the sense that the fire-power of modern weapons was devastating to the attacker. Neither in France nor in Britain had there been any effective comprehension of the consequences of the new fact that armoured vehicles could be made capable of withstanding artillery fire, and could advance a hundred miles a day. An illuminating book on this subject, published some years before by a Commander de Gaulle, had met with no response. The authority of the aged Marshal Pétain in the Conseil Supérieur de la Guerre had weighed heavily upon French military thought in closing the door to new ideas, and especially in discouraging what had been quaintly called 'offensive weapons'.

In the after-light the policy of the Maginot Line has often been condemned. It certainly engendered a defensive mentality. Yet it is always a wise precaution in defending a frontier of hundreds of miles to bar off as much as possible by fortifications, and thus economise in the use of troops in sedentary *rôles* and 'canalise' potential invasion. Properly used in the French scheme of war, the Maginot Line would have been of immense service to France. It could have been viewed as presenting a long succession of invaluable sally-ports, and above all as blocking off large sections of the front as a means of accumulating the general reserves or 'mass of manœuvre'. Having regard to the disparity of the population of France to that of Germany, the Maginot Line must be regarded as a wise and prudent measure. Indeed, it was extraordinary that it should not have been carried forward at least along the river Meuse. It could then have served as a trusty shield, freeing a heavy, sharp, offensive French sword. But Marshal Pétain had opposed this extension. He held strongly that the Ardennes could be ruled out as a channel of invasion on account of the nature of the ground. Ruled out accordingly it was. The offensive conceptions of the Maginot Line were explained to me by General Giraud when I visited Metz in 1937. They were however not carried into effect, and the Line not only absorbed very large numbers of highly-trained regular soldiers and technicians, but exercised an enervating effect both upon military strategy and national vigilance.

The new air-power was justly esteemed a revolutionary factor in all operations. Considering the comparatively small numbers of aircraft available on either side at this time, its effects were even exaggerated, and were held in the main to favour the defensive by hampering the concentrations and communications of great armies once launched in attack. Even the period of the French mobilisation was regarded by the French High Command as most critical on account of the possible destruction of railway centres, although the numbers of German aircraft, like those of the Allies, were far too few for such a task. These thoughts expressed by Air Chiefs followed correct lines, and were justified in the later years of the war, when the air strength had grown ten- or twenty-fold. At the outbreak they were premature.

*　　*　　*

It is a joke in Britain to say that the War Office is always preparing for the last war. But this is probably true of other departments and of other countries, and it was certainly true of the French Army. I also rested under the impression of the superior power of the defensive provided it were actively conducted. I had neither the responsibility nor the continuous information to make a new measurement. I knew that the carnage of the previous war had bitten deeply into the soul of the French people. The Germans had been given the time to build the Siegfried Line. How frightful to hurl the remaining manhood of France against this wall of fire and concrete! Elsewhere I have printed one kind of long-term method (called Cultivator No. 6) by which I then thought the fire-power of the defensive could be overcome. But in my mind's outlook in the opening months of this Second World War I did not dissent from the general view about the defensive, and I believed that anti-tank obstacles and field guns, cleverly posted and with suitable ammunition, could frustrate or break up tanks except in darkness or fog, real or artificial.

In the problems which the Almighty sets his humble servants things hardly ever happen the same way twice over, or if they seem to do so there is some variant which stultifies undue generalisation. The human mind, except when guided by extraordinary genius, cannot surmount the established conclusions amid which it has been reared. Yet we are to see, after eight months of inactivity on both sides, the Hitler inrush of a vast offensive, led by spear-point masses of cannon-proof or heavily-armoured vehicles, breaking up all defensive opposition, and for the first time for centuries, and even perhaps since the invention of gunpowder, making artillery for a while almost impotent on the battlefield. We are also to see that the increase of fire-power made the actual battles less bloody by enabling the necessary ground to be held with very small numbers of men, thus offering a far smaller human target.

*   *   *

No frontier has ever received the same strategic attention and experiment as that which stretches through the Low Countries between France and Germany. Every aspect of the ground, its heights and its waterways, has been studied for centuries in the light of the latest campaign by all the generals and military colleges in Western Europe. At this period there were two lines to which the Allies could advance if Belgium were invaded by Germany and they chose to come to her succour, or which they could occupy by a well-planned secret and sudden scheme, if invited by Belgium. The first of these lines was what may be called the line of the Scheldt. This was no great march from the French frontier and involved little serious risk. At the worst it would do no harm to hold it as a 'false front'. At the best it might be built up according to events. The second line was far more ambitious. It followed the Meuse through Givet, Dinant, and Namur by Louvain to Antwerp. If this adventurous line was seized by the Allies and held in hard battles the

German right-handed swing of invasion would be heavily checked; and if their armies were proved inferior it would be an admirable prelude to the entry and control of the vital centre of Germany's munitions production in the Ruhr.

Since the case of an advance through Belgium without Belgian consent was excluded on grounds of international morality, there only remained an advance from the common Franco-German frontier. An attack due eastwards across the Rhine north and south of Strasbourg, opened mainly into the Black Forest, which, like the Ardennes, was at that time regarded as bad ground for offensive operations. There was however the question of an advance from the front Strasbourg-Metz north-eastward into the Palatinate. Such an advance, with its right on the Rhine, might gain the control of that river as far north as Coblenz or Cologne. This led into good fighting country; and these possibilities, with many variants, had been a part of the war-games in the Staff Colleges of Western Europe for a good many years. In this sector however the Siegfried Line, with its well-built concrete pillboxes mutually supporting one another and organised in depth with masses of wire, was in September 1939 already formidable. The earliest date at which the French could have mounted a big attack was perhaps at the end of the third week of September. But by that time the Polish campaign had ended. By mid-October the Germans had seventy divisions on the Western Front. The fleeting French numerical superiority in the West was passing. A French offensive from their eastern frontier would have denuded their far more vital northern front. Even if an initial success had been gained by the French armies at the outset, within a month they would have had extreme difficulty in maintaining their conquests in the east, and would have been exposed to the whole force of the German counter-stroke to the north.

This is the answer to the question 'Why remain passive till Poland was destroyed?' But this battle had been lost some years before. In 1938 there was a good chance of victory while Czechoslovakia still existed. In 1936 there could have been no effective opposition. In 1933 a rescript from Geneva would have procured bloodless compliance. General Gamelin cannot be the only one to blame because in 1939 he did not run the risks which had so enormously increased since the previous crises, from which both the French and the British Governments had recoiled.

The British Chiefs of Staff Committee estimated that the Germans had by September 18 mobilised at least 116 divisions of all classes, distributed as follows: Western front, 42 divisions; Central Germany, 16 divisions; Eastern front, 58 divisions. We now know from enemy records that this estimate was almost exactly correct. Germany had in all from 108 to 117 divisions. Poland was attacked by 58 of the most matured. There remained 50 or 60 divisions of varying quality. Of these, along the Western front from Aix-la-Chapelle to the Swiss frontier there stood 42 German divisions (14 active, 25 reserve, and 3 Landwehr). The German armour was either engaged in Poland or had not yet come into being, and the great flow of tanks from the factories had hardly begun. The British Expeditionary Force was no more than a symbolic contribution. It was able to deploy two divisions by the first and two more by the second week in October. In spite of the enormous improvement since Munich in their relative strength, the German High Command regarded their situation in the West while Poland was unconquered with profound anxiety, and only Hitler's despotic authority, will-power, and five-times-vindicated political judgment about the unwillingness of France and Great Britain to fight induced or compelled them to run what they deemed an unjustified risk.

Hitler was sure that the French political system was rotten to the core, and that it had infected the French Army. He knew the power of the Communists in France, and that it would be used to weaken or paralyse action once Ribbentrop and Molotov had come to terms and Moscow had denounced the French and British Governments for entering upon a capitalist and imperialist war. He was convinced that Britain was pacifist and degenerate. In his view, though Mr. Chamberlain and M. Daladier had been brought to the point of declaring war by a bellicose minority in England, they would both wage as little of it as they could, and once Poland had been crushed would accept the accomplished fact, as they had done a year before in the case of Czechoslovakia. On the repeated occasions which have been set forth Hitler's instinct had been proved right and the arguments and fears of his generals wrong. He did not understand the profound change which takes place in Great Britain and throughout the British Empire once the signal for war has been given; nor how those who have been the most strenuous for peace turn overnight into untiring toilers for victory. He could not comprehend the mental or spiritual force of our Island people, who, however much opposed to war or military preparation, had through the centuries come to regard victory as their birthright. In any case, the British Army could be no factor at the outset, and he was certain that the French nation had not thrown its heart into the war. This was indeed true. He had his way, and his orders were obeyed.

*   *   *

It was thought by our officers that when Germany had completely defeated the Polish Army she would have to keep in Poland some 15 divisions, of which a large proportion might be of low category. If she had any doubts about the Russian pact this total might have to be increased to upwards of 30 divisions in the East. On the least favourable assumption Germany would therefore be able to draw over 40 divisions from the Eastern front, making 100 divisions available for the West. By that time the French would have mobilised 72 divisions in France, in addition to fortress troops equivalent to 12 or 14 divisions, and there would be 4 divisions of the British Expeditionary Force. Twelve French divisions would be required to watch the Italian frontier, making 76 against Germany. The enemy would thus have a superiority of four to three over the Allies, and might also be expected to form additional reserve divisions, bringing this total up to 130 in the near future. Against this the French had 14 additional divisions in North Africa, some of which could be drawn upon, and whatever further forces Great Britain could gradually supply.

In air-power our Chiefs of Staff estimated that Germany could concentrate, after the destruction of Poland, over 2,000 bombers in the West as against a combined Franco-British total of 950.* It was therefore clear that once Hitler had disposed of Poland he would be far more powerful on the ground and in the air than the British and French combined. There could therefore be no question of a French offensive against Germany. What then were the probabilities of a German offensive against France?

There were of course three methods open. First, invasion through Switzerland. This might turn the southern flank of the Maginot Line, but had many geographical and strategic difficulties. Secondly, invasion of France across the common frontier.

* Actually the German bomber strength at that date was 1,546.

This appeared unlikely, as the German Army was not believed to be fully equipped or armed for a heavy attack on the Maginot Line. And, thirdly, invasion of France through Holland and Belgium. This would turn the Maginot Line, and would not entail the losses likely to be sustained in a frontal attack against permanent fortifications. The Chiefs of Staff estimated that for this attack Germany would require to bring from the Eastern front twenty-nine divisions for the initial phase, with fourteen echelonned behind, as reinforcements to her troops already in the West. Such a movement could not be completed and the attack mounted with full artillery support under three weeks, and its preparation should be discernible by us a fortnight before the blow fell. It would be late in the year for the Germans to undertake so great an operation; but the possibility could not be excluded.

We should of course try to retard the German movement from east to west by air attack upon the communications and concentration areas. Thus a preliminary air battle to reduce or eliminate the Allied air forces by attacks on airfields and aircraft factories might be expected, and so far as England was concerned would not be unwelcome. Our next task would be to deal with the German advance through the Low Countries. We could not meet their attack so far forward as Holland, but it would be in the Allied interest to stem it, if possible, in Belgium. 'We understand,' wrote the Chiefs of Staff, 'that the French idea is that, provided the Belgians are still holding out on the Meuse, the French and British Armies should occupy the line Givet–Namur, the British Expeditionary Force operating on the left. *We consider it would be unsound to adopt this plan unless plans are concerted with the Belgians for the occupation of this line in sufficient time before the Germans advance. ... Unless the present Belgian attitude alters and plans can be prepared for early occupation of the Givet–Namur* [also called Meuse–Antwerp] *line, we are strongly of opinion that the German advance should be met in prepared positions on the French frontier.*' In this case it would of course be necessary to bomb Belgian and Dutch towns and railway centres used or occupied by German troops.

The subsequent history of this important issue must be recorded. It was brought before the War Cabinet on September 20, and after a brief discussion was remitted to the Supreme War Council. In due course the Supreme War Council invited General

Gamelin's comments. In his reply General Gamelin said merely
that the question of Plan D (*i.e.*, the advance to the Meuse–
Antwerp line) had been dealt with in a report by the French
Delegation. In this report the operative passage was, 'If the call
is made in time the Anglo-French troops will enter Belgium, but
not to engage in an encounter battle. Among the recognised lines
of defence are the line of the Scheldt and the line Meuse–Namur–
Antwerp'. After considering the French reply the British Chiefs
of Staff submitted another paper to the Cabinet, which discussed
the alternative of an advance to the Scheldt, but made no mention at all of the far larger commitments of an advance to the
Meuse–Antwerp line. When the second report was presented to
the Cabinet on October 4 by the Chiefs of Staff no reference
was made by them to the all-important alternative of Plan D.
It was therefore taken for granted by the War Cabinet that
the views of the British Chiefs of Staff had been met and that
no further action or decision was required. I was present at
both these Cabinets, and was not aware that any significant
issue was still pending. During October, there being no effective
arrangements with the Belgians, it was assumed that the advance
was limited to the Scheldt.

Meanwhile General Gamelin, negotiating secretly with the

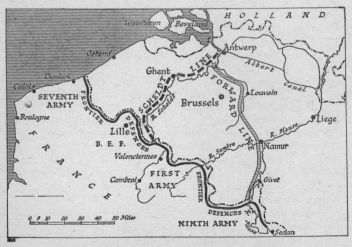

Diagram of Scheldt Line and Meuse-Antwerp Line

Belgians, stipulated, first, that the Belgian Army should be maintained at full strength, and, secondly, that Belgian defences should be prepared on the more advanced line from Namur to Louvain. By early November agreement was reached with the Belgians on these points, and from November 5 to 14 a series of conferences was held at Vincennes and La Ferté, at which, or at some of which, Ironside, Newall, and Gort were present. On November 15 General Gamelin issued his Instruction No. 8, confirming the agreements of the 14th, whereby support would be given to the Belgians 'if circumstances permitted' by an advance to the line Meuse–Antwerp. The Allied Supreme Council met in Paris on November 17. Mr. Chamberlain took with him Lord Halifax, Lord Chatfield, and Sir Kingsley Wood. I had not at that time reached the position where I should be invited to accompany the Prime Minister to these meetings. The decision was taken: 'Given the importance of holding the German forces as far east as possible, it is essential to make every endeavour to hold the line Meuse=Antwerp in the event of a German invasion of Belgium.' At this meeting Mr. Chamberlain and M. Daladier insisted on the importance which they attached to this resolution, and thereafter it governed action. This was, in fact, a decision in favour of Plan D, and it superseded the arrangements hitherto accepted of the modest forward move to the Scheldt.

As a new addition to Plan D there presently appeared the task of a Seventh French Army. The idea of an advance of this army on the seaward flank of the Allied armies first came to light early in November 1939. General Giraud, who was restless with a reserve army around Rheims, was put in command. The object of this excursion of Plan D was to move into Holland *via* Antwerp so as to help the Dutch, and secondly to occupy some parts of the Dutch islands Walcheren and Beveland. All this would have been good if the Germans had already been stopped on the Albert Canal. General Gamelin wanted it. General Georges thought it beyond our scope, and preferred that the troops involved should be brought into reserve behind the centre of the line. Of these differences we knew nothing.

In this posture therefore we passed the winter and awaited the spring. No new decisions of strategic principle were taken by the French and British Staffs or by their Governments in the six months which lay between us and the German onslaught.

CHAPTER 6

The Combat Deepens

Peace Suggestions – The Anglo-French Rejection – Soviet Absorption of the Baltic States – My Views on British Military Preparations – Possible Détente with Italy in the Mediterranean – The Home Front – The Sinking of the 'Royal Oak' – My Second Visit to Scapa Flow, October 31 – Decision about the Main Fleet Base – Mr. and Mrs. Chamberlain Dine at Admiralty House – The Loss of the 'Rawalpindi' – A False Alarm.

Hitler took advantage of his successes to propose his Peace Plan to the Allies. One of the unhappy consequences of our appeasement policy and generally of our attitude in the face of his rise to power had been to convince him that neither we nor France were capable of fighting a war. He had been unpleasantly surprised by the declaration of Great Britain and France on September 3, but he firmly believed that the spectacle of the swift and crashing destruction of Poland would make the decadent democracies realise that the day when they could exercise influence over the fate of Eastern and Central Europe was gone for ever. He felt very sure at this time of the Russians, gorged as they were with Polish territory and the Baltic States. Indeed, during this month of October he was able to send the captured American merchantman *City of Flint* into the Soviet port of Murmansk under a German prize crew. He had no wish at this stage to continue a war with France and Britain. He felt sure His Majesty's Government would be very glad to accept the decision reached by him in Poland, and that a peace offer would enable Mr. Chamberlain and his old colleagues, having vindicated their honour by a declaration of war, to get out of the scrape into which they had been forced by the war-mongering elements in Parliament. It never occurred to him for a moment that Mr. Chamberlain and the rest of the British Empire and Commonwealth of Nations now meant to have his blood or perish in the attempt.

The next step taken by Russia after partitioning Poland with Germany was to make three 'Mutual Assistance Pacts' with Esthonia, Latvia, and Lithuania. These Baltic States had broken themselves free from the Soviet Government in the War of Liberation of 1918 and 1920. Carrying through drastic land reform largely at the expense of the former German land-owners, these small countries evolved a nationalist and peasant way of life strongly anti-Communist in outlook. Ever fearful of their powerful Soviet neighbour, and desperately anxious to maintain their neutrality, these States attempted to avoid provocations in any direction. Their geographical situation made their task unenviable. Riga, for example, became a listening-post for news from Russia and an international anti-Bolshevik meeting-place. But the Germans had been content to throw them into their Russian deal, and the Soviet Government now advanced with pent-up hate and eager appetite upon their prey. These three States had formed a part of the Tsarist Empire, and were the old conquests of Peter the Great. They were immediately occupied by strong Russian forces, against which they had no means of effectual resistance. A ferocious liquidation of all anti-Communist and anti-Russian elements was carried through by the usual methods. Great numbers of people who for twenty years had lived in freedom in their native land and had represented the dominant majority of its people disappeared. A large proportion of these were transported to Siberia. The rest went farther. Such was the process described as 'Mutual Assistance'.

* * *

At home we busied ourselves with the expansion of the Army and the Air Force and with all the necessary measures to strengthen our naval power. I continued to submit my ideas to the Prime Minister, and pressed them upon other colleagues as might be acceptable.

First Lord to Prime Minister   1.x.39
This week-end I venture to write to you about several large issues.

1. When the peace offensive opens upon us it will be necessary to sustain the French. Although we have nearly a million men under arms, our contribution is, and must for many months remain, petty. We should tell the French that we are making as great a war effort, though in a different form, as in 1918 ; that we are constructing an Army of fifty-five divisions, which will be brought into action wherever needed, as fast as it can be trained and supplied, having regard to our great contribution in the air.

At present we have our Regular Army, which produces four or five divisions probably superior to anything in the field. But do not imagine that Territorial divisions will be able after six months' training or so to take their part without needless losses and bad results against German regular troops with at least two years' service and better equipment ; or stand at the side of French troops many of whom have had three years' service. The only way in which our forces in France can be rapidly expanded is by bringing the professional troops from India, and using them as the cadre upon which the Territorials and conscripts will form. I do not attempt to go into details now, but in principle 60,000 Territorials should be sent to India to maintain internal security and complete their training, and 40,000 or 45,000 Regular troops should *pari passu* be brought back to Europe. These troops should go into camps in the South of France, where the winter weather is more favourable to training than here, and where there are many military facilities, and become the nucleus and framework of eight or ten good field divisions. The texture of these troops would, by the late spring, be equal to those they will have to meet or stand beside. The fact of this force developing in France during the winter months would be a great encouragement and satisfaction to the French.

2. I was much concerned at the figures put forward by the Air Ministry of their fighting strength. They had 120 squadrons at the outbreak of war, but this actually boiled down to 96 able to go into action. One usually expects that on mobilisation there will be a large expansion. In this case there has been a severe contraction. What has happened is that a large number of squadrons have had to be gutted of trained air personnel, of mechanics, or spare parts, etc., in order to produce a fighting force, and that the débris of these squadrons has been thrown into a big pool called the Reserve. Into this pool will also flow, if the winter months pass without heavy attack, a great mass of new machines and large numbers of trained pilots. Even after making every deduction which is reasonable, we ought to be able to form at least six squadrons a month. It is much better to form squadrons which are held back in reserve than merely to have a large pool of spare pilots, spare machines, and spare parts. The disparity at the present time with Germany is shocking. I am sure this expansion could be achieved if you gave the word.

3. The A.R.P. [Air Raid Precautions] defences and expense are founded upon a wholly fallacious view of the degree of danger to each part of the country which they cover. Schedules should be made of the target areas and of the paths of flight by which they may be approached. In these areas there

must be a large proportion of whole-time employees. London is of course the chief [target], and others will readily occur. In these target areas the street-lighting should be made so that it can be controlled by the Air Wardens on the alarm signal being given; and while shelters should be hurried on with and strengthened, night and day, the people's spirits should be kept up by theatres and cinemas until the actual attack begins. Over a great part of the countryside modified lighting should be at once allowed, and places of entertainment opened. No paid A.R.P. personnel should be allowed in these [areas]. All should be on a voluntary basis, the Government contenting itself with giving advice and leaving the rest to local effort. In these areas, which comprise at least seven-eighths of the United Kingdom, gas-masks should be kept at home, and only carried in the target areas as scheduled. There is really no reason why orders to this effect should not be given during the coming week.

*   *   *

The disasters which had occurred in Poland and the Baltic States made me all the more anxious to keep Italy out of the war and to build up by every possible means some common interest between us. In the meantime the war went on, and I was busy over a number of administrative matters.

First Lord to Home Secretary   7.x.39
    In spite of having a full day's work usually here, I cannot help feeling anxious about the Home Front. You know my views about the needless, and in most parts of the country senseless, severities of these black-outs, entertainment restrictions, and the rest. But what about petrol? Have the Navy failed to bring in the supplies? Are there not more supplies on the water approaching and probably arriving than would have been ordered had peace remained unbroken? I am told that very large numbers of people and a large part of the business of the country is hampered by the stinting. Surely the proper way to deal with this is to have a ration at the standard price, and allow free purchasing, subject to a heavy tax, beyond it. People will pay for locomotion, the Revenue will benefit by the tax, more cars will come out with registration fees, and the business of the country can go forward.
    Then look at these rations, all devised by the Ministry of Food to win the war. By all means have rations, but I am told that the meat ration for instance is very little better than that of Germany. Is there any need of this when the seas are open?

If we have a heavy set-back from air attack or surface attack, it might be necessary to inflict these severities. Up to the present there is no reason to suppose that the Navy has failed in bringing in the supplies, or that it will fail.

Then what about all these people of middle age, many of whom served in the last war, who are full of vigour and experience, and who are being told by tens of thousands that they are not wanted, and that there is nothing for them except to register at the local Labour Exchange? Surely this is very foolish. Why do we not form a Home Guard of half a million men over forty (if they like to volunteer), and put all our elderly stars at the head and in the structure of these new formations? Let these five hundred thousand men come along and push the young and active out of all the home billets. If uniforms are lacking a brassard would suffice, and I am assured there are plenty of rifles at any rate. I thought from what you said to me the other day that you liked this idea. If so, let us make it work.

I hear continual complaints from every quarter of the lack of organisation on the Home Front. Can't we get at it?

* * *

Amidst all these preoccupations there burst upon us suddenly an event which touched the Admiralty in a most sensitive spot.

I have mentioned the alarm caused by the report that a U-boat was *inside Scapa Flow*, which had driven the Grand Fleet to sea on the night of October 17, 1914. That alarm was premature. Now, after exactly a quarter of a century almost to a day, it came true. At 1.30 a.m. on October 14, 1939, a German U-boat braved the tides and currents, penetrated our defences, and sank the battleship *Royal Oak* as she lay at anchor. At first, out of a salvo of torpedoes, only one hit the bow, and caused a muffled explosion. So incredible was it to the Admiral and captain on board that a torpedo could have struck them, safe in Scapa Flow, that they attributed the explosion to some internal cause. Twenty minutes passed before the U-boat, for such she was, had reloaded her tubes and fired a second salvo. Then three or four torpedoes, striking in quick succession, ripped the bottom out of the ship. In ten minutes she capsized and sank. Most of the men were at action stations, but the rate at which the ship turned over made it almost impossible for anyone below to escape.

An account based on a German report written at the time may be recorded.

At 01.30 on October 14, 1939, H.M.S. *Royal Oak*, lying at anchor in Scapa Flow, was torpedoed by U.47 (Lieutenant Prien). The operation had been carefully planned by Admiral Doenitz himself, the Flag Officer (Submarines). Prien left Kiel on October 8, a clear, bright autumn day, and passed through Kiel Canal—course N.N.W., Scapa Flow. On October 13, at 4 a.m., the boat was lying off the Orkneys. At 7 p.m.—surface ; a fresh breeze blowing, nothing in sight ; looming in the half darkness the line of the distant coast ; long streamers of Northern Lights flashing blue wisps across the sky. Course west. The boat crept steadily closer to Holm Sound, the eastern approach to Scapa Flow. Unfortunate it was that these channels had not been completely blocked. A narrow passage lay open between two sunken ships. With great skill Prien steered through the swirling waters. The shore was close. A man on a bicycle could be seen going home along the coast road. Then suddenly the whole bay opened out. Kirk Sound was passed. They were in. There under the land to the north could be seen the great shadow of a battleship lying on the water, with the great mast rising above it like a piece of filigree on a black cloth. Near, nearer —all tubes clear—no alarm, no sound but the lap of the water, the low hiss of air pressure and the sharp click of a tube lever. *Los!* [Fire!]—five seconds—ten seconds—twenty seconds. Then came a shattering explosion, and a great pillar of water rose in the darkness. Prien waited some minutes to fire another salvo. Tubes ready. Fire! The torpedoes hit amidships, and there followed a series of crashing explosions. H.M.S. *Royal Oak* sank, with the loss of 786 officers and men, including Rear-Admiral H. E. C. Blagrove (Rear-Admiral Second Battle Squadron). U.47 crept quietly away back through the gap. A blockship arrived twenty-four hours later.

This episode, which must be regarded as a feat of arms on the part of the German U-boat commander, gave a shock to public opinion. It might well have been politically fatal to any Minister who had been responsible for the pre-war precautions. Being a newcomer I was immune from such reproaches in these early months, and, moreover, the Opposition did not attempt to make capital out of the misfortune. On the contrary, Mr. A. V. Alexander was restrained and sympathetic. I promised the strictest inquiry.

On this occasion the Prime Minister also gave the House an account of the German air raids which had been made on October 16 upon the Firth of Forth. This was the first attempt the

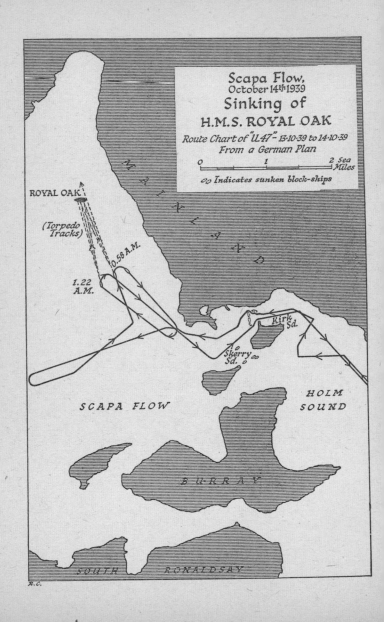

Scapa Flow,
October 14th 1939
Sinking of
H.M.S. ROYAL OAK

Route Chart of "U47" 13·10·39 to 14·10·39
From a German Plan

0   1   2 Sea
                        Miles

∽ Indicates sunken block-ships

ROYAL OAK

(Torpedo Tracks)

0.58 A.M.

1.22 A.M.

MAINLAND

Kirk Sd.

Skerry Sd.

SCAPA FLOW

HOLM SOUND

BURRAY

SOUTH RONALDSAY

R.C.

Germans had made to strike by air at our Fleet. Twelve or more machines in flights of two or three at a time had bombed our cruisers lying in the Firth. Slight damage was done to the cruisers *Southampton* and *Edinburgh* and to the destroyer *Mohawk*. Twenty-five officers and sailors were killed or wounded; but four enemy bombers were brought down, three by our fighter squadrons and one by the anti-aircraft fire. It might well be that only half the bombers had got home safely. This was an effective deterrent.

The following morning, the 17th, Scapa Flow was raided, and the old *Iron Duke*, now a demilitarised and disarmoured hulk used as a depot ship, was injured by near misses. She settled on the bottom in shallow water and continued to do her work throughout the war. Another enemy aircraft was shot down in flames. The Fleet was happily absent from the harbour. These events showed how necessary it was to perfect the defences of Scapa against all forms of attack before allowing it to be used. It was nearly six months before we were able to enjoy its commanding advantages.

*   *   *

The attack on Scapa Flow and the loss of the *Royal Oak* provoked instant reactions in the Admiralty. On October 31, accompanied by the First Sea Lord, I went to Scapa to hold a second conference on these matters in Admiral Forbes' flagship. The scale of defence for Scapa upon which we now agreed included reinforcement of the booms and additional blockships in the exposed eastern channels, as well as controlled minefields and other devices. These formidable deterrents would be reinforced by further patrol craft and guns sited to cover all approaches. Against air attack it was planned to mount eighty-eight heavy and forty light A.A. guns, together with numerous searchlights and increased barrage-balloon defences. Substantial fighter protection was organised both in the Orkneys and at Wick on the mainland. It was hoped that all these arrangements could be completed, or at least sufficiently advanced, to justify the return of the Fleet by March 1940. Meanwhile Scapa could be used as a destroyer refuelling base; but other accommodation had to be found for the heavy ships.

Experts differed on the rival claims of the possible alternative bases. Admiralty opinion favoured the Clyde, but Admiral Forbes demurred on the ground that this would involve an extra day's steaming each way to his main operational area. This in turn would require an increase in his destroyer forces and would necessitate the heavy ships working in two divisions. The other alternative was Rosyth, which had been our main base in the latter part of the previous war. It was more suitably placed geographically, but was more vulnerable to air attack. The decisions eventually reached at this conference were summed up in a minute which I prepared on my return to London.

On Friday, November 13, my relations with Mr. Chamberlain had so far ripened that he and Mrs. Chamberlain came to dine with us at Admiralty House, where we had a comfortable flat in the attics. We were a party of four. Although we had been colleagues under Mr. Baldwin for five years, my wife and I had never met the Chamberlains in such circumstances before. By happy chance I turned the conversation on to his life in the Bahamas, and I was delighted to find my guest expand in personal reminiscence to a degree I had not noticed before. He told us the whole story, of which I knew only the barest outline, of his six years' struggle to grow sisal on a barren West Indian islet near Nassau. His father, the great 'Joe', was firmly convinced that here was an opportunity at once to develop an Empire industry and fortify the family fortunes. His father and Austen had summoned him in 1890 from Birmingham to Canada, where they had long examined the project. About forty miles from Nassau in the Caribbean Gulf there was a small desert island, almost uninhabited, where the soil was reported to be suitable for growing sisal. After careful reconnaissance by his two sons, Mr. Joseph Chamberlain had acquired a tract on the island of Andros, and assigned the capital required to develop it. All that remained was to grow the sisal. Austen was dedicated to the House of Commons. The task therefore fell to Neville.

Not only in filial duty but with conviction and alacrity he obeyed, and the next five years of his life were spent in trying to grow sisal in this lonely spot, swept by hurricanes from time to time, living nearly naked, struggling with labour difficulties and every other kind of obstacle and with the town of Nassau as the only gleam of civilisation. He had insisted, he told us, on three months' leave in England each year. He built a small harbour and landing-stage and a short railroad or tramway. He used all the processes of fertilisation which were judged suitable to the soil and generally led a completely primitive, open-air existence. But no sisal! Or at any rate no sisal that would face the market. At the end of five years he was convinced that the plan could not succeed. He came home and faced his formidable parent, who was by no means contented with the result. I gathered that in the family the feeling was that though they loved him dearly they were sorry to have lost £50,000.

I was fascinated by the way Mr. Chamberlain warmed as he talked, and by the tale itself, which was one of gallant endeavour. I thought to myself, 'What a pity Hitler did not know when he met this sober English politician with his umbrella at Berchtesgaden, Godesberg, and Munich that he was actually talking to a hard-bitten pioneer from the outer marches of the British Empire!' This was really the only intimate social conversation that I can remember with Neville Chamberlain amid all the business we did together over nearly twenty years.

During dinner the war went on and things happened. With the soup an officer came up from the War Room below to report that a U-boat had been sunk. With the sweet he came again and reported that a second U-boat had been sunk ; and just before the ladies left the dining-room he came a third time reporting that a third U-boat had been sunk. Nothing like this had ever happened before in a single day, and it was more than a year before such a record was repeated. As the ladies left us, Mrs. Chamberlain, with a naïve and charming glance, said to me, 'Did you arrange all this on purpose?' I assured her that if she would come again we would produce a similar result.*

*   *   *

Our long, tenuous blockade-line north of the Orkneys, largely composed of armed merchant-cruisers with supporting warships at intervals, was of course always liable to a sudden attack by German capital ships, and particularly by their two fast and most powerful battle-cruisers, the *Scharnhorst* and the *Gneisenau*. We could not prevent such a stroke being made. Our hope was to bring the intruders to decisive action.

Late in the afternoon of November 23 the armed merchant-cruiser *Rawalpindi*, on patrol between Iceland and the Faroes, sighted an enemy warship which closed her rapidly. She believed the stranger to be the pocket-battleship *Deutschland*, and reported accordingly. Her commanding officer, Captain Kennedy, could have had no illusions about the outcome of such an encounter. His ship was but a converted passenger liner with a

---

* Alas, these hopeful reports are not confirmed by the post-war analysis.

broadside of four old 6-inch guns, and his presumed antagonist mounted six 11-inch guns, besides a powerful secondary armament. Nevertheless he accepted the odds, determined to fight his ship to the last. The enemy opened fire at 10,000 yards, and the *Rawalpindi* struck back. Such a one-sided action could not last long, but the fight continued until, with all her guns out of action, the *Rawalpindi* was reduced to a blazing wreck. She sank some time after dark, with the loss of her captain and 270 of her gallant crew. Only 38 survived, 27 of whom were made prisoners by the Germans, the remaining 11 being picked up alive after thirty-six hours in icy water by another British ship.

In fact it was not the *Deutschland* but the two battle-cruisers *Scharnhorst* and *Gneisenau* which were engaged. These ships had left Germany two days before to attack our Atlantic convoys, but having encountered and sunk the *Rawalpindi*, and fearing the consequences of the exposure, they abandoned the rest of their mission and returned at once to Germany. The *Rawalpindi*'s heroic fight was not therefore in vain. The cruiser *Newcastle*, near by on patrol, saw the gun-flashes, and responded at once to the *Rawalpindi*'s first report, arriving on the scene with the cruiser *Delhi* to find the burning ship still afloat. She pursued the enemy, and at 6.15 p.m. sighted two ships in gathering darkness and heavy rain. One of these she recognised as a battle-cruiser, but lost contact in the gloom, and the enemy made good his escape.

The hope of bringing these two vital German ships to battle dominated all concerned, and the Commander-in-Chief put to sea at once with his whole fleet. When last seen the enemy was retiring to the eastward, and strong forces, including submarines, were promptly organised to intercept him in the North Sea. However, we could not ignore the possibility that having shaken off the pursuit the enemy might renew his advance to the westward and enter the Atlantic. We feared for our convoys, and the situation called for the use of all available forces. Sea and air patrols were established to watch all the exits from the North Sea, and a powerful force of cruisers extended this watch to the coast of Norway. In the Atlantic the battleship *Warspite* left her convoy to search the Denmark Strait, and, finding nothing, continued round the north of Iceland to link up with the watchers in the North Sea. The *Hood*, the French battle-cruiser *Dunkerque*, and two French cruisers were dispatched to Icelandic waters, and the *Repulse* and *Furious* sailed from

Halifax for the same destination. By the 25th fourteen British cruisers were combing the North Sea, with destroyers and submarines co-operating and with the battle-fleet in support. But fortune was adverse; nothing was found, nor was there any indication of an enemy move to the west. Despite very severe weather the arduous search was maintained for seven days.

On the fifth day, while we were waiting anxiously in the Admiralty and still cherishing the hope that this splendid prize would not be denied us, a German U-boat was heard by our D.F. stations making a report. We judged from this that an attack had been made on one of our warships in the North Sea. Soon the German broadcast claimed that Captain Prien, the sinker of the *Royal Oak*, had sunk an 8-inch-gun cruiser to the eastward of the Shetlands. Admiral Pound and I were together when this news came in. British public opinion is extremely sensitive when British ships are sunk, and the loss of the *Rawalpindi*, after a gallant fight and with a heavy toll in life would tell seriously against the Admiralty if it remained unavenged. 'Why,' it would be demanded, 'was so weak a ship exposed without effective support? Could the German cruisers range at will even in the blockade zone in which our main forces were employed? Were the raiders to escape unscathed?'

We made a signal at once to clear up the mystery. When we met again an hour later without any reply, we passed through a very bad moment. I recall it because it marked the strong comradeship that had grown up between us and with Admiral Tom Phillips, who was also there. 'I take full responsibility,' I said, as was my duty. 'No, it is mine,' said Pound. We wrung each other's hands in lively distress. Hardened as we both were in war, it is not possible to sustain such blows without the most bitter pangs.

But it proved to be nobody's fault. Eight hours later it appeared that the *Norfolk* was the ship involved and that she was undamaged. She had not encountered any U-boat, but said that an air bomb had fallen close astern. However, Captain Prien was no braggart. What the *Norfolk* thought to be an air bomb from a clouded sky was in fact a German torpedo, which had narrowly missed its target and exploded in the ship's wake. Peering through the periscope, Prien had seen the great upheaval of water, blotting out the ship from his gaze. He dived to avoid an expected salvo. When, after half an hour, he rose for another peep the visibility was poor and no cruiser was to be seen. Hence his report. Our relief after the pain we had suffered took some of the sting out of the news that the *Scharnhorst* and the *Gneisenau* had safely re-entered the Baltic. It is now known that the *Scharnhorst* and *Gneisenau* passed through our cruiser line patrolling near the Norwegian coast on the morning of November 26. The weather was thick and neither saw the other. Modern Radar would have ensured contact, but then it was not available. Public impressions were unfavourable to the Admiralty. We could not bring home to the outside world the vastness of the seas or the intense exertions which the Navy was making in so many areas. After more than two months of war and several serious losses we had nothing to show on the other side. Nor could we yet answer the question, 'What is the Navy doing?'

CHAPTER 7

The Magnetic Mine

Conference with Admiral Darlan – The Anglo-French Naval Position – M. Campinchi – The Northern Barrage – The Magnetic Mine – A Devoted Deed – Technical Aspects – Minesweeping Methods – 'Degaussing' – The Magnetic Mining Attack Mastered and under Control – Retaliation – Fluvial Mines in the Rhine – Operation 'Royal Marine'.

In the first days of November I paid a visit to France for a conference on our joint operations with the French naval authorities. Admiral Pound and I drove out about forty miles from Paris to the French Marine Headquarters, which were established in the park around the ancient château of the Duc de Noailles. Before we went into the conference Admiral Darlan explained to me how Admiralty matters were managed in France. The Minister of Marine, M. Campinchi, was now allowed by him to be present when operational matters were under discussion. These fell into the purely professional sphere. I said that the First Sea Lord and I were one. Darlan said he recognised this, but in France it was different. 'However,' he said, 'Monsieur le Ministre will arrive for luncheon.' We then ranged over naval business for two hours with a great measure of agreement. At luncheon M. Campinchi turned up. He knew his place, and now presided affably over the meal. My son-in-law, Duncan Sandys, who was acting as my *aide*, sat next to Darlan. The Admiral spent most of luncheon explaining to him the limits to which the civilian Minister was restricted by the French system. Before leaving I called on the Duke in his château. He and his family seemed plunged in melancholy, but showed us their very beautiful house and its art treasures.

In the evening I gave a small dinner in a private room at the Ritz to M. Campinchi. I formed a high opinion of this man. His patriotism, his ardour, his acute intelligence, and above all his resolve to conquer or die, hit home. I could not help mentally comparing him with the Admiral, who, jealous of his position, was fighting on quite a different front from ours. Pound's valuation was the same as mine, although we both realised all that Darlan had done for the French Navy. One must not underrate Darlan, nor fail to understand the impulse that moved him. He deemed himself the French Navy, and the French Navy acclaimed him their chief and their reviver. For seven years he had held his office while shifting Ministerial phantoms had filled the office of Minister of Marine. It was his obsession to keep the politicians in their place as chatterboxes in the Chamber. Pound and I got on very well with Campinchi. This tough Corsican never flinched or failed. When he died, broken and under the scowl of Vichy, towards the beginning of 1941, his last words were of hope in me. I shall always deem them an honour.

Here is the statement summing up our naval position at this moment, which I made at the conference:

STATEMENT TO THE FRENCH ADMIRALTY BY THE FIRST LORD

The naval war alone has opened at full intensity. The U-boat attack on commerce, so nearly fatal in 1917, has been controlled by the Ango-French anti-submarine craft. We must expect a large increase in German U-boats (and possibly some will be lent to them by Russia). This need cause no anxiety provided that all our counter-measures are taken at full speed and on the largest scale. The Admiralty representatives will explain in detail our large programmes. But the full development of these will not come till late in 1940. In the meanwhile it is indispensable that every anti-submarine craft available should be finished and put in commission.

2. There is no doubt that our Asdic method is effective, and far better than anything known in the last war. It enables two torpedo-boats to do what required ten in 1917–18. But this applies only to hunting. For convoys numbers are still essential. One is only safe when escorted by vessels fitted with Asdics. This applies to warships equally with merchant convoys. The defeat of the U-boat will be achieved when it is certain that any attack on French or British vessels will be followed by an Asdic counter-attack.

The British Admiralty is prepared to supply and fit every French anti-submarine craft with Asdics. The cost is small, and accounts can be regulated later on. But any French vessels sent to England for fitting will be immediately taken in hand; and also we will arrange for the imparting of the method and for training to be given in each case. It would be most convenient to do this at Portland, the home of the

Asdics, where all facilities are available. We contemplate making provision for equipping fifty French vessels if desired.

3. But we earnestly hope that the French Marine will multiply their Asdic vessels, and will complete with the utmost rapidity all that can enter into action during 1940. After this is arranged for it will be possible six months hence to consider 1941. For the present let us aim at 1940, and especially at the spring and summer. The six large destroyers laid down in 1936 and 1937 will be urgently needed for ocean convoys before the climax of the U-boat warfare is reached in 1940. There are also fourteen small destroyers laid down in 1939, or now projected, which will play an invaluable part without making any great drain on labour and materials. Total, twenty vessels, which could be completed during 1940, and which, fitted with Asdics by us, would be weapons of high consequence in the destruction of the U-boat offensive of 1940. We also venture to mention as most desirable vessels the six sloop-minesweepers laid down in 1936, and twelve laid down in 1937, and also the sixteen submarine-chasers of the programme of 1938. For all these we offer Asdics and every facility. We will fit them as they are ready, as if it were a field operation. We cannot however consider these smaller vessels in the same order of importance as the large and small destroyers mentioned above.

4. It must not be forgotten that defeat of the U-boats carries with it the sovereignty of all the oceans of the world for the Allied Fleets, and the possibility of powerful neutrals coming to our aid, as well as the drawing of resources from every part of the French and British Empires, and the maintenance of trade, gathering with it the necessary wealth to continue the war.

5. At the British Admiralty we have drawn a sharp line between large vessels which can be finished in 1940 and those of later periods. In particular, we are straining every nerve to finish the *King George V* and the *Prince of Wales* battleships within that year, if possible by the autumn. This is necessary because the arrival of the *Bismarck* on the oceans before these two ships were completed would be disastrous in the highest degree, as it can neither be caught nor killed, and would therefore range freely throughout the oceans, rupturing all communications. But France has also a vessel of the highest importance in the *Richelieu*, which might be ready in the autumn of 1940 or even earlier, and will certainly be needed if the two new Italian ships should be finished by the dates in 1940 at which they profess to aim. Not to have these three capital ships in action before the end of 1940 would be an error in naval strategy of the gravest character, and might

entail not only naval but diplomatic consequences extremely
disagreeable. It is hoped therefore that every effort will be
made to complete the *Richelieu* at the earliest possible date.

With regard to later capital ships of the British and French
Navies, it would be well to discuss these in April or May
next year, when we shall see much more clearly the course
and character of the war.

6. The British Admiralty now express their gratitude to
their French colleagues and comrades for the very remarkable assistance which they have given to the common cause
since the beginning of this war. This assistance has gone far
beyond any promises or engagements made before the war.
In escorting home the convoys from Sierra Leone the French
cruisers and destroyers have played a part which could not
otherwise have been supplied, and which, if not forthcoming,
would simply have meant more slaughter of Allied merchantmen. The cruisers and contre-torpilleurs which, with the
Dunkerque, have covered the arrival of convoys in the Western Approaches were at the time the only means by which
the German raiders could be warded off. The maintenance
of the French submarines in the neighbourhood of Trinidad
has been a most acceptable service. Above all, the two destroyers which constantly escort the homeward- and outward-
bound convoys between Gibraltar and Brest are an important
relief to our resources, which, though large and ever-growing,
are at full strain.

Finally, we are extremely obliged by the facilities given to
the *Argus* aircraft-carrier to carry out her training of British
naval aircraft pilots under the favourable conditions of Mediterranean weather.

7. Surveying the more general aspects of the war: the
fact that the enemy have no line of .battle has enabled us to
disperse our naval forces widely over the oceans, and we have
seven or eight British hunting units, joined by two French
hunting units, each capable of catching and killing a *Deutschland*. We are now cruising in the North Atlantic, the South
Atlantic, and the Indian Oceans. The result has been that
the raiders have not chosen to inflict the losses upon the convoys which before the war it had been supposed they could
certainly do. The fact that certainly one, and perhaps two,
Deutschlands have been upon the main Atlantic trade routes
for several weeks without achieving anything makes us feel
easier about this form of attack, which had formerly been
rated extremely dangerous. We cannot possibly exclude its
renewal in a more energetic form. The British Admiralty think
it is not at all objectionable to keep large vessels in suitable
units ranging widely over the oceans where they are safe

from air attack, and make effective and apparent the control of the broad waters for the Allies.

8. We shall shortly be engaged in bringing the leading elements of the Canadian and Australian armies to France, and for this purpose a widespread disposition of all our hunting groups is convenient. It will also be necessary to give battleship escorts to many of the largest convoys crossing the Atlantic Ocean. We intend to maintain continually the Northern Blockade from Greenland to Scotland, in spite of the severities of the winter. Upon this blockade twenty-five armed merchant-cruisers will be employed in reliefs, supported by four 8-inch-gun 10,000-ton cruisers, and behind these we always maintain the main fighting forces of the British Navy, to wit, the latest battleships, and either the *Hood* or another great vessel, the whole sufficient to engage or pursue the *Scharnhorst* and the *Gneisenau* should they attempt to break out. We do not think it likely, in view of the situation in the Baltic, that these two vessels will be so employed. Nevertheless, we maintain continually the forces necessary to cope with them.

It is hoped that by a continuance of this strategy by the two Allied Navies no temptation will be offered to Italy to enter the war against us, and that the German power of resistance will certainly be brought to an end.

The French Admiralty in their reply explained that they were in fact proceeding with the completion of the vessels specified, and that they gladly accepted our Asdic offer. Not only would the *Richelieu* be finished in the summer of 1940, but also in the autumn the *Jean Bart*.

* * *

In mid-November Admiral Pound presented me with proposals for re-creating the minefield barrage between Scotland and Norway which had been established by the British and American Admiralties in 1917–18. I did not like this kind of warfare, which is essentially defensive, and seeks to substitute material on a vast scale for dominating action. However, I was gradually worn down and reconciled. I submitted the project to the War Cabinet on November 19.

THE NORTHERN BARRAGE

MEMORANDUM BY THE FIRST LORD OF THE ADMIRALTY

After much consideration I commend this project to my colleagues. There is no doubt that, as it is completed, it will impose a very great deterrent upon the exit and return of

U-boats and surface raiders. It appears to be a prudent provision against an intensification of the U-boat warfare, and an insurance against the danger of Russia joining our enemy. By this we coop the lot in, and have complete control of all approaches alike to the Baltic and the North Sea. The essence of this offensive minefield is that the enemy will be prevented by the constant vigilance of superior naval force from sweeping channels through it. When it is in existence we shall feel much freer in the outer seas than at present. Its gradual but remorseless growth, which will be known to the enemy, will exercise a depressive effect upon his morale. The cost is deplorably heavy, but a large provision has already been made by the Treasury, and the Northern Barrage is far the best method of employing this means of war [*i.e.*, mining].

This represented the highest professional advice and of course is just the kind of thing that passes easily through a grave, wise Cabinet. Events swept it away; but not until a great deal of money had been spent. The barrage mines came in handy later on for other tasks.

*　　*　　*

Presently a new and formidable danger threatened our life. During September and October nearly a dozen merchant ships were sunk at the entrance of our harbours, although these had been properly swept for mines. The Admiralty at once suspected that a magnetic mine had been used. This was no novelty to us; we had even begun to use it on a small scale at the end of the previous war. In 1936 an Admiralty committee had studied counter-measures against magnetic-firing devices, but their work had dealt chiefly with countering magnetic torpedoes or buoyant mines, and the terrible damage that could be done by large ground-mines laid in considerable depth by ships or aircraft had not been fully realised. Without a specimen of the mine it was impossible to devise the remedy. Losses by mines, largely Allied and neutral, in September and October had amounted to 56,000 tons, and in November Hitler was encouraged to hint darkly at his new 'secret weapon' to which there was no counter. One night when I was at Chartwell Admiral Pound came down to see me in serious anxiety. Six ships had been sunk in the approaches to the Thames. Every day hundreds of ships went in and out of British harbours, and our survival depended on their movement. Hitler's experts may well have told him that this form of attack would compass our ruin. Luckily he began on a small scale, and with limited stocks and manufacturing capacity.

Fortune also favoured us more directly. On November 22 between 9 and 10 p.m. a German aircraft was observed to drop a large object attached to a parachute into the sea near Shoeburyness. The coast here is girdled with great areas of mud which uncover with the tide, and it was immediately obvious that whatever the object was it could be examined and possibly recovered at low water. Here was our golden opportunity. Before midnight that same night two highly-skilled officers, Lt.-Commanders Ouvry and Lewis, from H.M.S. *Vernon*, the naval establishment responsible for developing underwater weapons, were called to the Admiralty, where the First Sea Lord and I interviewed them and heard their plans. By 1.30 in the morning they were on their way by car to Southend to undertake the hazardous task of recovery. Before daylight on the 23rd, in pitch-darkness, aided only by a signal lamp, they found the mine some 500 yards below high-water mark, but as the tide was then rising they could only inspect it and make their preparations for attacking it after the next high water.

The critical operation began early in the afternoon, by which time it had been discovered that a second mine was also on the mud near the first. Ouvry with Chief Petty Officer Baldwin tackled the first, whilst their colleagues, Lewis and Able Seaman Vearncombe, waited at a safe distance in case of accidents. After each prearranged operation Ouvry would signal to Lewis, so that the knowledge gained would be available when the second mine came to be dismantled. Eventually the combined efforts of all four men were required on the first, and their skill and devotion were amply rewarded. That evening some of the party came to the Admiralty to report that the mine had been recovered intact and was on its way to Portsmouth for detailed examination. I received them with enthusiasm. I gathered together eighty or a hundred officers and officials in our largest room, and a thrilled audience listened to the tale, deeply conscious of all that was at stake. From this moment the whole position was transformed. Immediately the knowledge derived from past research could be applied to devising practical measures for combating the particular characteristics of the mine.

The whole power and science of the Navy were now applied ; and it was not long before trial and experiment began to yield practical results. Rear-Admiral Wake-Walker was appointed to co-ordinate all technical measures which the occasion demanded. We worked all ways at once, devising first active means of attacking the mine by new methods of minesweeping and fuse-provocation, and secondly, passive means of defence for all ships against possible mines in unswept, or ineffectually swept, channels. For this second purpose a most effective system of demagnetising ships by girdling them with an electric cable was developed. This was called 'degaussing', and was at once applied to ships of all types. Merchant ships were thus equipped in all our major ports without appreciably delaying their turn-round. In the Fleet progress was simplified by the presence of the highly-trained technical staffs of the Royal Navy. The reader who does not shrink from technical details would find an account of these developments most interesting.

* * *

Serious casualties continued. The new cruiser *Belfast* was mined in the Firth of Forth on November 21, and on December 4 the battleship *Nelson* was mined whilst entering Loch Ewe. Both ships were however able to reach a dockyard port. Two destroyers were lost, and two others, besides the minelayer *Adventure*, were damaged on the East Coast during this period. It is remarkable that German Intelligence failed to pierce our security measures covering the injury to the *Nelson* until the ship had been repaired and was again in service. Yet from the first many thousands in England had to know the true facts.

Experience soon gave us new and simpler methods of degaussing. The moral effect of its success was tremendous, but it was on the faithful, courageous, and persistent work of the minesweepers and the patient skill of the technical experts, who devised and provided the equipment they used, that we relied chiefly to defeat the enemy's efforts. From this time onward, despite many anxious periods, the mine menace was always under control, and eventually the danger began to recede. By Christmas Day I was able to write to the Prime Minister:

December 25, 1939

Everything is very quiet here, but I thought you would like to know that we have had a marked success against the magnetic mines. The first two devices for setting them off which we have got into action have both proved effective. Two mines were blown up by the magnetic sweep and two by lighters carrying heavy coils. This occurred at Port A [Loch Ewe], where our interesting invalid [the *Nelson*] is still waiting for a clear passage to be swept for her to the convalescent home at Portsmouth. It also looks as if the demagnetisation of warships and merchant ships can be accomplished by a simple, speedy, and inexpensive process. All our best devices are now approaching [completion]. The aeroplanes and the magnetic ship—the *Borde*—will be at work within the next ten days, and we all feel pretty sure that the danger from magnetic mines will soon be out of the way.

We are also studying the possible varying of this form of attack, viz., acoustic mines and supersonic mines. Thirty ardent experts are pursuing these possibilities, but I am not yet able to say that they have found a cure....

It is well to ponder this side of the naval war. In the event a significant proportion of our whole war effort had to be devoted to combating the mine. A vast output of material and money was diverted from other tasks, and many thousands of men risked their lives night and day in the minesweepers alone. The peak figure was reached in June 1944, when nearly sixty thousand were thus employed. Nothing daunted the ardour of the Merchant Navy, and their spirits rose with the deadly complications of the mining attack and our effective measures for countering it. Their toils and tireless courage were our salvation. The sea traffic on which we depended for our existence proceeded without interruption.

*   *   *

The first impact of the magnetic mine had stirred me deeply, and, apart from all the protective measures which had been enforced upon us, I sought for a means of retaliation. My visit to the Rhine on the eve of the war had focused my mental vision upon this supreme and vital German artery. Even in September I had raised discussion in the Admiralty about the launching or dropping of fluvial mines in the Rhine. Considering that this river was used by the traffic of many neutral nations, we could not of course take action unless and until the Germans had taken the initiative in this form of indiscriminate warfare against us. Now that they had done so, it seemed to me that the proper retort for indiscriminate sinkings by mines at the mouths of the British harbours was a similar and if possible more effective mining attack upon the Rhine.

Accordingly on November 19 I issued several minutes, of which the following gives the most precise account of the plan:

Controller [*and others*]

1. As a measure of retaliation it may become necessary to feed large numbers of floating mines into the Rhine. This can easily be done at any point between Strasbourg and the Lauter, where the left bank is French territory. General Gamelin was much interested in this idea, and asked me to work it out for him.

2. Let us clearly see the object in view. The Rhine is traversed by an enormous number of very large barges, and is the main artery of German trade and life. These barges, built only for river work, have not got double keels or any large subdivision by bulkheads. It is easy to check these details. In addition there are at least twelve bridges of boats recently thrown across the Rhine upon which the German armies concentrated in the Saarbruck-Luxemburg area depend.

3. The type of mine required is therefore a small one, perhaps no bigger than a football. The current of the river is at most about seven miles an hour, and three or four at ordinary times, but it is quite easy to verify this. There must therefore be a clockwork apparatus in the mine which makes it dangerous only after it has gone a certain distance, so as to be clear of French territory and also so as to spread the terror farther down the Rhine to its confluence with the Moselle and beyond. The mine should automatically sink, or preferably explode, by this apparatus before reaching Dutch territory. After the mine has proceeded the required distance, which can be varied, it should explode on a light contact. It would be a convenience if, in addition to the above, the mine could go off if stranded after a certain amount of time, as it might easily spread alarm on either of the German banks.

4. It would be necessary in addition that the mine should float a convenient distance beneath the surface so as to be invisible in the turgid waters. A hydrostatic valve actuated by a small cylinder of compressed air should be devised. I have not made the calculations, but I should suppose 48 hours would be the maximum for which it would have to work. An alternative would be to throw very large numbers of camouflage globes—tin shells—into the river, which would spread confusion and exhaust remedial activities.

5. What can they do against this? Obviously nets would be put across; but wreckage passing down the river would

break these nets, and except at the frontier they would be a great inconvenience to the traffic. Anyhow, when our mine fetched up against them it would explode, breaking a large hole in the nets, and after a dozen or more of these explosions the channel would become free again, and other mines would jog along. Specially large mines might be used to break the nets. I cannot think of any other method of defence, but perhaps some may occur to the officers entrusted with this study.

6. Finally, as very large numbers of these mines would be used and the process kept up night after night for months on end, so as to deny the use of the waterway, it is necessary to bear in mind the simplification required for mass production.

The War Cabinet liked this plan. It seemed to them only right and proper that when the Germans were using the magnetic mine to waylay and destroy all traffic, Allied or neutral, entering British ports we should strike back by paralysing, as we might well do, the whole of their vast traffic on the Rhine. The necessary permissions and priorities were obtained, and work started at full speed. In conjunction with the Air Ministry we developed a plan for mining the Ruhr section of the Rhine by discharge from aeroplanes. I entrusted all this work to Rear-Admiral FitzGerald, serving under the First Sea Lord. This brilliant officer, who perished later in command of an Atlantic convoy, made an immense personal contribution. The technical problems were solved. A good supply of mines was assured ; and several hundred ardent British sailors and marines were organised to handle them when the time should come. All this was in November, and we could not be ready before March. It is always agreeable in peace or war to have something positive coming along on your side.

CHAPTER 8

The Action off the River Plate

Surface Raiders – The German Pocket Battleship – Orders of the German Admiralty – British Hunting Groups – The American Three-Hundred-Mile Limit – Offer of Our Asdics to the United States – Anxieties at Home – Caution of the 'Deutschland' – Daring of the 'Graf Spee' – Captain Langsdorff's Manœuvres – Commodore Harwood's Squadron off the Plate – His Foresight and Fortune – Collision on December 13 – Langsdorff's Mistake – The 'Exeter' Disabled – Retreat of the German Pocket-Battleship – Pursuit by 'Ajax' and 'Achilles' – The 'Spee' Takes Refuge in Montevideo – My Letter of December 17 to the Prime Minister – British Concentration on Montevideo – Langsdorff's Orders from the Fuehrer – Scuttling of the 'Spee' – Langsdorff's Suicide – End of the First Surface Challenge to British Commerce – The 'Altmark' – The 'Exeter' – Effects of the Action off the Plate – My Telegram to President Roosevelt.

Although it was the U-boat menace from which we suffered most and ran the greatest risks, the attack on our ocean commerce by surface raiders would have been even more formidable could it have been sustained. The three German pocket-battleships permitted by the Treaty of Versailles had been designed with profound thought as commerce-destroyers. Their six 11-inch guns, their 26-knot speed, and the armour they carried had been compressed with masterly skill into the limits of a 10,000-ton displacement. No single British cruiser could match them. The German 8-inch gun cruisers were more modern than ours, and if employed as commerce-raiders would also be a formidable threat. Besides this the enemy might use disguised heavily-armed merchantmen. We had vivid memories of the depredations of the *Emden* and *Koenigsberg* in 1914, and of the thirty or more warships and armed merchantmen they had forced us to combine for their destruction.

There were rumours and reports before the outbreak of the new war that one or more pocket-battleships had already sailed from Germany. The Home Fleet searched but found nothing. We now know that both the *Deutschland* and the *Admiral Graf*

Spee sailed from Germany between August 21 and 24, and were already through the danger zone and loose in the oceans before our blockade and northern patrols were organised. On September 3 the *Deutschland*, having passed through the Denmark Straits, was lurking near Greenland. The *Graf Spee* had crossed the North Atlantic trade route unseen and was already far south of the Azores. Each was accompanied by an auxiliary vessel to replenish fuel and stores. Both at first remained inactive and lost in the ocean spaces. Unless they struck they won no prizes. Until they struck they were in no danger.

The orders of the German Admiralty issued on August 4 were well conceived:

Task in the Event of War

Disruption and destruction of enemy merchant shipping by all possible means. . . . Enemy naval forces, even if inferior, are only to be engaged if it should further the principal task. . . .

Frequent changes of position in the operational areas will create uncertainty and will restrict enemy merchant shipping, even without tangible results. A temporary departure into distant areas will also add to the uncertainty of the enemy.

If the enemy should protect his shipping with superior forces so that direct successes cannot be obtained, then the mere fact that his shipping is so restricted means that we have greatly impaired his supply situation. Valuable results will also be obtained if the pocket-battleships continue to remain in the convoy area.

With all this wisdom the British Admiralty would have been in rueful agreement.

*　　*　　*

On September 30 the British liner *Clement*, of 5,000 tons, sailing independently, was sunk by the *Graf Spee* off Pernambuco. The news electrified the Admiralty. It was the signal for which we had been waiting. A number of hunting groups were immediately formed, comprising all our available aircraft-carriers, supported by battleships, battle-cruisers, and cruisers. Each group of two or more ships was judged to be capable of catching and destroying a pocket-battleship.

In all, during the ensuing months the search for two raiders entailed the formation of nine hunting groups, comprising twenty-three powerful ships. We were also compelled to provide three battleships and two cruisers as additional escorts with the important North Atlantic convoys. These requirements represented a very severe drain on the resources of the Home and Mediterranean Fleets, from which it was necessary to withdraw twelve ships of the most powerful types, including three aircraft-carriers. Working from widely-dispersed bases in the Atlantic and Indian Oceans, the hunting groups could cover the main focal areas traversed by our shipping. To attack our trade the enemy must place himself within reach of at least one of them. To give an idea of the scale of these operations, I set out on page 102 the full list of the hunting groups at their highest point.

*   *   *

At this time it was the prime objective of the American Government to keep the war as far from their shores as possible. On October 3 delegates of twenty-one American republics, assembled at Panama, decided to declare an American Security Zone, proposing to fix a belt of from three hundred to six hundred miles from their coasts within which no warlike act should be committed. We were anxious to help in keeping the war out of American waters—to some extent, indeed, this was to our advantage. I therefore hastened to inform President Roosevelt that if America asked all belligerents to respect such a zone we should immediately declare our readiness to fall in with their wishes—subject of course to our rights under international law. We should not mind how far south the Security Zone went, provided that it was effectively maintained. We should have found great difficulty in accepting a Security Zone which was to be policed only by some weak neutral; but if the United States Navy was to take care of it we should feel no anxiety. The more United States warships there were cruising along the South American coast the better we should be pleased; for the German raider which we were hunting might then prefer to leave American waters for the South African trade route, where we were ready to deal with him. But if a surface raider operated from the American Security Zone or took refuge in it we should expect either to be protected or to be allowed to protect ourselves from the mischief which he might do.

At this date we had no definite knowledge of the sinking of three ships on the Cape of Good Hope route which occurred between October 5 and 10. All three were sailing homeward independently. No distress messages were received, and suspicion was only aroused when they became overdue. It was some time before it could be assumed that they had fallen victims to a raider.

The necessary dispersion of our forces caused me and others anxiety, especially as our main Fleet was sheltering on our west coast.

First Sea Lord, D.C.N.S., Controller   23.ix.39

The appearance of *Scheer* off Pernambuco and subsequent mystery of her movements, and why she does not attack trade, make one ask, did the Germans want to provoke a widespread dispersion of our surplus vessels, and if so why? As the First Sea Lord has observed, it would be more natural they should wish to concentrate them in home waters in order to have targets for air attack. Moreover, how could they have foreseen the extent to which we should react on the rumour of *Scheer* in South Atlantic? It all seems quite purposeless ; yet the Germans are not the people to do things without reason. Are you sure it was *Scheer* and not a plant, or a fake?

I see the German wireless boast they are driving the Fleet out of the North Sea. At present this is less mendacious than most of their stuff. There may therefore be danger on the East Coast from surface ships. Could not submarine flotillas of our own be disposed well out at sea across a probable line of hostile advance? They would want a parent destroyer perhaps to scout for them. They should be well out of our line of watching trawlers. It may well be there is something going to happen, now that we have retired to a distance to gain time.

I should be the last to raise those 'invasion scares', which I combated so constantly during the early days of 1914–15. Still, it might be well for the Chiefs of Staff to consider what would happen if, for instance, 20,000 men were run across and landed, say, at Harwich, or at Webburn Hook, where there is deep water close inshore. These 20,000 men might make the training of Mr. Hore-Belisha's masses very much more realistic than is at present expected. The long dark nights would help such designs. Have any arrangements been made by the War Office to provide against this contingency? Remember how we stand in the North Sea at the present time. I do not think it likely, but it is physically possible.

The *Deutschland*, which was to have harassed our lifeline across the North-west Atlantic, interpreted her orders with

ORGANISATION OF HUNTING GROUPS—OCTOBER 31st, 1939

FORCE	COMPOSITION			AREA
	BATTLESHIPS AND BATTLE-CRUISERS	CRUISERS	AIRCRAFT-CARRIERS	
F		*Berwick* *York*		North America and West Indies
G		*Cumberland* *Exeter* *Ajax* *Achilles*		East coast of South America
H		*Sussex* *Shropshire*		Cape of Good Hope
I		*Cornwall* *Dorsetshire*	*Eagle*	Ceylon
	Malaya		*Glorious*	Gulf of Aden
K	*Renown*		*Ark Royal*	Pernambuco–Freetown
L	*Repulse*		*Furious*	Atlantic convoys
X		Two French 8–inch cruisers	*Hermes*	Pernambuco–Dakar
Y	*Strasbourg*	*Neptune*		Pernambuco–Dakar
		One French 8–inch cruiser		

Additional escorts with North Atlantic convoys:

Battleships:	*Revenge* *Resolution* *Warspite*
Cruisers:	*Emerald* *Enterprise*

comprehending caution. At no time during her two and a half months' cruise did she approach a convoy. Her determined efforts to avoid British forces prevented her from making more than two kills, one being a small Norwegian ship. A third ship, the United States *City of Flint*, carrying a cargo for Britain, was captured, but was eventually released by the Germans from a Norwegian port. Early in November the *Deutschland* slunk back to Germany, passing again through Arctic waters. The mere presence of this powerful ship upon our main trade route had however imposed, as was intended, a serious strain upon our escorts and hunting groups in the North Atlantic. We should in fact have preferred her activity to the vague menace she embodied.

The *Graf Spee* was more daring and imaginative and soon became the centre of attention in the South Atlantic. In this vast area powerful Allied forces came into play by the middle of October. One group consisted of the aircraft-carrier *Ark Royal* and the battle-cruiser *Renown*, working from Freetown, in conjunction with a French group of two heavy cruisers and the British aircraft-carrier *Hermes*, based on Dakar. At the Cape of Good Hope were the two heavy cruisers *Sussex* and *Shropshire*, while on the east coast of South America, covering the vital traffic with the River Plate and Rio de Janeiro, ranged Commodore Harwood's group, comprising the *Cumberland, Exeter, Ajax,* and *Achilles*. The *Achilles* was a New Zealand ship manned mainly by New Zealanders.

The *Spee*'s practice was to make a brief appearance at some point, claim a victim, and vanish again into the trackless ocean wastes. After a second appearance farther south on the Cape route, in which she sank only one ship, there was no further sign of her for nearly a month, during which our hunting groups were searching far and wide in all areas, and special vigilance was enjoined in the Indian Ocean. This was in fact her destination, and on November 15 she sank a small British tanker in the Mozambique Channel, between Madagascar and the mainland. Having thus registered her appearance as a feint in the Indian Ocean, in order to draw the hunt in that direction, her captain—Langsdorff, a high-class person—promptly doubled back and, keeping well south of the Cape, re-entered the Atlantic. This move had not been unforeseen ; but our plans to intercept him were foiled by the quickness of his withdrawal. It was by no means clear to the Admiralty whether in fact one raider was on the prowl or two, and exertions were made both in the Indian and Atlantic Oceans. We also thought that the *Spee* was her sister ship, the *Scheer*. The disproportion between the strength of the enemy and the counter-measures forced upon us was vexatious. It recalled to me the anxious weeks before the action at Coronel and later at the Falkland Islands in December 1914, when we had to be prepared at seven or eight different points, in the Pacific and South Atlantic, for the arrival of Admiral von Spee with the earlier edition of the *Scharnhorst* and *Gneisenau*. A quarter of a century had passed, but the puzzle was the same. It was with a definite sense of relief that we learnt that the *Spee* had appeared once more on the Cape-Freetown route, sinking two more ships on December 2 and one on the 7th.

*   *   *

From the beginning of the war Commodore Harwood's special care and duty had been to cover British shipping off the River Plate and Rio de Janeiro. He was convinced that sooner or later the *Spee* would come towards the Plate, where the richest prizes were offered to her. He had carefully thought out the tactics which he would adopt in an encounter. Together, his 8-inch cruisers *Cumberland* and *Exeter*, and his 6-inch cruisers *Ajax* and *Achilles*, could not only catch but kill. However, the needs of fuel and refit made it unlikely that all four would be present 'on the day'. If they were not the issue was disputable. On hearing that the *Doric Star* had been sunk on December 2, Harwood guessed right. Although she was over 3,000 miles away he assumed that the *Spee* would come towards the Plate. He estimated with luck and wisdom that she might arrive by the 13th. He ordered all his available forces to concentrate there by December 12. Alas, the *Cumberland* was refitting at the Falklands; but on the morning of the 13th *Exeter, Ajax,* and *Achilles* were in company at the centre of the shipping routes off the mouth of the river. Sure enough, at 6.14 a.m. smoke was sighted to the east. The longed-for collision had come.

Harwood, in the *Ajax,* disposing his forces so as to attack the pocket-battleship from widely-divergent quarters and thus confuse her fire, advanced at the utmost speed of his small squadron. Captain Langsdorff thought at the first glance that he had only to deal with one light cruiser and two destroyers, and he too went full speed ahead; but a few moments later he recognised the quality of his opponents, and knew that a mortal action impended. The two forces were now closing at nearly fifty miles an hour. Langsdorff had but a minute to make up his mind. His right course would have been to turn away immediately so as to keep his assailants as long as possible under the superior range and weight of his 11-inch guns, to which the British could not at first have replied. He would have thus gained for his undisturbed firing the difference between adding speeds and subtracting them. He might well have crippled one of his foes before any could fire at him. He decided, on the contrary, to hold on his course and make for the *Exeter*. The action therefore began almost simultaneously on both sides.

Commodore Harwood's tactics proved advantageous. The 8-inch salvoes from the *Exeter* struck the *Spee* from the earliest stages of the fight. Meanwhile the 6-inch cruisers were also hitting hard and effectively. Soon the *Exeter* received a hit

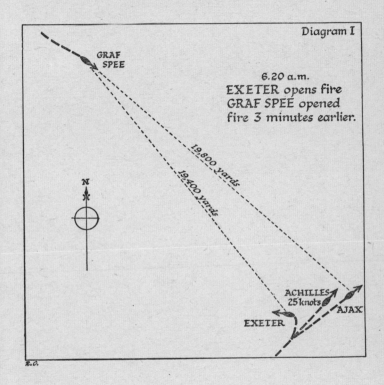

Diagram I

GRAF
SPEE

6.20 a.m.
EXETER opens fire
GRAF SPEE opened
fire 3 minutes earlier.

19,800 yards

19,400 yards

N

ACHILLES
25 knots

AJAX

EXETER

which, besides knocking out B turret, destroyed all the communications on the bridge, killed or wounded nearly all upon it, and put the ship temporarily out of control. By this time however the 6-inch cruisers could no longer be neglected by the enemy, and the *Spee* shifted her main armament to them, thus giving respite to the *Exeter* at a critical moment. The German battleship, plastered from three directions, found the British attack too hot, and soon afterwards turned away under a smoke-screen with the apparent intention of making for the River Plate. Langsdorff had better have done this earlier.

After this turn the *Spee* once more engaged the *Exeter*, hard hit by the 11-inch shells. All her forward guns were out of

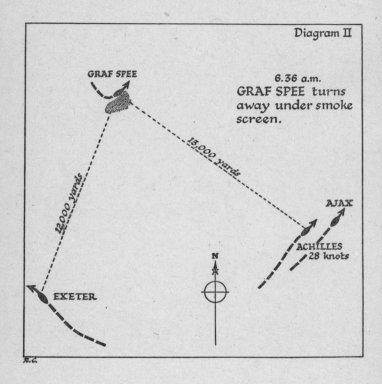

Diagram II

GRAF SPEE

6.36 a.m.
GRAF SPEE turns away under smoke screen.

13,000 yards

12,000 yards

AJAX

ACHILLES
28 knots

N

EXETER

R.C.

action. She was burning fiercely amidships and had a heavy list. Captain Bell, unscathed by the explosion on the bridge, gathered two or three officers round him in the after control-station, and kept his ship in action with her sole remaining turret, until at 7.30 failure of pressure put this too out of action. He could do no more. At 7.40 the *Exeter* turned away to effect repairs and took no further part in the fight.

The *Ajax* and *Achilles*, already in pursuit, continued the action in the most spirited manner. The *Spee* turned all her heavy guns upon them. By 7.25 the two after-turrets in the *Ajax* had been knocked out, and the *Achilles* had also suffered damage. These two light cruisers were no match for the enemy

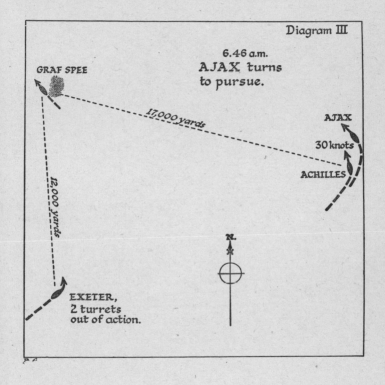

in gun-power, and, finding that his ammunition was running low, Harwood in the *Ajax* decided to break off the fight till dark, when he would have better chances of using his lighter armament effectively, and perhaps his torpedoes. He therefore turned away under cover of smoke, and the enemy did not follow. This fierce action had lasted an hour and twenty minutes. During all the rest of the day the *Spee* made for Montevideo, the British cruisers hanging grimly on her heels, with only

Diagram IV

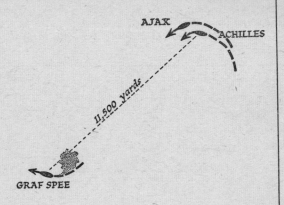

AJAX

ACHILLES

11,500 yards

GRAF SPEE

N

7.30 a.m.
GRAF SPEE screened
by smoke. AJAX turns
towards the enemy.
Two turrets out of
action at 7.25

To Falkland
Islands,
1000 miles.

EXETER
turning away at 7.40

R.C.

occasional interchanges of fire. Shortly after midnight the *Spee* entered Montevideo, and lay there repairing damage, taking in stores, landing wounded, transhipping personnel to a German merchant ship, and reporting to the Fuehrer. *Ajax* and *Achilles* lay outside, determined to dog her to her doom should she ven-

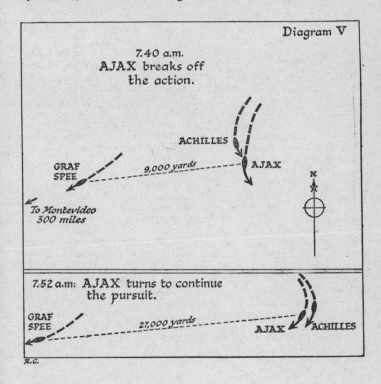

Diagram V

7.40 a.m.
AJAX breaks off
the action.

ACHILLES

GRAF
SPEE   9,000 yards ---------- AJAX

N

To Montevideo
300 miles

7.52 a.m. AJAX turns to continue
the pursuit.

GRAF
SPEE   27,000 yards ---------- AJAX ACHILLES

R.C.

ture forth. Meanwhile on the night of the 14th the *Cumberland*, which had been steaming at full speed from the Falklands, took the place of the utterly crippled *Exeter*. The arrival of this 8-inch-gun cruiser restored to its narrow balance a doubtful situation.

It had been most exciting to follow the drama of this brilliant action from the Admiralty War Room, where I spent a large part of the 13th. Our anxieties did not end with the day. Mr.

Chamberlain was at that time in France on a visit to the Army. On the 17th I wrote to him:

December .17, 1939

If the *Spee* breaks out as she may do to-night we hope to renew the action of the 13th with the *Cumberland,* an eight 8-inch-gun ship, in the place of the six-gun *Exeter.* The *Spee* knows now that *Renown* and *Ark Royal* are oiling at Rio, so this is her best chance. The *Dorsetshire* and *Shropshire,* who are coming across from the Cape, are still three and four days away respectively. It is fortunate that the *Cumberland* was handy at the Falklands, as *Exeter* was heavily damaged. She was hit over a hundred times, one turret smashed, three guns knocked out, and sixty officers and men killed and twenty wounded. Indeed, the *Exeter* fought one of the finest and most resolute actions against superior range and metal on record. Every conceivable precaution has been taken to prevent the *Spee* slipping out unobserved, and I have told Harwood [who is now an Admiral and a K.C.B.] that he is free to attack her anywhere outside the three-mile limit. We should prefer however that she should be interned, as this will be less creditable to the German Navy than being sunk in action. Moreover, a battle of this kind is full of hazard, and needless bloodshed must never be sought.

The whole of the Canadians came in safely this morning under the protection of the main fleet, and [are] being welcomed by Anthony, Massey, and I trust a good part of the people of Greenock and Glasgow. We plan to give them a cordial reception. They are to go to Aldershot, where no doubt you will go and see them presently.

There have been ten air attacks to-day on individual ships along the East Coast from Wick to Dover, and some of the merchant ships have been machine-gunned out of pure spite, some of our people being hit on their decks.

I am sure you must be having a most interesting time at the Front, and I expect you will find that change is the best kind of rest.

From the moment when we heard that action was joined we instantly ordered powerful forces to concentrate off Montevideo, but our hunting groups were naturally widely dispersed and none was within two thousand miles of the scene. In the north Force K, comprising the *Renown* and *Ark Royal*, was completing a sweep which had begun at Capetown ten days before and was now six hundred miles east of Pernambuco and 2,500 miles from Montevideo. Farther north still the cruiser *Neptune,*

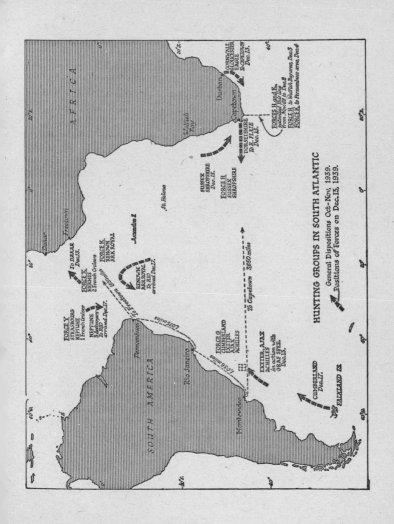

HUNTING GROUPS IN SOUTH ATLANTIC
General Dispositions Oct-Nov, 1939.
Positions of Forces on Dec.13, 1939.

with three destroyers, had just parted company with the French
Force X and was coming south to join Force K. All these were
ordered to Montevideo ; they had first to fuel at Rio. However,
we succeeded in creating the impression that they had already
left Rio and were approaching Montevideo at thirty knots.

On the other side of the Atlantic Force H was returning to the
Cape for fuel after an extended sweep up the African coast.
Only the *Dorsetshire* was immediately available at Capetown,
and she was ordered at once to join Admiral Harwood, but
she had nearly 4,000 miles to travel. She was followed later by
the *Shropshire*. In addition, to guard against the possible escape
of the *Spee* to the eastward, Force I, now comprising the *Corn-
wall, Gloucester,* and the aircraft-carrier *Eagle* from the East
Indies station, which at this time was at Durban, was placed at
the disposal of the C.-in-C. South Atlantic.

*   *   *

Meanwhile Captain Langsdorff telegraphed on December 16
to the German Admiralty as follows:

> Strategic position off Montevideo. Besides the cruisers and
> destroyers, *Ark Royal* and *Renown*. Close blockade at night ;
> escape into open sea and break-through to home waters
> hopeless. ... Request decision on whether the ship should
> be scuttled in spite of insufficient depth in the estuary of the
> Plate, or whether internment is to be preferred.

At a conference presided over by the Fuehrer, at which
Raeder and Jodl were present, the following answer was decided
on:

> Attempt by all means to extend the time in neutral waters.
> ... Fight your way through to Buenos Aires if possible. No
> internment in Uruguay. Attempt effective destruction if ship
> is scuttled.

As the German envoy in Montevideo reported later that further attempts to extend the time-limit of seventy-two hours
were fruitless, these orders were confirmed by the German
Supreme Command.

Accordingly during the afternoon of the 17th the *Spee* transferred more than seven hundred men, with baggage and pro-
visions, to the German merchant ship in the harbour. Shortly
afterwards Admiral Harwood learnt that she was weighing
anchor. At 6.15 p.m., watched by immense crowds, she left

harbour and steamed slowly seawards, awaited hungrily by the British cruisers. At 8.54 p.m., as the sun sank, the *Ajax*'s aircraft reported: '*Graf Spee* has blown herself up.' The *Renown* and *Ark Royal* were still a thousand miles away.

Langsdorff was broken-hearted by the loss of his ship. In spite of the full authority he had received from his Government, he wrote on December 19:

> I can now only prove by my death that the fighting services of the Third Reich are ready to die for the honour of the flag. I alone bear the responsibility for scuttling the pocket-battleship *Admiral Graf Spee*. I am happy to pay with my life for any possible reflection on the honour of the flag. I shall face my fate with firm faith in the cause and the future of the nation and of my Fuehrer.

That night he shot himself.

Thus ended the first surface challenge to British trade on the oceans. No other raider appeared until the spring of 1940, when a new campaign opened, utilising disguised merchant ships. These could more easily avoid detection, but on the other hand could be mastered by lesser forces than those required to destroy a pocket-battleship.

* * *

As soon as the news arrived of the end of the *Spee* I was impatient to bring our widely-scattered hunting groups home. The *Spee*'s auxiliary, the *Altmark*, was however still afloat, and it was believed that she had on board the crews of the nine ships which had been sunk by the raider.

First Sea Lord 17.XII.39

Now that the South Atlantic is practically clear except for the *Altmark*, it seems of high importance to bring home the *Renown* and *Ark Royal*, together with at least one of the 8-inch-gun cruisers. This will give us more easement in convoy work and enable refits and leave to be accomplished. I like your plan of the two small ships anchoring to-morrow in Montevideo inner harbour, but I do not think it would be right to send Force K so far south. Moreover, perhaps so many warships would not be allowed in at one time. It would be very convenient if, as you proposed, *Neptune* relieved *Ajax* as soon as the triumphal entry into [Montevideo harbour] is over ; and it would be very good if all the returning forces could scrub and search the South Atlantic on their way home for the *Altmark*. I feel that we ought to bring home all that are not absolutely needed. The Northern Patrol will require constant support in two, or better still three, reliefs from the Clyde as long as we stay there. I agree with Captain Tennant that the German Admiralty will be most anxious to do something to get their name back.

Perhaps you will let me know what you think about these ideas.

I was also most anxious about the *Exeter*, and could not accept the proposals made to me to leave her unrepaired in the Falkland Islands till the end of the war.

First Sea Lord, Controller, and others   17.XII.39

This preliminary report of damage to *Exeter* shows the tremendous fire to which she was exposed and the determination with which it was fought. It also reflects high credit on the Constructors' Department that she should have been able to stand up to such a prolonged and severe battering. This story will have to be told as soon as possible, omitting anything undesirable [*i.e.,* what the enemy should not know].

What is proposed about repair? What can be done at the Falklands? I presume she will be patched up sufficiently to come home for long refit.

First Sea Lord, D.C.N.S., Controller   23.XII.39

We ought not readily to accept the non-repair during the war of *Exeter*. She should be strengthened and strutted internally as far as possible, and should transfer her ammunition, or the bulk of it, to some merchant ship or tender. Perhaps she might be filled up in part with barrels or empty oil-drums, and come home with reduced crew under escort either to the Mediterranean or to one of our dockyards. If nothing can be done with her then, she should be stripped of all useful guns and appliances, which can be transferred to new construction.

The above indicates only my general view. Perhaps you will let me know how it can be implemented.

Controller and First Sea Lord   29.XII.39

I have not seen the answer to the telegram from the Rear-Admiral South America about its not being worth while to repair *Exeter,* on which I minuted in the contrary sense. How does this matter now stand? I gathered from you verbally that we were all in agreement she should come home and be thoroughly repaired, and that this need not take so long as the R.A. thought.

Top: Polish Uhlans cross a river in the Polish Corridor. *Bottom:* Mechanised units of the mobilised Polish Army

Top: Polish partisans taken prisoner and guarded by German soldiers.
Bottom: Personnel of the Soviet Embassy in Warsaw, who escaped after
the Russian invasion of Poland, reach the German lines

Top: Wreck of the first German bomber forced down over Great Britain, near Humble in Scotland. *Bottom:* The famous German pocket battleship *Admiral Graf Spee,* the sinking of which (in December 1939) was Britain's first success of the war

Top: Finnish soldiers in their white camouflage suits. *Bottom:* Husky dogs who acted as transport for the Finnish Army

Part of the notorious Mannerheim Line, showing tank traps in the thick snow

Allied underground munition stores in the Maginot Line

Top: Churchill, at the British headquarters in France, in conversation with Lord Gort. *Bottom:* British troops enter a French casemate

River Plate, which they claimed to be a violation of the American Security Zone. It also happened about this time that two German merchant ships were intercepted by our cruisers near the coast of the United States. One of these, the liner *Columbus*, of 32,000 tons, was scuttled and survivors were rescued by an American cruiser; the other escaped into territorial waters in Florida. President Roosevelt reluctantly complained about these vexations near the coast of the Western Hemisphere, and in my reply I took the opportunity of stressing the advantages which our action off the Plate had brought to all the South American Republics. Their trade had been hampered by the activities of the German raider and their ports had been used for his supply ships and as information centres. By the laws of war the raider had been entitled to capture all merchant ships trading with us in the South Atlantic, or to sink them after providing for their crews; and this had inflicted grave injury on American commercial interests, particularly in the Argentine. The South American Republics should greet the action off the Plate as a deliverance from all this annoyance. The whole of the South Atlantic was now clear, and might perhaps remain clear, of warlike operations. This relief should be highly valued by the South American States, who might now in practice enjoy for a long period the advantages of a Security Zone of three thousand, rather than three hundred, miles.

I could not forbear from adding that the Royal Navy was carrying a very heavy burden in enforcing respect for international law at sea. The presence of even a single raider in the North Atlantic called for the employment of half our battle-fleet to give sure protection to the world's commerce. The unlimited laying of magnetic mines by the enemy was adding to the strain upon our flotillas and small craft. If we should break under this strain the South American Republics would soon have many worse worries than the sound of one day's distant seaward cannonade; and in quite a short time the United States would also face more direct cares. I therefore felt entitled to ask that full consideration should be given to the burden which we were carrying at this crucial period, and that the best construction should be placed on action which was indispensable if the war was to be ended within reasonable time and in the right way.

CHAPTER 9

Scandinavia. Finland

The Norway Peninsula – Swedish Iron Ore – Neutrality and the Norwegian Corridor – An Error Corrected – Behind the German Veil – Admiral Von Raeder and Herr Rosenberg – Vidkun Quisling – Hitler's Decision, December 14, 1939 – Soviet Action against the Baltic States – Stalin's Demands upon Finland – The Russians Declare War on Finland, November 28, 1939 – Gallant Finnish Resistance – The Soviet Failure and Rebuff – World-wide Satisfaction – Aid to Finland and Norwegian and Swedish Neutrality – The Case for Mining the 'Leads' – The Moral Issue.

The thousand-mile-long peninsula stretching from the mouth of the Baltic to the Arctic Circle had an immense strategic significance. The Norwegian mountains run into the ocean in a continuous fringe of islands. Between these islands and the mainland there was a corridor in territorial waters through which Germany could communicate with the outer sea to the grievous injury of our blockade. German war industry was mainly based upon supplies of Swedish iron ore, which in the summer were drawn from the Swedish port of Luleå, at the head of the Gulf of Bothnia, and in the winter, when this was frozen, from Narvik, on the west coast of Norway. To respect the corridor would be to allow the whole of this traffic to proceed under the shield of neutrality in the face of our superior sea-power. The Admiralty Staff were seriously perturbed at this important advantage being presented to Germany, and at the earliest opportunity I raised the issue in the Cabinet.

My recollection of the previous war was that the British and American Governments had had no scruples about mining the 'Leads', as these sheltered waters were called. The great mine barrage which was laid in 1917–18 across the North Sea from Scotland to Norway could not have been fully effective if German commerce and German U-boats had only to slip round the end of it unmolested. I found however that neither of the Allied Fleets had laid any minefields in Norwegian territorial waters. Their admirals had complained that the barrage, on which enormous quantities of labour and money had been spent, would be ineffective unless this corridor was closed, and all the Allied Governments had therefore put the strongest pressure on Norway to close it themselves. The immense barrage took a long time to lay, and by the time it was finished there was not much doubt how the war would end or that Germany no longer possessed the power to invade Scandinavia. It was not however till the end of September 1918 that the Norwegian Government were persuaded to take action. Before they actually carried out their undertaking the war came to an end.

When eventually I presented this case in the House of Commons, in April 1940, I said:

> During the last war, when we were associated with the United States, the Allies felt themselves so deeply injured by this covered way, then being used especially for U-boats setting out on their marauding expeditions, that the British, French, and United States Governments together induced the Norwegians to [undertake to] lay a minefield in their territorial waters across the covered way in order to prevent the abuse by U-boats of this channel. It was only natural that the Admiralty since this war began should have brought this precedent—although it is not exactly on all fours and there are some differences—this modern and highly respectable precedent, to the notice of His Majesty's Government, and should have urged that we should be allowed to lay a minefield of our own in Norwegian territorial waters in order to compel this traffic which was passing in and out to Germany to come out into the open sea and take a chance of being brought into the Contraband Control or being captured as enemy prize by our blockading squadrons and flotillas. It was only natural and it was only right that His Majesty's Government should have been long reluctant to incur the reproach of even a technical violation of international law.

They certainly were long in reaching a decision.

At first the reception of my case was favourable. All my colleagues were deeply impressed with the evil; but strict respect for the neutrality of small States was a principle of conduct to which we all adhered.

First Lord to First Sea Lord and others   19.IX.39
   I brought to the notice of the Cabinet this morning the importance of stopping the Norwegian transportation of Swedish iron ore from Narvik, which will begin as soon as the ice forms in the Gulf of Bothnia. I pointed out that we

had laid a minefield across the 3-mile limit in Norwegian territorial waters in 1918, with the approval and co-operation of the United States. I suggested that we should repeat this process very shortly. [This, as is explained above, was not an accurate statement, and I was soon apprised of the fact.] The Cabinet, including the Foreign Secretary, appeared strongly favourable to this action.

It is therefore necessary to take all steps to prepare it.

1. The negotiations with the Norwegians for the chartering of their tonnage must be got out of the way first.

2. The Board of Trade would have to make arrangements with Sweden to buy the ore in question, as it is far from our wish to quarrel with the Swedes.

3. The Foreign Office should be made acquainted with our proposals, and the whole story of Anglo-American action in 1918 must be carefully set forth, together with a reasoned case.

4. The operation itself should be studied by the Admiralty Staff concerned. The Economic Warfare Department should be informed as and when necessary.

Pray let me be continually informed of the progress of this plan, which is of the highest importance in crippling the enemy's war industry.

A further Cabinet decision will be necessary when all is in readiness.

On the 29th, at the invitation of my colleagues, and after the whole subject had been minutely examined at the Admiralty, I drafted a paper for the Cabinet upon this subject, and on the chartering of neutral tonnage, which was linked with it.

NORWAY AND SWEDEN

MEMORANDUM BY THE FIRST LORD OF THE ADMIRALTY

Chartering Norwegian Tonnage   *September* 29, 1939

1. The Norwegian Delegation is approaching, and in a few days the President of the Board of Trade hopes to make a bargain with them by which he charters all their spare tonnage, the bulk of which consists of tankers.

The Admiralty consider the chartering of this tonnage most important, and Lord Chatfield has written strongly urging it upon them.

German Supplies of Iron Ore from Narvik

2. At the end of November the Gulf of Bothnia normally freezes, so that Swedish iron ore can be sent to Germany

only through Oxelosund, in the Baltic, or from Narvik, at the north of Norway. Oxelosund can export only about one-fifth of the weight of ore Germany requires from Sweden. In winter normally the main trade is from Narvik, whence ships can pass down the west coast of Norway, and make the whole voyage to Germany without leaving territorial waters until inside the Skagerrak.

It must be understood that an adequate supply of Swedish iron ore is vital to Germany, and the interception or prevention of these Narvik supplies during the winter months, *i.e.*, from October to the end of April, will greatly reduce her power of resistance. For the first three weeks of the war no iron ore ships left Narvik owing to the reluctance of crews to sail and other causes outside our control. Should this satisfactory state of affairs continue, no special action would be demanded from the Admiralty. Furthermore, negotiations are proceeding with the Swedish Government which in themselves may effectively reduce the supplies of Scandinavian ore to Germany.

Should however the supplies from Narvik to Germany start moving again, more drastic action will be needed.

Relations with Sweden

3. Our relations with Sweden require careful consideration. Germany acts upon Sweden by threats. Our sea-power gives us also powerful weapons, which, if need be, we must use to ration Sweden. Nevertheless, it should be proposed, as part of the policy outlined in paragraph 2, to assist the Swedes so far as possible to dispose of their ore in exchange for our coal ; and, should this not suffice, to indemnify them, partly at least, by other means. This is the next step.

Charter and Insurance of all available Neutral Tonnage

4. The above considerations lead to a wider proposal. Ought we not to secure the control, by charter or otherwise, of all the free neutral shipping we can obtain, as well as the Norwegian, and thus give the Allies power to regulate the greater part of the sea transport of the world and recharter it, profitably, to those who act as we wish?

And ought we not to extend to neutral shipping not under our direct control the benefit of our convoy system?

The results so far achieved by the Royal Navy against the U-boat attack seem, in the opinion of the Admiralty, to justify the adoption of this latter course. This would mean that we should offer safe convoy to all vessels of all countries traversing our sea routes, provided they conform to our rules of contraband and pay the necessary premiums in foreign devisen. They would therefore be able to contract themselves out of the war risk, and with the success of our anti-U-boat campaign we may well hope to make a profit to offset its heavy expense. Thus not only vessels owned by us or controlled by us, but independent neutral ships, would all come to enjoy the British protection of the high seas, or be indemnified in case of accidents. It is not believed at the Admiralty that this is beyond our strength. Had some such scheme for the chartering and insurance of neutral shipping been in force from the early days of the last war, there is little doubt that it would have proved a highly profitable speculation. In this war it might well prove to be the foundation of a League of Free Maritime Nations to which it was profitable to belong.

5. It is therefore asked that the Cabinet, if they approve in principle of these four main objectives, should remit the question to the various departments concerned in order that detailed plans may be made for prompt action.

Before circulating this paper to the Cabinet and raising the issue there, I called upon the Admiralty Staff for a thorough re-check of the whole position.

First Lord to the Assistant Chief of the Naval Staff   29.IX.39
Please reconvene the meeting on iron ore we held on Thursday to-morrow morning, while Cabinet is sitting, in order to consider the draft print which I have made. It is no use my asking the Cabinet to take the drastic action suggested against a neutral country unless the results are in the first order of importance.

I am told that there are hardly any German or Swedish ships trying to take ore south from Narvik. Also that the Germans have been accumulating ore by sea at Oxelosund against the freezing up, and so will be able to bring good supplies down the Baltic via the Kiel Canal to the Ruhr during the winter months. Are these statements true? It would be very unpleasant if I went into action on mining the Norwegian territorial waters and was answered that it would not do the trick.

At the same time, assuming that the west coast traffic of Norway in ore is a really important factor worth making an exertion to stop, at what point would you stop it?

Pray explore in detail the coast and let me know the point. Clearly it should be north at any rate of Bergen, thus leaving the southern part of the West Norwegian coast open for any traffic that may come from Norway or out of the Baltic in the Norwegian convoy across to us. All this has to be more explored before I can present my case to the Cabinet. I shall not attempt to do so until Monday or Tuesday.

When all was agreed and settled at the Admiralty I brought the matter a second time before the Cabinet. Again there was general agreement upon the need; but I was unable to obtain assent to action. The Foreign Office arguments about neutrality were weighty, and I could not prevail. I continued, as will be seen, to press my point by every means and on all occasions. It was not however until April 1940 that the decision that I asked for in September 1939 was taken. By that time it was too late.

* * *

Almost at this very moment, as we now know, German eyes were turned in the same direction. On October 3 Admiral Raeder, Chief of the Naval Staff, submitted a proposal to Hitler headed 'Gaining of Bases in Norway'. He asked, 'That the Fuehrer be informed as soon as possible of the opinions of the Naval War Staff on the possibilities of extending the operational base to the north. It must be ascertained whether it is possible to gain bases in Norway under the combined pressure of Russia and Germany, with the aim of improving our strategic and operational position.' He framed therefore a series of notes, which he placed before Hitler on October 10. 'In these notes,' he wrote, 'I stressed the disadvantages which an occupation of Norway by the British would have for us: the control of the approaches to the Baltic, the outflanking of our naval operations and of our air attacks on Britain, the end of our pressure on Sweden. I also stressed the advantages for us of the occupation of the Norwegian coast: outlet to the North Atlantic, no possibility of a British mine barrier, as in the year 1917–18. ... The Fuehrer saw at once the significance of the Norwegian problem; he asked me to leave the notes, and stated that he wished to consider the question himself.'

Rosenberg, the foreign affairs expert of the Nazi Party, and in charge of a special bureau to deal with propaganda activities in foreign countries, shared the Admiral's view. He dreamed of 'converting Scandinavia to the idea of a Nordic community embracing the northern peoples under the natural leadership of Germany'. Early in 1939 he thought he had discovered an instrument in the extreme Nationalist Party in Norway, which was led by a former Norwegian Minister of War named Vidkun

Quisling. Contacts were established, and Quisling's activity was linked with the plans of the German Naval Staff through Rosenberg's organisation and the German Naval Attaché in Oslo.

Quisling and his assistant, Hagelin, went to Berlin on December 14, and were taken by Raeder to Hitler, to discuss a political stroke in Norway. Quisling arrived with a detailed plan. Hitler, careful of secrecy, affected reluctance to increase his commitments, and said he would prefer a neutral Scandinavia. Nevertheless, according to Raeder, it was on this very day that he gave the order to the Supreme Command to prepare for a Norwegian Operation.

Of all this we of course knew nothing.

*   *   *

Meanwhile the Scandinavian peninsula became the scene of an unexpected conflict which aroused strong feeling in Britain and France, and powerfully affected the discussion about Norway. As soon as Germany was involved in war with Great Britain and France, Soviet Russia, in the spirit of her pact with Germany, proceeded to block the lines of entry into the Soviet Union from the west. One passage led from East Prussia through the Baltic States ; another led across the waters of the Gulf of Finland ; the third route was through Finland itself and across the Karelian Isthmus to a point where the Finnish frontier was only twenty miles from the suburbs of Leningrad. The Soviets had not forgotten the dangers which Leningrad had faced in 1919. Even the White Russian Government of Kolchak had informed the Peace Conference in Paris that bases in the Baltic States and Finland were a necessary protection for the Russian capital. Stalin had used the same language to the British and French Missions in the summer of 1939 ; and we have seen in earlier chapters how the natural fears of these small States had been an obstacle to an Anglo-French Alliance with Russia, and had paved the way for the Molotov-Ribbentrop agreement.

Stalin had wasted no time. On September 24 the Esthonian Foreign Minister had been called to Moscow, and four days later his Government signed a Pact on Mutual Assistance which gave the Russians the right to garrison key bases in Esthonia. By October 21 the Red Army and Air Force were installed. The same procedure was used simultaneously in Latvia, and Soviet garrisons also appeared in Lithuania. Thus the southern road to Leningrad and half the Gulf of Finland had been swiftly barred against potential German ambitions by the armed forces of the Soviets. There remained only the approach through Finland.

Early in October Mr. Paasikivi, one of the Finnish statesmen who had signed the peace of 1921 with the Soviet Union, went to Moscow. The Soviet demands were sweeping: the Finnish frontier on the Karelian Isthmus must be moved back a considerable distance so as to remove Leningrad from the range of hostile artillery. The cession of certain Finnish islands in the Gulf of Finland; the lease of the Rybathy Peninsula, together with Finland's only ice-free port in the Arctic Sea, Petsamo; and, above all, the leasing of the port of Hango, at the entrance of the Gulf of Finland, as a Russian naval and air base, completed the Soviet requirements. The Finns were prepared to make concessions on every point except the last. With the keys of the Gulf in Russian hands the strategic and national security of Finland seemed to them to vanish. The negotiations broke down on November 13, and the Finnish Government began to mobilise, and strengthen their troops on the Karelian frontier. On November 28 Molotov denounced the Non-Aggression Pact between Finland and Russia; two days later the Russians attacked at eight points along Finland's thousand-mile frontier, and on the same morning the capital, Helsingfors, was bombed by the Red Air Force.

The brunt of the Russian attack fell at first upon the frontier defences of the Finns in the Karelian Isthmus. These comprised a fortified zone about twenty miles in depth running north and south through forest country, deep in snow. This was called the 'Mannerheim Line', after the Finnish Commander-in-Chief and saviour of Finland from Bolshevik subjugation in 1917. The indignation excited in Britain, France, and even more vehemently in the United States, at the unprovoked attack by the enormous Soviet Power upon a small, spirited, and highly-civilised nation was soon followed by astonishment and relief. The early weeks of fighting brought no success to the Soviet forces, which in the first instance were drawn almost entirely from the Leningrad garrison. The Finnish Army, whose total fighting strength was only about 200,000 men, gave a good account of themselves. The Russian tanks were encountered with audacity and a new type of hand-grenade, soon nicknamed 'the Molotov Cocktail'.

It is probable that the Soviet Government had counted on a

Russian Attack on Finland, December 1939

walk-over. Their early air raids on Helsingfors and elsewhere, though not on a heavy scale, were expected to strike terror. The troops they used at first, though numerically much stronger, were inferior in quality and ill-trained. The effect of the air raids and of the invasion of their land roused the Finns, who rallied to a man against the aggressor and fought with absolute determination and the utmost skill. It is true that the Russian division which carried out the attack on Petsamo had little difficulty in throwing back the 700 Finns in that area. But the

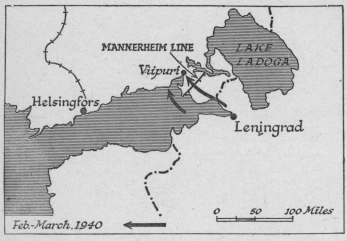

Breaking the Mannerheim Line, March 1940

attack on the 'Waist' of Finland proved disastrous to the invaders. The country here is almost entirely pine forests, gently undulating and at the time covered with a foot of hard snow. The cold was intense. The Finns were well equipped with skis and warm clothing, of which the Russians had neither. Moreover, the Finns proved themselves aggressive individual fighters, highly trained in reconnaissance and forest warfare. The Russians relied in vain on numbers and heavier weapons. All along this front the Finnish frontier posts withdrew slowly down the roads, followed by the Russian columns. After these had penetrated about thirty miles they were set upon by the Finns. Held in front at Finnish defence lines constructed in the forests, violently attacked in flank by day and night, their communications severed behind them, the columns were cut to pieces, or, if lucky got back after heavy loss whence they came. By the end of December the whole Russian plan for driving in across the 'Waist' had broken down.

Meanwhile the attacks against the Mannerheim Line in the Karelian Isthmus fared no better. North of Lake Ladoga a turning movement attempted by about two Soviet divisions met the same fate as the operations farther north. Against the Line itself a series of mass attacks by nearly twelve divisions was launched in early December, and continued throughout the month. The Russian artillery bombardments were inadequate; their tanks were mostly light, and a succession of frontal attacks were repulsed with heavy losses and no gains. By the end of the year failure all along the front convinced the Soviet Government that they had to deal with a very different enemy from what they had expected. They determined upon a major effort. Realising that in the forest warfare of the north they could not overcome by mere weight of numbers the superior tactics and training of the Finns, they decided to concentrate on piercing the Mannerheim Line by methods of siege warfare in which the power of massed heavy artillery and heavy tanks could be brought into full play. This required preparation on a large scale, and from the end of the year fighting died down all along the Finnish front, leaving the Finns so far victorious over their mighty assailant. This surprising event was received with equal satisfaction in all countries, belligerent or neutral, throughout the world. It was a pretty bad advertisement for the Soviet Army. In British circles many people congratulated themselves that we had not gone out of our way to bring the Soviets in on our side, and preened themselves on their foresight. The conclusion was drawn too hastily that the Russian Army had been ruined by the purge, and that the inherent rottenness and degradation of their system of government and society was now proved. It was not only in England that this view was taken. There is no doubt that Hitler and his generals meditated profoundly upon the Finnish exposure, and that it played a potent part in influencing the Fuehrer's thought.

All the resentment felt against the Soviet Government for the Ribbentrop-Molotov pact was fanned into flame by this latest exhibition of brutal bullying and aggression. With this was also mingled scorn for the inefficiency displayed by the Soviet troops and enthusiasm for the gallant Finns. In spite of the Great War which had been declared, there was a keen desire to help the Finns by aircraft and other precious war material and by volunteers from Britain, from the United States, and still more from France. Alike for the munitions supplies and the volunteers there was only one possible route to Finland. The iron ore port of Narvik, with its railroad over the mountains to the Swedish iron mines, acquired a new sentimental if not strategic significance. Its use as a line of supply for the Finnish armies affected the neutrality both of Norway and Sweden. These two States, in equal fear of Germany and Russia, had no aim but to keep out of the wars by which they were encircled and might be engulfed. For them this seemed the only chance of survival. But whereas the British Government were naturally reluctant to commit even a technical infringement of Norwegian territorial waters by laying mines in the Leads for their own advantage against Germany, they moved upon a generous emotion, only indirectly connected with our war problem, towards a far more serious demand upon both Norway and Sweden for the free passage of men and supplies to Finland.

I sympathised ardently with the Finns and supported all proposals for their aid ; and I welcomed this new and favourable breeze as a means of achieving the major strategic advantage of cutting off the vital iron ore supplies of Germany. If Narvik was to become a kind of Allied base to supply the Finns, it would certainly be easy to prevent the German ships loading ore at the port and sailing safely down the Leads to Germany. Once Norwegian and Swedish protestations were overborne, for whatever reason, the greater measures would include the less. The Admiralty's eyes were also fixed at this time upon the movements of a large and powerful Russian ice-breaker which was to be sent from Murmansk to Germany, ostensibly for repairs, but much more probably to open the now frozen Baltic port of Luleå for the German ore-ships. I therefore renewed my efforts to win consent to the simple and bloodless operation of mining the Leads, for which a certain precedent from the previous war existed. As the question raises moral issues, I feel it right to set the case in its final form as I made it after prolonged reflection and debate.

NORWAY—IRON ORE TRAFFIC

16.XII.39

1. The effectual stoppage of the Norwegian ore supplies to Germany ranks as a major offensive operation of war. No other measure is open to us for many months to come which gives so good a chance of abridging the waste and destruction of the conflict, or of perhaps preventing the vast slaughters which will attend the grapple of the main armies.

2. If the advantage is held to outweigh the obvious and serious objections, the whole process of stoppage must be enforced. The ore from Luleå is already stopped by the winter ice, which must not be [allowed to be] broken by the Soviet ice-breaker, should the attempt be made. The ore from Narvik must be stopped by laying successively a series of small minefields in Norwegian territorial waters at the two or three suitable points on the coast, which will force the ships carrying ore to Germany to quit territorial waters and come on to the high seas where, if German, they will be taken as prize, or, if neutral, be subject to our contraband control. The ore from Oxelosund, the main ice-free port in the Baltic, must also be prevented from leaving by methods which will be neither diplomatic nor military. All these three ports must be dealt with in various appropriate ways as soon as possible.

3. Thus it is not a question of denying Germany a mere million tons between now and May, but of cutting off her whole winter supply, except the negligible amounts that can be got from Gavle, or other minor ice-free Baltic ports. Germany would therefore undergo a severe deprivation, tending to crisis before the summer. But when the ice melts in the Gulf of Bothnia the abundant supply from Luleå would again be open, and Germany is no doubt planning not only to get as much as she can during the winter, but to make up the whole $9\frac{1}{2}$ million tons which she needs, or even more, between May 1 and December 15, 1940. After this she might hope to organise Russian supplies and be able to wage a very long war.

4. It may well be that, should we reach the month of May with Germany starving for ore for her industries and her munitions, the prevention of the reopening of Luleå may become [for us] a principal naval objective. The laying of a declared minefield, including magnetic mines, off Luleå by British submarines would be one way. There are others. If Germany can be cut from all Swedish ore supplies from now onwards till the end of 1940 a blow will have been struck at her war-making capacity equal to a first-class victory in the

field or from the air, and without any serious sacrifice of life. It might indeed be immediately decisive.

5. To every blow struck in war there is a counter. If you fire at the enemy he will fire back. It is most necessary therefore to face squarely the counter-measures which may be taken by Germany, or constrained by her from Norway or Sweden. As to Norway, there are three pairs of events which are linked together. First, the Germans, conducting war in a cruel and lawless manner, have violated the territorial waters of Norway, sinking without warning or succour a number of British and neutral vessels. To that our response is to lay the minefields mentioned above. It is suggested that Norway, by way of protest, may cancel the valuable agreement we have made with her for chartering her tankers and other shipping. But then she would lose the extremely profitable bargain she has made with us, and this shipping would become valueless to her in view of our contraband control. Her ships would be idle, and her owners impoverished. It would not be in Norwegian interests for her Government to take this step; and interest is a powerful factor. Thirdly, Norway could retaliate by refusing to export to us the aluminium and other war materials which are important to the Air Ministry and the Ministry of Supply. But here again her interests would suffer. Not only would she not receive the valuable gains which this trade brings her, but Great Britain, by denying her bauxite and other indispensable raw materials, could bring the whole industry of Norway, centring upon Oslo and Bergen, to a complete standstill. In short, Norway, by retaliating against us, would be involved in economic and industrial ruin.

6. Norwegian sympathies are on our side, and her future independence from German overlordship hangs upon the victory of the Allies. It is not reasonable to suppose that she will take either of the counter-measures mentioned above (although she may threaten them), unless she is compelled to do so by German brute force.

7. This will certainly be applied to her anyway, and whatever we do, if Germany thinks it her interest to dominate forcibly the Scandinavian peninsula. In that case the war would spread to Norway and Sweden, and with our command of the seas there is no reason why French and British troops should not meet German invaders on Scandinavian soil. At any rate, we can certainly take and hold whatever islands or suitable points on the Norwegian coast we choose. Our northern blockade of Germany would then become absolute. We could, for instance, occupy Narvik and Bergen, and keep them open for our own trade while closing them completely to Germany. It cannot be too strongly emphasised that British

control of the Norwegian coast-line is a strategic objective of first-class importance. It is not therefore seen how, even if retaliation by Germany were to run its full course, we should be worse off for the action now proposed. On the contrary, we have more to gain than lose by a German attack upon Norway or Sweden. This point is capable of more elaboration than is necessary here.

There is no reason why we should not manage to secure a large and long-continued supply of iron ore from Sweden through Narvik while at the same time diverting all supplies of ore from Germany. This must be our aim.

I concluded as follows:

8. The effect of our action against Norway upon world opinion and upon our own reputation must be considered. We have taken up arms in accordance with the principles of the Covenant of the League in order to aid the victims of German aggression. No technical infringement of international law, so long as it is unaccompanied by inhumanity of any kind, can deprive us of the good wishes of neutral countries. No evil effect will be produced upon the greatest of all neutrals, the United States. We have reason to believe that they will handle the matter in the way most calculated to help us. And they are very resourceful.

9. The final tribunal is our own conscience. We are fighting to re-establish the reign of law and to protect the liberties of small countries. Our defeat would mean an age of barbaric violence, and would be fatal not only to ourselves, but to the independent life of every small country in Europe. Acting in the name of the Covenant, and as virtual mandatories of the League and all it stands for, we have a right, and indeed are bound in duty, to abrogate for a space some of the conventions of the very laws we seek to consolidate and reaffirm. Small nations must not tie our hands when we are fighting for their rights and freedom. The letter of the law must not in supreme emergency obstruct those who are charged with its protection and enforcement. It would not be right or rational that the Aggressor Power should gain one set of advantages by tearing up all laws, and another set by sheltering behind the innate respect for law of its opponents. Humanity, rather than legality, must be our guide.

Of all this history must be the judge. We now face events.

* * *

My memorandum was considered by the Cabinet on December 22, and I pleaded the case to the best of my ability. I could not obtain any decision for action. Diplomatic protest might be made to Norway about the misuse of her territorial waters by Germany, and the Chiefs of Staff were instructed to consider the military consequences of commitments on Scandinavian soil. They were authorised to plan for landing a force at Narvik for the sake of Finland, and also a possible German occupation of Southern Norway. But no executive orders could be issued to the Admiralty. In a paper which I circulated on December 24 I summarised the Intelligence reports which showed the possibilities of a Russian design upon Norway. The Soviet were said to have three divisions concentrated at Murmansk preparing for a seaborne expedition. 'It may be,' I concluded, 'that this theatre will become the scene of early activities.' This proved only too true ; but from a different quarter.

CHAPTER 10

A Dark New Year

The Trance Continues – 'Catherine': The Final Phase – Tension with Russia – Mussolini's Misgivings – Mr. Hore-Belisha Leaves the War Office – Impediments to Action – A Twilight Mood in the Factories – The Results in May – Capture of the German Plans Against Belgium – Work and Growth of the British Expeditionary Force – No Armoured Division – Deterioration of the French Army – Communist Intrigues – German Plans for the Invasion of Norway – The Supreme War Council of February 5 – My First Attendance – The 'Altmark' Incident – Captain Philip Vian – Rescue of the British Prisoners – Mr. Chamberlain's Effective Defence – Hitler Appoints General von Falkenhorst to Command Against Norway – Norway Before France – German Air Attack on Our East Coast Shipping – Counter-measures – Satisfactory Results of the First Six Months' Sea War – Navy Estimates Speech, February 27, 1940.

The end of the year 1939 left the war still in its sinister trance. An occasional cannon-shot or reconnoitring patrol alone broke the silence of the Western Front. The armies gaped at each other from behind their rising fortifications across an undisputed 'No-man's-land'.

There is a certain similarity [I wrote to Pound on Christmas Day] between the position now and at the end of the year 1914. The transition from peace to war has been accomplished. The outer seas, for the moment at any rate, are clear from enemy surface craft. The lines in France are static. But in addition on the sea we have repelled the first U-boat attack, which previously did not begin till February 1915, and we can see our way through the magnetic mine novelty. Moreover, in France the lines run along the frontiers instead of six or seven of the French provinces and Belgium being in the enemy's hands. Thus I feel we may compare the position now very favourably with that of 1914. And also I have the feeling (which may be corrected at any moment) that the Kaiser's Germany was a much tougher customer than Nazi Germany.

This is the best I can do for a Christmas card in these hard times.

I was by now increasingly convinced that there could be no Operation 'Catherine' in 1940. 'The sending of a superior surface fleet into the Baltic,' I wrote to Pound (January 6), 'though eminently desirable, is not essential to the seizure and retention of the ironfields. While therefore every preparation to send the Fleet in should continue, and strong efforts should be made, it would be wrong to try it unless we can see our way to maintaining it under air attack, and still more wrong to make the seizure of the ironfields dependent upon the sending of a surface fleet. Let us advance with confidence and see how the naval side develops as events unfold.'

And again a week later:

First Lord to First Sea Lord   14.1.40

1. I have carefully considered all the papers you have been good enough to send me in reply to my various minutes about 'Catherine'. I have come reluctantly but quite definitely to the conclusion that the operation we outlined in the autumn will not be practicable this year. We have not yet obtained sufficient mastery over U-boats, mines, and raiders to enable us to fit for their special duties the many smaller vessels required. The problem of making our ships comparatively secure against air attack has not been solved. The dive-bomber remains a formidable menace. The Rocket [called for secrecy 'the U.P. weapon', *i.e.*, unrotated projectile], though progressing rapidly towards the production stage, will not be available in sufficient quantities, even if all goes well, for many months to come. We have not been able so far to give the additional armour protection to our larger ships. The political situation in the Baltic is as baffling as ever. On the other hand, the arrival of the *Bismarck* in September adds greatly to the scale of the surface resistance to be encountered.

2. But the war may well be raging in 1941, and no one can tell what opportunities may present themselves then. I wish therefore that all the preparations of various ships and auxiliaries outlined in your table and marked as 'beneficial' should continue as opportunity offers, and that when ships come into the dockyards for repair or refit everything should be done to them which will not delay their return to service. And it would surely be only common prudence, in view of the attitude of Russia, to go on warming our destroyers for service in winter seas. I am glad to feel that we are agreed in this.

*   *   *

So far no ally had espoused our cause. The United States

was cooler than in any other period. I persevered in my correspondence with the President, but with little response. The Chancellor of the Exchequer groaned about our dwindling dollar resources. We had already signed a pact of mutual assistance with Turkey, and were considering what aid we could give her from our narrow margins. The stresses created by the Finnish war had worsened our relations, already bad, with the Soviets. Any action we might undertake to help the Finns might lead to war with Russia. The fundamental antagonisms between the Soviet Government and Nazi Germany did not prevent the Kremlin actively aiding by supplies and facilities the development of Hitler's power. Communism in France and any that existed in Britain denounced the 'Imperialist-Capitalist' war, and did what they could to hamper work in the munitions factories. They certainly exercised a depressing and subversive influence within the French Army, already wearied by inaction. We continued to court Italy by civilities and favourable contracts, but we could feel no security, or progress towards friendship. Count Ciano was polite to our Ambassador. Mussolini stood aloof.

The Italian Dictator was not however without his own misgivings. On January 3 he wrote a revealing letter to Hitler expressing his distaste for the German agreement with Russia:

No one knows better than I, with forty years' political experience, that policy—particularly a revolutionary policy—has its tactical requirements. I recognised the Soviets in 1924. In 1934 I signed with them a treaty of commerce and friendship. I therefore understood that, *especially as Ribbentrop's forecast about the non-intervention of Britain and France has not come off,* you are obliged to avoid the Second Front. You have had to pay for this in that Russia has, without striking a blow, been the greater profiteer in the war in Poland and the Baltic.

But I who was born a revolutionary and have not modified my revolutionary mentality tell you that you cannot permanently sacrifice the principles of *your* revolution to the tactical requirements of a given moment. ... I have also the definite duty to add that a further step in the relations with Moscow would have catastrophic repercussions in Italy, where the unanimity of anti-Bolshevist feeling is absolute, granite-hard, and unbreakable. Permit me to think that this will not happen. The solution of your *Lebensraum* is in Russia, and nowhere else. ... The day when we shall have demolished Bolshevism we shall have kept faith with both our revolutions.

Then it will be the turn of the great democracies, who will not be able to survive the cancer which gnaws them. . . .

*   *   *

On January 6 I again visited France, to explain my two mechanical projects, Cultivator No. 6 and the fluvial mine (Operation 'Royal Marine') to the French High Command. In the morning, before I left, the Prime Minister sent for me and told me he had decided to make a change at the War Office, and that Mr. Hore-Belisha would give place to Mr. Oliver Stanley. Late that night Mr. Hore-Belisha called me on the telephone at our Embassy in Paris and told me what I knew already. I pressed him, but without success, to take one of the other offices which were open to him. The Government was itself in low water at this time, and almost the whole Press of the country declared that a most energetic and live figure had been lost to the Government. He quitted the War Office amid a chorus of newspaper tributes. Parliament does not take its opinion from the newspapers ; indeed, it often reacts in the opposite sense. When the House of Commons met a week later Mr. Hore-Belisha had few champions, and refrained from making any statement. I wrote to him as follows :

January 10, 1940

I much regret that our brief association as colleagues has ended. In the last war I went through the same experience as you have suffered, and I know how bitter and painful it is to anyone with his heart in the job. I was not consulted in the changes that were proposed. I was only informed after they had been decided. At the same time, I should fail in candour if I did not let you know that I thought it would have been better if you had gone to the Board of Trade or the Ministry of Information, and I am very sorry that you did not see your way to accept the first of these important offices.

The outstanding achievement of your tenure of the War Office was the passage of conscription in time of peace. You may rest with confidence upon this, and I hope that it will not be long before we are colleagues again, and that this temporary set-back will prove no serious obstacle to your opportunities of serving the country.

It was not possible for me to realise my hope until, after the break-up of the National Coalition, I formed the so-called 'Caretaker Government' in May 1945. Belisha then became Minister of National Insurance. In the interval he had been one

of our severe critics ; but I was very glad to be able to bring so
able a man back into the Administration.

*   *   *

All January the Finns stood firm, and at the end of the month
the growing Russian armies were still held in their positions.
The Red Air Force continued to bomb Helsingfors and Viipuri,
and the cry from the Finnish Government for aircraft and war
materials grew louder. As the Arctic nights shortened the Soviet
air offensive would increase, not only upon the towns of Finland,
but upon the communications of their armies. Only a trickle
of war material and only a few thousand volunteers from the
Scandinavian countries had reached Finland so far. A bureau
for recruiting was opened in London in January, and several
scores of British aircraft were sent to Finland, some direct by
air. Nothing in fact of any use was done.

The delays about Narvik continued interminably. Although
the Cabinet were prepared to contemplate pressure upon Norway and Sweden to allow aid to pass to Finland, they remained
opposed to the much smaller operation of mining the Leads.
The first was noble, the second merely tactical. Besides, everyone could see that Norway and Sweden would refuse facilities
for aid, so nothing would come of the project anyway.

In my vexation after one of our Cabinets I wrote to a colleague:

January 15, 1940

My disquiet was due mainly to the awful difficulties which
our machinery of war-conduct presents to positive action. I
see such immense walls of prevention, all built and building,
that I wonder whether any plan will have a chance of climbing
over them. Just look at the arguments which have had to
be surmounted in the seven weeks we have discussed this
Narvik operation. First, the objections of the Economic Departments, Supply, Board of Trade, etc. Secondly, the Joint
Planning Committee. Thirdly, the Chiefs of Staff Committee.
Fourthly, the insidious argument, 'Don't spoil the big plan
for the sake of the small,' when there is really very little chance
of the big plan being resolutely attempted. Fifthly, the juri-
dical and moral objections, all gradually worn down. Sixthly,
the attitude of neutrals, and above all the United States. But
see how well the United States have responded to our *dé-
marche*! Seventhly, the Cabinet itself, with its many angles
of criticism. Eighthly, when all this has been smoothed out,

the French have to be consulted. Finally, the Dominions and their consciences have to be squared, they not having gone through the process by which opinion has advanced at home. All this makes me feel that under the present arrangements we shall be reduced to waiting upon the terrible attacks of the enemy, against which it is impossible to prepare in every quarter simultaneously without fatal dissipation of strength.

I have two or three projects moving forward, but all, I fear, will succumb before the tremendous array of negative arguments and forces. Pardon me, therefore, if I showed distress. One thing is absolutely certain, namely, that victory will never be found by taking the line of least resistance.

However, all this Narvik story is for the moment put on one side by the threat to the Low Countries. If this materialises the position will have to be studied in the light of entirely new events. . . . Should a great battle engage in the Low Countries the effects upon Norway and Sweden may well be decisive. Even if the battle ends only in a stalemate they may feel far more free, and to us a diversion may become even more needful.

* * *

There were other causes for uneasiness. Progress in converting our industries to war production was not up to the pace required. In a speech at Manchester on January 27 I urged the immense importance of expanding our labour supply and of bringing great numbers of women into industry to replace the men taken for the armed forces and to augment our strength. I continued:

We have to make a huge expansion, especially of those capable of performing skilled or semi-skilled operations. Here we must specially count for aid and guidance upon our Labour colleagues and trade union leaders. I can speak with some knowledge about this, having presided over the former Ministry of Munitions in its culminating phase. Millions of new workers will be needed, and more than a million women must come boldly forward into our war industries—into the shell plants, the munitions works, and into the aircraft factories. Without this expansion of labour and without allowing the women of Britain to enter the struggle as they desire to do, we should fail utterly to bear our fair share of the burden which France and Britain have jointly assumed.

Little was however done, and the sense of extreme emergency seemed lacking. There was a 'twilight' mood in the ranks of Labour and of those who directed production as well as in the military operations. It was not till the beginning of May that a survey of employment in the engineering, motor, and aircraft group of industries which was presented to the Cabinet revealed the facts in an indisputable form. This paper was searchingly examined by my statistical department under Professor Lindemann. In spite of the distractions and excitements of the Norwegian hurly-burly then in progress, I found time to address the following note to my colleagues:

NOTE BY THE FIRST LORD OF THE ADMIRALTY

May 4, 1940

This report suggests that in this fundamental group, at any rate, we have hardly begun to organise man-power for the production of munitions.

In [previous papers] it was estimated that a very large expansion, amounting to 71.5 per cent. of the number engaged in the metal industry, would be needed in the first year of war. Actually the engineering, motor, and aircraft group, which covers three-fifths of the metal industry and which is discussed in this survey, has only expanded by 11.1 per cent. (122,000) between June 1939 and April 1940. This is less than one-sixth of the expansion stated to be required. Without any Government intervention, by the mere improvement of trade, the number increased as quickly as this in the year 1936-37.

Although 350,000 boys leave school each year, there is an increase of only 25,000 in the number of males under 21 employed in this group. Moreover, the proportion of women and young persons has only increased from 26.6 per cent. to 27.6 per cent. In the engineering, motor, and aircraft group we now have only one woman for every twelve men. During the last war the ratio of women to men in the metal industries increased from one woman for every ten men to one woman for every three men. In the first year of the last war, July 1914 to July 1915, the new workers drafted into the metal industries amounted to 20 per cent. of those already there. In the group under survey, which may fairly be taken as typical of the whole metal industry, only 11 per cent. have been added in the last ten months.

Admiralty establishments, in which employment has been increased by nearly 27 per cent., have not been considered here, as no figures of the different types of labour are given.

*   *   *

On January 10 anxieties about the Western Front received confirmation. A German staff major of the 7th Air Division had been ordered to take some documents to headquarters in Cologne. He missed his train and decided to fly. His machine overshot the mark and made a forced landing in Belgium, where Belgian troops arrested him and impounded his papers, which he tried desperately to destroy. These contained the entire and actual scheme for the invasion of Belgium, Holland, and France on which Hitler had resolved. Shortly the German major was released to explain matters to his superiors. I was told about all this at the time, and it seemed to me incredible that the Belgians would not make a plan to invite us in. But they did nothing about it. It was argued in all three countries concerned that probably it was a plant. But this could not be true. There could be no sense in the Germans trying to make the Belgians believe that they were going to attack them in the near future. This might make them do the very last thing the Germans wanted, namely, make a plan with the French and British Armies to come forward privily and quickly one fine night. I therefore believed in the impending attack.

On January 13 Admiral Keyes telephoned to me that the King of the Belgians might be able to persuade his Ministers to invite French and British troops into Belgium 'at once' if we would agree to give certain far-reaching guarantees. 'At once' was taken by us to mean immediately and not 'as soon as Germany invades'. The War Cabinet decided to reply that we could give no guarantees other than those implicit in a military alliance, and that the invitation to enter Belgium must be given soon enough to enable the Allied troops to forestall a German invasion, which the Belgian Government apparently thought was imminent. Admiral Keyes telegraphed on January 15 that the King thought this reply would have a very bad effect if he communicated it to his Government, that if Allied troops entered 'at once' Belgium and Holland would be immediately involved in war, and that it would be better that the onus of breaking Belgian neutrality should rest on Germany. A similar reply was given by the Belgian Government to M. Daladier, and the French Ambassador in London also told us that the Belgian Government thought that if Germany were left to commit an act of aggression Anglo-French help would 'acquire a moral character' which 'would increase the chance of success'.

Thus the Belgian King and his Army staff merely waited,

hoping that all would turn out well. In spite of the German major's papers no further action of any kind was taken by the Allies or the threatened States. Hitler, on the other hand, as we know, summoned Goering to his presence, and on being told that the captured papers were in fact the complete plans for invasion, ordered, after venting his anger, new variants to be prepared.

It was thus clear at the beginning of 1940 that Hitler had a detailed plan involving both Belgium and Holland for the invasion of France. Should this begin at any moment, General Gamelin's Plan D would be put in operation, including the movement of the Seventh French Army and the British Army. Plan D had been worked out in exact detail, and required only one single word to set it in motion. This course, though deprecated at the outset of the war by the British Chiefs of Staff, had been definitely and formally confirmed in Paris on November 17, 1939. On this basis the Allies awaited the impending shock, and Hitler the campaigning season, for which the weather might well be favourable from April onwards.

During the winter and spring the B.E.F. were extremely busy setting themselves to rights, fortifying their line and preparing for war, whether offensive or defensive. From the highest rank to the lowest all were hard at it, and the good showing that they eventually made was due largely to the full use made of the opportunities provided during the winter. The British was a far better army at the end of the 'Twilight War'. It was also larger. The 42nd and 44th Divisions arrived in France in March, and went on to the frontier line in the latter half of April 1940. In that month there also arrived the 12th, 23rd, and 46th Divisions. These were sent to complete their training in France and to augment the labour force for all the work in hand. They were short even of the ordinary unit weapons and equipment, and had no artillery. Nevertheless they were inevitably drawn into the fighting when it began, and acquitted themselves well.

The awful gap, reflecting on our pre-war arrangements, was *the absence of even one armoured division in the British Expeditionary Force*. Britain, the cradle of the tank in all its variants, had between the wars so far neglected the development of this weapon, soon to dominate the battlefields, that eight months after the declaration of war our small but good Army had only with it, when the hour of trial arrived, the 1st Army Tank Brigade, comprising 17 light tanks and 100 'Infantry' tanks. Only 23 of the latter carried even the 2-pdr. gun, the rest machine-guns only. There were also seven cavalry and Yeomanry regiments equipped with carriers and light tanks which were in process of being formed into two light armoured brigades. Apart from the lack of armour, the progress in the efficiency of the B.E.F. was marked.

*   *   *

Developments on the French front were less satisfactory. In a great national conscript force the mood of the people is closely reflected in its army, the more so when that army is quartered in the homeland and contacts are close. It cannot be said that France in 1939–40 viewed the war with uprising spirit, or even with much confidence. The restless internal politics of the past decade had bred disunity and discontents. Important elements, in reaction to growing Communism, had swung towards Fascism, lending a ready ear to Goebbels' skilful propaganda and passing it on in gossip and rumour. So also in the Army the disintegrating influences of both Communism and Fascism were at work ; the long winter months of waiting gave time and opportunity for the poisons to be established.

Very many factors go to the building up of sound morale in an army, but one of the greatest is that the men be fully employed at useful and interesting work. Idleness is a dangerous breeding-ground. Throughout the winter there were many tasks that needed doing: training demanded continuous attention ; defences were far from satisfactory or complete—even the Maginot Line lacked many supplementary field works ; physical fitness demands exercise. Yet visitors to the French Front were often struck by the prevailing atmosphere of calm aloofness, by the seemingly poor quality of the work in hand, by the lack of visible activity of any kind. The emptiness of the roads behind the line was in great contrast to the continual coming and going which extended for miles behind the British sector.

There can be no doubt that the quality of the French Army was allowed to deteriorate during the winter, and that it would have fought better in the autumn than in the spring. Soon it was to be stunned by the swiftness and violence of the German assault. It was not until the last phases of that brief campaign that the true fighting qualities of the French soldier rose uppermost in defence of his country against the age-long enemy. But then it was too late.

*   *   *

Meanwhile the German plans for a direct assault on Norway and a lightning occupation of Denmark also were advancing. General Keitel drew up a memorandum on this subject on January 27, 1940:

The Fuehrer and Supreme Commander of the Armed Forces wishes that Study N should be further worked on under my direct and personal guidance, and in the closest conjunction with the general war policy. For these reasons the Fuehrer has commissioned me to take over the direction of further preparations.

The detailed planning for this operation proceeded through the normal channels.

* * *

In early February, when the Prime Minister was going to the Supreme War Council in Paris, he invited me for the first time to go with him. I suggested that we should go by sea, which I could arrange ; so we all sailed from Dover in a destroyer, and reached Paris in time for a meeting in the evening. On the way over Mr. Chamberlain showed me the reply he had given to the peace suggestions which Mr. Sumner Welles had gathered. This struck me favourably, and when I had read it in his presence I said to him: 'I am proud to serve in your Government.' He seemed pleased at this.

The main subject of discussion on February 5 was 'Aid to Finland', and plans were approved to prepare three or four divisions and persuade Norway and Sweden to let us send supplies and reinforcements to the Finns, and incidentally to get control of the Gällivare ore-field. As might be expected, the Swedes did not agree to this, and, though extensive preparations were made, the whole project fell to the ground. Mr. Chamberlain conducted the proceedings himself on our behalf, and only minor interventions were made by the various British Ministers attending. I am not recorded as having said a word.

The next day, when we came to re-cross the Channel, an amusing incident occurred. We sighted a floating mine. So I said to the captain, 'Let's blow it up by gunfire.' It burst with a good bang, and a large piece of wreckage sailed over towards us and seemed for an instant as if it were going to settle on the bridge, where all the politicians and some of the other swells were clustered. However, it landed on the forecastle, which was happily bare, and no one was hurt. Thus everything passed off pleasantly. From this time onwards I was invited by the Prime Minister to accompany him, with others, to the meetings of the Supreme War Council. But I could not provide an equal entertainment each time.

* * *

The Council decided that it was of the first importance that Finland should be saved; that she could not hold out after the spring without reinforcements of thirty to forty thousand trained men; that the present stream of heterogeneous volunteers was not sufficient; and that the destruction of Finland would be a major defeat for the Allies. It was therefore necessary to send Allied troops either through Petsamo or through Narvik and/or other Norwegian ports. The operation through Narvik was preferred, as it would enable the Allies to 'kill two birds with one stone' (*i.e.*, help Finland and cut off the iron ore). Two British divisions due to start for France in February should be retained in England and prepared for fighting in Norway. Meanwhile every effort should be made to procure the assent and if possible the co-operation of the Norwegians and Swedes. The issue of what to do if Norway and Sweden refused, as seemed probable, was never faced.

A vivid episode now sharpened everything in Scandinavia. The reader will remember my concern that the *Altmark*, the auxiliary of the *Spee*, should be captured. This vessel was also a floating prison for the crews of our sunk merchant-ships. British captives released by Captain Langsdorff according to international law in Montevideo harbour told us that nearly three hundred British merchant seamen were on board the *Altmark*. This vessel hid in the South Atlantic for nearly two months, and then, hoping that the search had died down, her captain made a bid to return to Germany. Luck and the weather favoured her, and not until February 14, after passing between Iceland and the Faroes, was she sighted by our aircraft in Norwegian territorial waters.

First Lord to First Sea Lord   16.II.40

On the position as reported to me this morning, it would seem that the cruiser and destroyers should sweep northward during the day up the coast of Norway, not hesitating to arrest *Altmark* in territorial waters should she be found. This ship is violating neutrality in carrying British prisoners of war to Germany. Surely another cruiser or two should be sent to rummage the Skagerrak to-night? The *Altmark* must be regarded as an invaluable trophy.

In the words of an Admiralty communiqué, 'certain of His Majesty's ships which were conveniently disposed were set in motion'. A destroyer flotilla, under the command of Captain Philip Vian, of H.M.S. *Cossack*, intercepted the *Altmark*, but did not immediately molest her. She took refuge in Jösing Fiord, a narrow inlet about a mile and a half long surrounded by high snow-clad cliffs. Two British destroyers were told to board her for examination. At the entrance to the fiord they were met by two Norwegian gunboats, who informed them that the ship was unarmed, and had been examined the previous day, and had received permission to proceed to Germany, making use of Norwegian territorial waters. Our destroyers thereupon withdrew.

When this information reached the Admiralty I intervened, and, with the concurrence of the Foreign Secretary, ordered our ships to enter the fiord. I did not often act so directly ; but I now sent Captain Vian the following order :

February 16, 1940, 5.25 p.m.
Unless Norwegian torpedo-boat undertakes to convoy *Altmark* to Bergen with a joint Anglo-Norwegian guard on board, and a joint escort, you should board *Altmark*, liberate the prisoners, and take possession of the ship pending further instructions. If Norwegian torpedo-boat interferes, you should warn her to stand off. If she fires upon you, you should not reply unless attack is serious, in which case you should defend yourself, using no more force than is necessary, and ceasing fire when she desists.

Vian did the rest. That night in the *Cossack* with searchlights burning he entered the fiord through the icefloes. He first went on board the Norwegian gunboat *Kjell* and requested that the *Altmark* should be taken to Bergen under a joint escort, for inquiry according to international law. The Norwegian captain repeated his assurance that the *Altmark* had been twice searched, that she was unarmed, and that no British prisoners had been found. Vian then stated that he was going to board her, and invited the Norwegian officer to join him. This offer was eventually declined.

Meanwhile the *Altmark* got under way, and in trying to ram

the *Cossack* ran herself aground. The *Cossack* forced her way alongside and a boarding party sprang across, after grappling the two ships together. A sharp hand-to-hand fight followed, in which four Germans were killed and five wounded ; part of the crew fled ashore and the rest surrendered. The search began for the British prisoners. They were soon found in their hundreds, battened down, locked in storerooms, and even in an empty oil-tank. Then came the cry, 'The Navy's here!' The doors were broken in and the captives rushed on deck. Altogether 299 prisoners were released and transferred to our destroyers. It was also found that the *Altmark* carried two pom-poms and four machine-guns, and that, despite having been boarded twice by the Norwegians, she had not been searched. The Norwegian gunboats remained passive observers throughout. By midnight Vian was clear of the fiord, and making for the Forth.

Admiral Pound and I sat up together in some anxiety in the Admiralty War Room. I had put a good screw on the Foreign Office, and was fully aware of the technical gravity of the measures taken. To judge them fairly it must be remembered that up to that date Germany had sunk 218,000 tons of Scandinavian shipping, with a loss of 555 Scandinavian lives. But what mattered at home and in the Cabinet was whether British prisoners were found on board or not. We were delighted when at three o'clock in the morning news came that three hundred had been found and rescued. This was a dominating fact.

On the assumption that the prisoners were in a pitiable condition from starvation and confinement, we directed ambulances, doctors, the Press, and photographers to the port of Leith to receive them. As however it appeared that they were in good health, had been well looked after on the destroyers, and came ashore in a hearty condition, no publicity was given to this aspect. Their rescue and Captain Vian's conduct aroused a wave of enthusiasm in Britain almost equal to that which followed the sinking of the *Graf Spee*. Both these events strengthened my hand and the prestige of the Admiralty. 'The Navy's here!' was passed from lip to lip.

Every allowance must be made for the behaviour of the Norwegian Government, which was of course quivering under the German terror and exploiting our forbearance. They protested vehemently against the entry of their territorial waters. Mr. Chamberlain's speech in the House of Commons contained the essence of the British reply :

According to the views expressed by Professor Koht [the Norwegian Foreign Minister], the Norwegian Government see no objection to the use of Norwegian territorial waters for hundreds of miles by a German warship for the purpose of escaping capture on the high seas and of conveying British prisoners to a German prison camp. Such a doctrine is at variance with international law as His Majesty's Government understand it. It would in their view legalise the abuse by German warships of neutral waters and create a position which His Majesty's Government could in no circumstances accept.

* * *

Hitler's decision to invade Norway had, as we have seen, been taken on December 14, and the staff work was proceeding under Keitel. The incident of the *Altmark* no doubt gave a spur to action. At Keitel's suggestion, on February 20 Hitler summoned urgently to Berlin General von Falkenhorst, who was at that time in command of an Army Corps at Coblenz. Falkenhorst had taken part in the German campaign in Finland in 1918, and upon this subject the interview with the Fuehrer opened. The General described the conversation at the Nuremberg trials.

Hitler reminded me of my experience in Finland, and said to me, 'Sit down and tell me what you did.' After a moment the Fuehrer interrupted me. He led me to a table covered with maps. 'I have a similar thing in mind,' he said 'the occupation of Norway; because I am informed that the English intend to land there, and I want to be there before them.'

Then, marching up and down, he expounded to me his reasons. 'The occupation of Norway by the British would be a strategic turning movement which would lead them into the Baltic, where we have neither troops nor coastal fortifications. The success which we have gained in the East and which we are going to win in the West would be annihilated, because the enemy would find himself in a position to advance on Berlin and to break the backbone of our two fronts. In the second and third place, the conquest of Norway will ensure the liberty of movement of our Fleet in the Bay of Wilhelmshaven, and will protect our imports of Swedish ore.' . . . Finally he said to me, 'I appoint you to the command of the expedition.'

That afternoon Falkenhorst was summoned again to the Chancellery to discuss with Hitler, Keitel, and Jodl the detailed operational plans for the Norwegian expedition. The question of priorities was of supreme importance. Would Hitler commit himself in Norway before or after the execution of 'Case Yellow'—the attack on France? On March 1 he made his decision: Norway was to come first. The entry in Jodl's diary for March 3 reads: 'The Fuehrer decides to carry out "Weser Exercise" before "Case Yellow", with a few days' interval.'

*   *   *

A vexatious air attack had recently begun on our shipping all along the East Coast. Besides ocean-going vessels destined for the large ports there were on any given day about 320 ships of between 500 and 2,000 tons either at sea or in harbour on the coast, many engaged in coal transport to London and the south. Only a few of these small vessels had yet been provided with an anti-aircraft gun, and the enemy aircraft therefore concentrated upon this easy prey. They even attacked the lightships. These faithful servants of the seamen, moored in exposed positions near the shoals along our coasts, were of use to all, even the marauding U-boat itself, and had never been touched in any previous war. Several were now sunk or damaged, the worst case being off the Humber, where a fierce machine-gun attack killed eight out of the lightship's crew of nine.

As a defence against air attack the convoy system proved as effective as it had against the U-boats, but everything was now done to find some kind of weapon for each ship. In our dearth of ack-ack guns all sorts of contrivances were used. Even a life-saving rocket brought down an air bandit. The spare machine-guns from the Home Fleet were distributed to British and Allied merchant ships on the East Coast with naval gunners. These men and their weapons were shifted from ship to ship for each voyage through the danger zone. By the end of February the Army was able to help, and thus began an organisation later known as the Maritime Royal Artillery. At the height of the war in 1944 more than 38,000 officers and men from the regular forces were employed in this task, of which 14,000 were found by the Army. Over considerable sections of the East Coast convoy route air fighter protection from the nearest airfields could soon be given on call. Thus the efforts of all three Services were combined. An increasing toll was taken of the raiders. Shooting up ordinary defenceless shipping of all countries turned out to be more costly than had been expected, and the attacks diminished.

Not all the horizon was dark. In the outer seas there had been no further signs of raider activity since the destruction of the *Graf Spee* in December, and the work of sweeping German shipping from the seas continued. During February six German ships left Spain in an attempt to reach Germany. Only one succeeded; of the remainder three were captured, one scuttled herself, and one was wrecked in Norway. Seven other German ships attempting to run the blockade were intercepted by our patrols during February and March. All except one of these were scuttled by their captains. Altogether by the beginning of April 1940 seventy-one ships, of 340,000 tons, had been lost to the Germans by capture or scuttling, while 215 German ships still remained cooped in neutral ports. Finding our merchant ships armed, the U-boats had abandoned the gun for the torpedo. Their next descent had been from the torpedo to the lowest form of warfare—the undeclared mine. We have seen how the magnetic mine attack had been met and mastered. Nevertheless more than half our losses in January were from this cause, and more than two-thirds of the total fell on neutrals.

On the Navy Estimates at the end of February I reviewed the salient features of the war at sea. The Germans, I surmised, had lost half the U-boats with which they had entered the war. Contrary to expectation, few new ones had yet made their appearance. Actually, as we now know, sixteen U-boats had been sunk and nine added up to the end of February. The enemy's main effort had not yet developed. Our programme of small-ship building, both in the form of escort vessels and in replacement of merchant ships, was very large. The Admiralty had taken over control of merchant ship-building, and Sir James Lithgow, the Glasgow ship-builder, had joined the Board for this purpose. In the first six months of this new war, after making allowance for gains through new construction and transfers from foreign flags, our net loss had been less than 200,000 tons, compared with 450,000 tons in the single deadly month of April 1917. Meanwhile we had continued to capture more cargoes in tonnage destined for the enemy than we had lost ourselves.

Each month [I said in ending my speech] there has been a steady improvement in imports. In January the Navy carried safely into British harbours, despite U-boats and mines and the winter gales and fog, considerably more than four-fifths of the peace-time average for the three preceding years. ...

When we consider the great number of British ships which have been withdrawn for naval service or for the transport of our armies across the Channel or of troop convoys across the globe, there is nothing in these results, to put it mildly, which should cause despondency or alarm.

CHAPTER 11

Before the Storm

The Fleet Returns to Scapa Flow – Our Voyage through the Minches – 'Mines Reported in the Fairway' – An Air Alarm – Improvements at Scapa – Hitler's Plans as Now Known – Desperate Plight of Finland – M. Daladier's Vain Efforts – The Russo-Finnish Armistice Terms – New Dangers in Scandinavia – Operation 'Royal Marine' – The Fluvial Mines Ready – M. Daladier's Opposition – The Fall of the Daladier Government – My Letter to the New Premier, M. Reynaud – Meeting of Supreme War Council, March 28 – Mr. Chamberlain's Survey – Decision to Mine the Norwegian Leads at Last – Seven Months' Delay – Various Offensive Proposals and Devices – Mr. Chamberlain's Speech of April 5, 1940 – Signs of Impending German Action.

March 12 was the long-desired date for the reoccupation and use of Scapa as the main base of the Home Fleet. I thought I would give myself the treat of being present on this occasion in our naval affairs, and embarked accordingly in Admiral Forbes' flagship at the Clyde.

The fleet comprised five capital ships, a cruiser squadron, and perhaps a score of destroyers. The twenty-hour voyage lay through the Minches. We were to pass the Northern Straits at dawn and reach Scapa about noon. The *Hood* and other ships from Rosyth, moving up the East Coast, would be there some hours before us. The navigation of the Minches is intricate, and the northern exit barely a mile wide. On every side are rocky shores and reefs, and three U-boats were reported in these enclosed waters. We had to proceed at high speed and by zigzag. All the usual peace-time lights were out. This was therefore a task in navigation which the Navy keenly appreciated. However, just as we were about to start after luncheon the Master of the Fleet, navigating officer of the flagship, on whom the prime direct responsibility lay, was suddenly stricken by influenza. So a very young-looking lieutenant who was his assistant came up on to the bridge to take charge of the movement of the fleet. I was struck by this officer, who without any notice had to undertake so serious a task, requiring such perfect science, accuracy, and judgment. His composure did not entirely conceal his satisfaction.

I had many things to discuss with the Commander-in-Chief, and it was not until after midnight that I went up on to the bridge. All was velvet black. The air was clear, but no stars were to be seen, and there was no moon. The great ship ploughed along at about 16 knots. One could just see astern the dark mass of the following battleship. Here were nearly thirty vessels steaming in company and moving in order with no lights of any kind except their tiny stern-lights, and constantly changing course in accordance with the prescribed anti-U-boat ritual. It was five hours since they had had any observation of the land or the heavens. Presently the Admiral joined me, and I said to him, 'Here is one of the things I should be very sorry to be made responsible for carrying out. How are you going to make sure you will hit the narrow exit from the Minches at daylight?' 'What would you do, sir,' he said, 'if you were at this moment the only person who could give an order?' I replied at once, 'I should anchor and wait till morning. "Anchor, Hardy," as Nelson said.' But the Admiral answered, 'We have nearly a hundred fathoms of water beneath us now.' I had of course complete confidence, gained over many years, in the Navy, and I only tell this tale to bring home to the general reader the marvellous skill and precision with which what seem to landsmen to be impossible feats of this kind are performed as a matter of course when necessary.

It was eight o'clock before I woke, and we were in the broad waters north of the Minches, steering round the western extremity of Scotland towards Scapa Flow. We were perhaps half an hour's steaming from the entrance to Scapa when a signal reached us saying that several German aircraft had dropped mines in the main entrance we were about to use. Admiral Forbes thereupon decided that he must stand out to the westward for twenty-four hours until the channel had been reported clear, and on this the whole fleet began to change its course. 'I can easily put you ashore in a destroyer if you care to tranship,' he said. 'The *Hood* is already in harbour and can look after you.' As I had snatched these three days from London with difficulty, I accepted this offer. Our baggage was rapidly brought on deck, the flagship reduced her speed to three or four knots, and a cutter manned by twelve men in their lifebelts was lowered from the davits. My small party was already in it, and I was taking leave of the Admiral, when an air-raid alarm sounded, and the whole ship flashed into activity as all the ackack batteries were manned and other measures taken.

I was worried that the ship should have had to slow down in waters where we knew there were U-boats, but the Admiral said it was quite all right, and pointed to five destroyers which were circling round her at high speed, while a sixth waited for us. We were a quarter of an hour rowing across the mile that separated us from our destroyer. It was like in the olden times, except that the sailors had not so much practice with the oars. The flagship had already regained her speed and was steaming off after the rest of the fleet before we climbed on board. All the officers were at their action stations on the destroyer, and we were welcomed by the surgeon, who took us into the wardroom, where all the instruments of his profession were laid out on the table ready for accidents. But no air raid occurred, and we immediately proceeded at high speed into Scapa. We entered through Switha Sound, which is a small and subsidiary channel and was not affected by the mine-dropping. 'This is the tradesmen's entrance,' said Thompson, my Flag Commander. It was in fact the one assigned to the storeships. 'It's the only one,' said the destroyer lieutenant stiffly, 'that the flotillas are allowed to use.' To make everything go well I asked him if he could remember Kipling's poem about

> 'Mines reported in the fairway,
> Warn all traffic and detain.
> 'Sent up . . .'

and here I let him carry on, which he did correctly:

> 'Unity, Claribel, Assyrian, Stormcock, and Golden Gain.'*

We soon found our way to the Hood, where Admiral Whitworth received us, having gathered most of his captains, and I passed a pleasant night on board before the long round of inspections which filled the next day. This was the last time I set foot upon the Hood, although she had nearly two years of war service to perform before her destruction by the Bismarck in 1941.

More than six months of constant exertion and the highest priorities had repaired the peace-time neglect at Scapa. The three main entrances were defended with booms and mines, and

* Quoted from 'Mine Sweepers', from Sea Warfare, by permission of Mrs. Bambridge and Messrs. Macmillan & Co., Ltd.

three additional blockships, among others, had already been placed in Kirk Sound, through which Prien's U-boat had slipped to destroy the *Royal Oak*. Many more blockships were yet to come. A large garrison guarded the base and the still-growing batteries. We had planned for over 120 ack-ack guns, with numerous searchlights and a balloon barrage, to command the air over the fleet anchorage. Not all these measures were yet complete, but the air defences were already formidable. Many small craft patrolled the approaches in ceaseless activity, and two or three squadrons of Hurricane fighters from the airfields in Caithness could be guided to an assailant in darkness or daylight by one of the finest Radar installations then in existence. At last the Home Fleet had a home. It was the famous home from which in the previous war the Royal Navy had ruled the seas.

*   *   *

Although, as we now know, May 10 was already chosen for the invasion of France and the Low Countries, Hitler had not yet fixed the actual date of the prior Norway onslaught. Much was to precede it. On March 14 Jodl wrote in his diary:

> The English keep vigil in the North Sea with fifteen to sixteen submarines; doubtful whether reason to safeguard own operations or prevent operations by Germans. Fuehrer has not yet decided what reason to give for Weser Exercise.

There was a hum of activity in the planning sections of the German war machine. Preparations both for the attack on Norway and the invasion of France continued simultaneously and efficiently. On March 20 Falkenhorst reported that his side of the 'Weser' operation plan was ready. The Fuehrer held a Military Conference on the afternoon of March 16, and D-Day was provisionally fixed, apparently for April 9. Admiral Raeder reported to the conference:

> ... In my opinion the danger of a British landing in Norway is no longer acute at present. ... The question of what the British will do in the North in the near future can be answered as follows: They will make further attempts to disrupt German trade in neutral waters and to cause incidents in order perhaps to create a pretext for action against Norway. One object has been and still is to cut off Germany's imports from Narvik. These will be cut off at least for a time however, even if the Weser operation is carried out.

Sooner or later Germany will be faced with the necessity of carrying out the Weser operation. Therefore it is advisable to do so as soon as possible, by April 15 at the latest, since after that date the nights are too short ; there will be a new moon on April 7. The operational possibilities of the Navy will be restricted too much if the Weser operation is postponed any longer. The submarines can remain in position only for two to three weeks more. Weather of the type favourable for operation 'Gelb' [Yellow] is not to be waited for in the case of the Weser operation ; overcast, foggy weather is more satisfactory for the latter. The general state of preparedness of the naval forces and ships is at present good.

*　　*　　*

From the beginning of the year the Soviets had brought their main power to bear on the Finns. They redoubled their efforts to pierce the Mannerheim Line before the melting of the snows. Alas, this year the spring and its thaw, on which the hard-pressed Finns based their hopes, came nearly six weeks late. The great Soviet offensive on the isthmus, which was to last forty-two days, opened on February 1, combined with heavy air bombing of base depots and railway junctions behind the lines. Ten days of heavy bombardment from Soviet guns, massed wheel to wheel, heralded the main infantry attack. After a fortnight's fighting the line was breached. The air attacks on the key fort and base of Viipuri increased in intensity. By the end of the month the Mannerheim defence system had been disorganised and the Russians were able to concentrate against the Gulf of Viipuri. The Finns were short of ammunition and their troops exhausted.

The honourable correctitude which had deprived us of any strategic initiative equally hampered all effective measures for sending munitions to Finland. We had been able so far only to send from our own scanty store contributions insignificant to the Finns. In France, however a warmer and deeper sentiment prevailed, and this was strongly fostered by M. Daladier. On March 2, without consulting the British Government, he agreed to send fifty thousand volunteers and a hundred bombers to Finland. We could certainly not act on this scale, and in view of the documents found on the German major in Belgium, and of the ceaseless Intelligence reports of the steady massing of German troops on the Western Front, it went far beyond what prudence would allow. However, it was agreed to send fifty

British bombers. On March 12 the Cabinet again decided to revive the plans for military landings at Narvik and Trondheim, to be followed at Stavanger and Bergen, as a part of the extended help to Finland into which we had been drawn by the French. These plans were to be available for action on March 20, although the need of Norwegian and Swedish permission had not been met. Meanwhile on March 7 Mr. Paasikivi had gone again to Moscow, this time to discuss armistice terms. On the 12th the Russian terms were accepted by the Finns. All our plans for military landings were again shelved, and the forces which were being collected were to some extent dispersed. The two divisions which had been held back in England were now allowed to proceed to France, and our striking power towards Norway was reduced to eleven battalions.

*   *   *

Meanwhile Operation 'Royal Marine' had ripened. Five months of intensive effort with Admiralty priorities behind it had brought its punctual fruition. Admiral FitzGerald and his trained detachments of British naval officers and marines, each man aflame with the idea of a novel stroke in the war, were established on the upper reaches of the Rhine, ready to strike when permission could be obtained. In March all preparations were perfected, and I at length appealed both to my colleagues and to the French. The War Cabinet were very ready to let me begin this carefully-prepared offensive plan, and left it to me, with Foreign Office support, to do what I could with the French. In all their wars and troubles in my lifetime I have been bound up with the French, and I believed that they would do as much for me as for any other foreigner alive. But in this phase of the Twilight War I could not move them. When I pressed very hard they used a method of refusal which I never met before or since. M. Daladier told me with an air of exceptional formality that 'The President of the Republic himself had intervened, and that no aggressive action must be taken which might only draw reprisals upon France.' This idea of not irritating the enemy did not commend itself to me. Hitler had done his best to strangle our commerce by the indiscriminate mining of our harbours. We had beaten him by defensive means alone. Good, decent, civilised people, it appeared, must never themselves strike till after they have been struck dead. In these days

the fearful German volcano and all its subterranean fires drew
near to their explosion-point. There were still months of pre-
tended war. On the one side endless discussions about trivial
points, no decisions taken, or if taken rescinded, and the rule
'Don't be unkind to the enemy ; you will only make him angry.'
On the other, doom preparing—a vast machine grinding forward ready to break upon us!

* * *

The military collapse of Finland led to further repercussions.
On March 18 Hitler met Mussolini at the Brenner Pass. Hitler
deliberately gave the impression to his Italian host that there
was no question of Germany launching a land offensive in the
West. On the 19th Mr. Chamberlain spoke in the House of Commons. In view of growing criticism he reviewed in some detail
the story of British aid to Finland. He rightly emphasised that
our main consideration had been the desire to respect the neutrality of Norway and Sweden, and he also defended the
Government for not being hustled into attempts to succour the
Finns, which had offered little chance of success. The defeat
of Finland was fatal to the Daladier Government, whose
chief had taken such marked, if tardy, action, and who had
personally given disproportionate prominence to this part of
our anxieties. On March 21 a new Cabinet was formed, under M.
Reynaud, pledged to an increasingly vigorous conduct of the war.

My relations with M. Reynaud stood on a different footing
from any I had established with M. Daladier. Reynaud, Mandel, and I had felt the same emotions about Munich. Daladier
had been on the other side. I therefore welcomed the change
in the French Government, and I also hoped that my fluvial
mines would now have a better chance of acceptance.

Mr. Churchill to M. Reynaud   *March* 22, 1940
   I cannot tell you how glad I am that all has been accomplished so successfully and speedily, and especially that Daladier has been rallied to your Cabinet. This is much admired
over here, and also Blum's self-effacing behaviour.
   I rejoice that you are at the helm, and that Mandel is with
you, and I look forward to the very closest and most active
co-operation between our two Governments. I share, as you
know, all the anxieties you expressed to me the other night
about the general course of the war, and the need for strenuous and drastic measures ; but I little thought when we spoke
that events would so soon take a decisive turn for you. We

have thought so much alike during the last three or four years that I am most hopeful that the closest understanding will prevail, and that I may contribute to it.

I now send you the letter which I wrote to Gamelin upon the business which brought me to Paris last week, and I beg you to give the project your immediate sympathetic consideration. Both the Prime Minister and Lord Halifax have become very keen upon this operation ['Royal Marine'], and we were all three about to press it strongly upon your predecessor. It seems a great pity to lose this valuable time. I have now upwards of 6,000 mines ready and moving forward in an endless flow—alas, only on land—and of course there is always danger of secrecy being lost when delays occur.

I look forward to an early meeting of the Supreme Council, where I trust concerted action may be arranged between French and English *colleagues*—for that is what we are.

Pray give my kind regards to Mandel, and believe me, with the warmest wishes for your success, in which our common safety is deeply involved . . .

The French Ministers came to London for a meeting of the Supreme War Council on March 28. Mr. Chamberlain opened with a full and clear description of the scene as he saw it. To my great satisfaction he said his first proposal was that 'a certain operation, generally known as the "Royal Marine", should be put into operation immediately'. He described how this project would be carried out, and stated that stocks had been accumulated for effective and continuous execution. There would be complete surprise. The operation would take place in that part of the Rhine used almost exclusively for military purposes. No similar operation had ever been carried out before, nor had equipment previously been designed capable of taking advantage of river conditions and working successfully against the barrages and types of craft found in rivers. Finally, owing to the design of the weapons, neutral waters would not be affected. The British anticipated that this attack would create the utmost consternation and confusion. It was well known that no people were more thorough than the Germans in preparation and planning ; but equally no people could be more completely upset when their plans miscarried. They could not improvise. Again, the war had found the German railways in a precarious state, and therefore their dependence on their inland waterways had increased. In addition to the floating mines other weapons had been designed to be dropped from aircraft in canals within Germany itself, where there was no current. He urged that surprise depended upon speed. Secrecy would be endangered by delay, and the river conditions were about to be particularly favourable. As to German retaliation, if Germany thought it worth while to bomb French or British cities she would not wait for a pretext. Everything was ready. It was only necessary for the French High Command to give the order.

He then said that Germany had two weaknesses: her supplies of iron ore and of oil. The main sources of supply of these were situated at the opposite ends of Europe. The iron ore came from the North. He unfolded with precision the case for intercepting the German iron ore supplies from Sweden. He dealt also with the Roumanian and Baku oilfields, which ought to be denied to Germany, if possible by diplomacy. I listened to this powerful argument with increasing pleasure. I had not realised how fully Mr. Chamberlain and I were agreed.

M. Reynaud spoke of the impact of German propaganda upon French morale. The German radio blared each night that the Reich had no quarrel with France; that the origin of the war was to be found in the blank cheque given by Britain to Poland; that France had been dragged into war at the heels of the British, and even that she was not in a position to sustain the struggle. Goebbels' policy towards France seemed to be to let the war run on at the present reduced tempo, counting upon growing discouragement among the five million Frenchmen now called up and upon the emergence of a French Government willing to come to compromise terms with Germany at the expense of Great Britain.

The question, he said, was widely asked in France, 'How can the Allies win the war?' The number of divisions 'despite British efforts', was increasing faster on the German side than on ours. When therefore could we hope to secure that superiority in manpower required for successful action in the West? We had no knowledge of what was going on in Germany in material equipment. There was a general feeling in France that the war had reached a deadlock, and that Germany had only to wait. Unless some action were taken to cut the enemy's supply of oil and other raw material 'the feeling might grow that blockade was not a weapon strong enough to secure victory for the Allied cause'. About the operation 'Royal Marine' he said that, though good in itself, it could not be decisive, and that any reprisals would fall upon France. However, if other things were settled he would make a special effort to secure French concurrence. He was far more responsive about cutting off supplies of Swedish iron ore, and he stated that there was an exact relation between the supplies of Swedish iron ore to Germany and the output of the German iron and steel industry. His conclusion was that the Allies should lay mines in the territorial waters along the Norwegian coast and later obstruct by similar action ore being carried from the port of Luleå to Germany. He emphasised the importance of hampering German supplies of Roumanian oil.

It was at last decided that, after addressing communications in general terms to Norway and Sweden, we should lay minefields in Norwegian territorial waters on April 15, and that, *subject to the concurrence of the French War Committee*, 'Royal Marine' should be begun by launching the fluvial mines in the Rhine on April 4, and on April 15 upon the German canals from the air. It was also agreed that if Germany invaded Belgium the Allies should immediately move into that country without waiting for a formal invitation ; and that if Germany invaded Holland, and Belgium did not go to her assistance, the Allies should consider themselves free to enter Belgium for the purpose of helping Holland.

Finally, as an obvious point on which all were at one, the communiqué stated that the British and French Governments had agreed on the following solemn declaration :

That during the present war they would neither negotiate nor conclude an armistice or treaty of peace except by mutual agreement.

This pact later acquired high importance.

*   *   *

On April 3 the British Cabinet implemented the resolve of the Supreme War Council, and the Admiralty was authorised to mine the Norwegian Leads on April 8. I called the actual mining operation 'Wilfred', because by itself it was so small and innocent. As our mining of Norwegian waters might provoke a German retort, it was also agreed that a British brigade and a French contingent should be sent to Narvik to clear the port and advance to the Swedish frontier. Other forces should be despatched to Stavanger, Bergen, and Trondheim, in order to deny these bases to the enemy.

It is worth while looking back on the stages by which at last the decision to mine the Leads was reached.* I had asked for it on September 29, 1939. Nothing relevant had altered in the meanwhile. The moral and technical objections on the score of neutrality, the possibility of German retaliation against Norway, the importance of stopping the flow of iron ore from Narvik to Germany, the effect on neutral and world-wide opinion—all were exactly the same. But at last the Supreme War Council was convinced, and at last the War Cabinet were reconciled to the scheme, and indeed resolved upon it. Once had they given consent and withdrawn it. Then their mind had been overlaid by the complications of the Finnish war. On sixty days 'Aid to Finland' had been part of the Cabinet agenda. Nothing had come of it all. Finland had been crushed into submission by Russia. Now after all this vain boggling, hesitation, changes of policy, arguments between good and worthy people unending, we had at last reached the simple point on which action had been demanded seven months before. But in war seven months is a long time. Now Hitler was ready, and ready with a far more powerful and well-prepared plan. One can hardly find a more perfect example of the impotence and fatuity of waging war by committee, or rather by groups of committees. It fell to my lot in the weeks which followed to bear much of the burden and some of the odium of the ill-starred Norwegian campaign, the course of which will presently be described. Had I been allowed to act with freedom and design when I first demanded permission a far more agreeable conclusion might have been reached in this key theatre, with favourable consequences in every direction. But now all was to be disaster.

> He that will not when he may,
> When he will he shall have nay.

* * *

* September 29, 1939. First Lord calls attention of the Cabinet to the value of Swedish iron ore to the German economy.
    November 27, 1939. First Lord addresses a minute to the First Sea Lord asking for examination of proposal to mine the Leads.
    December 15, 1939. First Lord raises in Cabinet the question of iron ore shipments to Germany.
    December 16, 1939. Circulation of detailed memorandum on the subject to the Cabinet.
    December 22, 1939. Memorandum considered by the Cabinet.
    February 5, 1940. Detailed discussion of issue in connection with aid to Finland at Supreme War Council in Paris (W.S.C. present).
    February 19, 1940. Renewed discussion of mining of Leads in British Cabinet. Admiralty authorised to make preparations.
    February 29, 1940. Authorisation cancelled.
    March 28, 1940. Resolution of Supreme War Council that minefields should be laid.
    April 3, 1940. Final decision taken by British Cabinet.
    April 8, 1940. The minefields laid.

It may here be right to set forth the various offensive proposals and devices which in my subordinate position I put forward during the Twilight War. The first was the entry and domination of the Baltic, which was the sovereign plan if it were possible. It was vetoed by the growing realisation of air-power. The second was the creation of a Close Action squadron of naval tortoises not too much afraid of the air-bomb or torpedo, by the reconstruction of the *Royal Sovereign* class of battleships. This fell by the way through the movement of the war and the priorities which had to be given to aircraft-carriers. The third was the simple tactical operation of laying mines in the Norwegian Leads to cut off the vital German iron ore supplies. Fourthly comes 'Cultivator No. 6'—namely a long-term means of breaking the deadlock on the French front without a repetition of the slaughter of the previous war. This was superseded by the onrush of German armour turning our own invention of tanks to our undoing, and proving the ascendancy of the offensive in this new war. The fifth was the operation 'Royal Marine'— namely, the paralysing of traffic on the Rhine by the dropping and discharge of fluvial mines. This played its limited part and proved its virtue from the moment when it was permitted. It was however swept away in the general collapse of the French resistance. In any case it required prolonged application to cause major injury to the enemy.

To sum up: In the war of armies on the ground I was under the thrall of defensive fire-power. On the sea I strove persistently within my sphere to assert the initiative against the enemy as a relief from the terrible ordeal of presenting our enormous target of sea commerce to his attack. But in this prolonged trance of the Twilight or 'Phoney' War, as it was commonly called in the United States, neither France nor Britain was capable of meeting the German vengeance thrust. It was only after France had been flattened out that Britain, thanks to her island advantage, developed out of the pangs of defeat and the menace of annihilation a national resolve equal to that of Germany.

*   *   *

Ominous items of news of varying credibility now began to come in. At the meeting of the War Cabinet on April 3 the Secretary of State for War told us that a report had been received at the War office that the Germans had been collecting strong forces of troops at Rostock with the intention of taking Scandinavia if necessary. The Foreign Secretary said that the news from Stockholm tended to confirm this report. According to the Swedish Legation in Berlin, 200,000 tons of German shipping were now concentrated at Stettin and Swinemünde, with troops on board which rumour placed at 400,000. It was suggested that these forces were in readiness to deliver a counterstroke against a possible attack by us upon Narvik or other Norwegian ports, about which the Germans were said to be still nervous.

Soon we learnt that the French War Committee would not agree to the launching of 'Royal Marine'. They were in favour of mining the Norwegian Leads, but opposed to anything that might draw retaliation on France. Through the French Ambassador Reynaud expressed his regret. Mr. Chamberlain, who was much inclined to aggressive action of some kind at this stage, was vexed at this refusal, and in a conversation with M. Corbin he linked the two operations together. The British would cut off the ore supplies of Germany as the French desired, provided that at the same time the French allowed us to retaliate by means of 'Royal Marine' for all the injuries we had suffered and were enduring from the magnetic mine. Keen as I was on 'Royal Marine', I had not expected him to go so far as this. Both operations were methods of making offensive war upon the enemy, and bringing to an end the twilight period, from the prolongation of which I now believed Germany was the gainer. However, if a few days would enable us to bring the French into agreement upon the punctual execution of the two projects, I was agreeable to postponing 'Wilfred' for a few days.

The Prime Minister was so favourable to my views at this juncture that we seemed almost to think as one. He asked me to go over to Paris and see what I could do to persuade M. Daladier, who was evidently the stumbling-block. I met M. Reynaud and several other of his Ministers at dinner on the night of the 4th at the British Embassy, and we seemed in pretty good agreement. Daladier had been invited to attend, but professed a previous engagement. It was arranged that I should see him the next morning. While meaning to do my utmost to persuade Daladier, I asked permission from the Cabinet to make it clear that we would go forward with 'Wilfred' even if 'Royal Marine' was vetoed.

I visited Daladier at the Rue St. Dominique at noon on the 5th and had a serious talk with him. I commented on his absence from our dinner the night before. He pleaded his previous engagement. It was evident to me that a considerable gulf existed between the new and the former Premier. Daladier argued that in three months' time the French aviation would be sufficiently improved for the necessary measures to be taken to meet German reactions to 'Royal Marine'. For this he was prepared to give a firm date in writing. He made a strong case about the defenceless French factories. Finally he assured me that the period of political crises in France was over, and that he would work in harmony with M. Reynaud. On this we parted.

I reported by telephone to the War Cabinet, who were agreed that 'Wilfred' should go forward notwithstanding the French refusal of 'Royal Marine', but wished this to be the subject of a formal communication. At their meeting on April 5 the Foreign Secretary was instructed to inform the French Government that notwithstanding the great importance we had throughout attached to carrying out the 'Royal Marine' operation at an early date, and simultaneously with the proposed operation in Norwegian territorial waters, we were nevertheless prepared as a concession to their wishes to proceed with the latter alone. The date was thus finally fixed for April 8.

* * *

On Thursday, April 4, 1940, the Prime Minister addressed the Central Council of the National Union of Conservative and Unionist Associations in a spirit of unusual optimism:

> After seven months of war I feel ten times as confident of victory as I did at the beginning. ... I feel that during the seven months our relative position towards the enemy has become a great deal stronger than it was.
> Consider the difference between the ways of a country like Germany and our own. Long before the war Germany was making preparations for it. She was increasing her armed forces on land and in the air with feverish haste, she was devoting all her resources to turning out arms and equipment and to building up huge reserves of stocks ; in fact, she was turning herself into a fully armed camp. On the other hand, we, a peaceful nation, were carrying on with our peaceful pursuits. It is true that we had been driven by what was going on in Germany to begin to build up again those defences which we had so long left in abeyance, but we postponed as long as

any hope of peace remained—we continually postponed—those drastic measures which were necessary if we were to put the country on a war footing.

The result was that when war did break out German preparations were far ahead of our own, and it was natural then to expect that the enemy would take advantage of his initial superiority to make an endeavour to overwhelm us and France before we had time to make good our deficiencies. Is it not a very extraordinary thing that no such attempt was made? Whatever may be the reason—whether it was that Hitler thought he might get away with what he had got without fighting for it, or whether it was that after all the preparations were not sufficiently complete—however, one thing is certain: he missed the bus.

And so the seven months that we have had have enabled us to make good and remove our weaknesses, to consolidate, and to tune up every arm, offensive and defensive, and so enormously to add to our fighting strength that we can face the future with a calm and steady mind whatever it brings.

Perhaps you may say, 'Yes, but has not the enemy too been busy?' I have not the slightest doubt he has. I would be the last to underrate the [his] strength or determination to use that strength without scruple and without mercy if he thinks he can do so without getting his blows returned with interest. I grant that. But I say this too: the very completeness of his preparations has left him very little margin of strength still to call upon.

This proved an ill-judged utterance. Its main assumption that we and the French were relatively stronger than at the beginning of the war was not reasonable. As has been previously explained the Germans were now in the fourth year of vehement munitions manufacture, whereas we were at a much earlier stage, probably comparable in fruitfulness to the second year. Moreover, with every month that had passed the German Army, now four years old, was becoming a mature and perfected weapon, and the former advantage of the French Army in training and cohesion was steadily passing away. The Prime Minister showed no premonition that we were on the eve of great events, whereas it seemed almost certain to me that the land war was about to begin. Above all, the expression 'Hitler missed the bus' was unlucky.

All lay in suspense. The various minor expedients I had been able to suggest had gained acceptance; but nothing of a major character had been done by either side. Our plans, such as they were, rested upon enforcing the blockade by the mining of the Norwegian corridor in the north and by hampering German oil supplies from the south-east. Complete immobility and silence reigned behind the German front. Suddenly the passive or small-scale policy of the Allies was swept away by a cataract of violent surprises. We were to learn what total war means.

CHAPTER 12

The Clash at Sea

Lord Chatfield's Retirement – The Prime Minister Invites Me to Preside over the Military Co-ordination Committee – An Awkward Arrangement – 'Wilfred' – Oslo – The German Seizure of Norway – Tragedy of Neutrality – All the Fleets at Sea – The 'Glowworm' – The 'Renown' Engages the 'Scharnhorst' and 'Gneisenau' – The Home Fleet off Bergen – Action by British Submarines – Warburton-Lee's Flotilla at Narvik – Supreme War Council Meets in London, April 9 – Its Conclusions – My Minute to the First Sea Lord, April 10 – Anger in England – Debate in Parliament, April 11 – The 'Warspite' and her Flotilla Exterminate the German Destroyers at Narvik – Letter from the King.

Before resuming the narrative I must explain the alterations in my position which occurred during the month of April 1940.

Lord Chatfield's office as Minister for the Co-ordination of Defence had become redundant, and on the 3rd Mr. Chamberlain accepted his resignation, which he proffered freely. On the 4th a statement was issued from No. 10 Downing Street that it was not proposed to fill the vacant post, but that arrangements were being made for the First Lord of the Admiralty, as the senior Service Minister concerned, to preside over the Military Co-ordination Committee. Accordingly I took the chair at its meetings, which were held daily, and sometimes twice daily, from the 8th to 15th of April. I had therefore an exceptional measure of responsibility, but no power of effective direction. Among the other Service Ministers who were also members of the War Cabinet I was 'first among equals'. I had however no power to take or to enforce decisions. I had to carry with me both the Service Ministers and their professional chiefs. Thus many important and able men had a right and duty to express their views on the swiftly-changing phases of the battle—for battle it was—which now began.

The Chiefs of Staff sat daily together after discussing the

whole situation with their respective Ministers. They then arrived at their own decisions, which obviously became of dominant importance. I learned about these either from the First Sea Lord, who kept nothing from me, or by the various memoranda or *aide-mémoires* which the Chiefs of Staff Committee issued. If I wished to question any of these opinions I could of course raise them in the first instance at my Co-ordinating Committee, where the Chiefs of Staff, supported by their departmental Ministers, whom they had usually carried along with them, were all present as individual members. There was a copious flow of polite conversation at the end of which a tactful report was drawn up by the secretary in attendance and checked by the three Service departments to make sure there were no discrepancies. Thus we had arrived at those broad, happy uplands where everything is settled for the greatest good of the greatest number by the common sense of most after the consultation of all. But in war of the kind we were now to feel the conditions were different. Alas, I must write it: the actual conflict had to be more like one ruffian bashing the other on the snout with a club, a hammer, or something better. All this is deplorable, and it is one of the many good reasons for avoiding war, and having everything settled by agreement in a friendly manner, with full consideration for the rights of minorities and the faithful recording of dissentient opinions.

The Defence Committee of the War Cabinet sat almost every day to discuss the reports of the Military Co-ordination Committee and those of the Chiefs of Staff; and their conclusions or divergences were again referred to frequent Cabinets. All had to be explained and re-explained; and by the time this process was completed the whole scene had often changed. At the Admiralty, which is of necessity in war-time a battle headquarters, decisions affecting the Fleet were taken on the instant, and only in the gravest cases referred to the Prime Minister, who supported us on every occasion. Where the action of the other Services was involved the procedure could not possibly keep pace with events. However, at the beginning of the Norway campaign the Admiralty in the nature of things had three-quarters of the executive business in its own hands.

I do not pretend that, whatever my powers, I should have been able to take better decisions or reach good solutions of the problems with which we were now confronted. The impact of the events about to be described was so violent and the conditions so chaotic that I soon perceived that only the authority of the Prime Minister could reign over the Military Co-ordination Committee. Accordingly on the 15th I requested Mr. Chamberlain to take the chair, and he presided at practically every one of our subsequent meetings during the campaign in Norway. He and I continued in close agreement, and he gave his supreme authority to the views which I expressed. I was most intimately involved in the conduct of the unhappy effort to rescue Norway when it was already too late. The change in chairmanship was announced to Parliament by the Prime Minister in reply to a question as follows:

I have agreed at the request of the First Lord of the Admiralty to take the chair myself at the meetings of the Co-ordination Committee when matters of exceptional importance relating to the general conduct of the war are under discussion.

Loyalty and goodwill were forthcoming from all concerned. Nevertheless both the Prime Minister and I were acutely conscious of the formlessness of our system, especially when in contact with the surprising course of events. Although the Admiralty was at this time inevitably the prime mover, obvious objections could be raised to an organisation in which one of the Service Ministers attempted to concert all the operations of the other Services, while at the same time managing the whole business of the Admiralty and having a special responsibility for the naval movements. These difficulties were not removed by the fact that the Prime Minister himself took the chair and backed me up. But while one stroke of misfortune after another, the results of want of means or of indifferent management, fell upon us almost daily, I nevertheless continued to hold my position in this fluid, friendly, but unfocused circle.

*   *   *

On the evening of Friday, April 5, the German Minister in Oslo invited distinguished guests, including members of the Government, to a film show at the Legation. The film depicted the German conquest of Poland, and culminated in a crescendo of horror scenes during the German bombing of Warsaw. The caption read: 'For this they could thank their English and French friends.' The party broke up in silence and dismay. The Norwegian Government was however chiefly concerned with the activities of the British. Between 4.30 and 5 a.m. on April 8 four British destroyers laid our minefield off the entrance to West Fiord, the channel to the port of Narvik. At 5 a.m. the news was broadcast from London, and at 5.30 a note from His Majesty's Government was handed to the Norwegian Foreign Minister. The morning in Oslo was spent in drafting protests to London. But later that afternoon the Admiralty informed the Norwegian Legation in London that German warships had been sighted off the Norwegian coast proceeding northwards, and presumably bound for Narvik. About the same time reports reached the Norwegian capital that a German troopship, the *Rio de Janeiro*, had been sunk off the south coast of Norway by the Polish submarine *Orzel*, that large numbers of German soldiers had been rescued by the local fishermen, and that they said they were bound for Bergen to help the Norwegians defend their country against the British and French. More was to come. Germany had broken into Denmark, but the news did not reach Norway until after she herself was invaded. Thus she received no formal warning. Denmark was easily overrun after a resistance in which a few faithful soldiers were killed.

That night German warships approached Oslo. The outer batteries opened fire. The Norwegian defending force consisted of a mine-layer, the *Olav Tryggvason*, and two minesweepers. After dawn two German minesweepers entered the mouth of the fiord to disembark troops in the neighbourhood of the shore batteries. One was sunk by the *Olav Tryggvason*, but the German troops were landed and the batteries taken. The gallant minelayer however held off two German destroyers at the mouth of the fiord and damaged the cruiser *Emden*. An armed Norwegian whaler mounting a single gun also went into action at once and without special orders against the invaders. Her gun was smashed and the commander had both legs shot off. To avoid unnerving his men, he rolled himself overboard and died nobly. The main German force, led by the heavy cruiser *Bluecher*, now entered the fiord, making for the narrows defended by the fortress of Oscarsborg. The Norwegian batteries opened, and two torpedoes fired from the shore at 500 yards scored a decisive strike. The *Bluecher* sank rapidly, taking with her the senior officers of the German administrative staff and detachments of the Gestapo. The other German ships, including the *Luetzow*, retired. The damaged *Emden* took no further part in the fighting at sea. Oslo was ultimately taken, not from the sea, but by troop-carrying aeroplanes and by landing in the fiord.

Hitler's plan immediately flashed into its full scope. German forces descended at Kristiansand, at Stavanger, and to the north at Bergen and Trondheim.

The most daring stroke was at Narvik. For a week supposedly empty German ore-ships returning to that port in the ordinary course had been moving up the corridor sanctioned by Norwegian neutrality, filled with supplies and ammunition. Ten German destroyers, each carrying two hundred soldiers and supported by the *Scharnhorst* and *Gneisenau*, had left Germany some days before, and reached Narvik early on the 9th.

Two Norwegian warships, *Norge* and *Eidsvold*, lay in the fiord. They were prepared to fight to the last. At dawn destroyers were sighted approaching the harbour at high speed, but in the prevailing snow-squalls their identity was not at first established. Soon a German officer appeared in a motor launch and demanded the surrender of the *Eidsvold*. On receiving from the commanding officer the curt reply, 'I attack,' he withdrew, but almost at once the ship was destroyed with nearly all hands by a volley of torpedoes. Meanwhile the *Norge* opened fire, but in a few minutes she too was torpedoed and sank instantly.

In this gallant but hopeless resistance 287 Norwegian seamen perished, less than a hundred being saved from the two ships. Thereafter the capture of Narvik was easy. It was a strategic key—for ever to be denied us.

*   *   *

Surprise, ruthlessness, and precision were the characteristics of the onslaught upon innocent and naked Norway. Nowhere did the initial landing forces exceed two thousand men. Seven army divisions were employed, embarking principally from Hamburg and Bremen and for the follow-up from Stettin and Danzig. Three divisions were used in the assault phase, and four supported them through Oslo and Trondheim. Eight hundred operational aircraft and 250 to 300 transport planes were the salient and vital features of the design. Within forty-eight hours all the main ports of Norway were in the German grip.

*   *   *

On the night of Sunday, the 7th, our air reconnaissance reported that a German fleet, consisting of a battle-cruiser, two light cruisers, fourteen destroyers, and another ship, probably a transport, had been seen the day before moving towards the Naze across the mouth of the Skaggerak. We found it hard at the Admiralty to believe that this force was going to Narvik. In spite of a report from Copenhagen that Hitler meant to seize that port, it was thought by the Naval Staff that the German ships would probably turn back into the Skaggerak. Nevertheless the following movement was at once ordered. The Home Fleet, comprising *Rodney, Repulse, Valiant*, two cruisers, and ten destroyers, was already under steam, and left Scapa at 8.30 p.m. on April 7; the Second Cruiser Squadron, of two cruisers and fifteen destroyers, started from Rosyth at 10 p.m. on the same night. The First Cruiser Squadron, which had been embarking troops at Rosyth for the possible occupation of Norwegian ports in the event of a German attack, was ordered to march the soldiers ashore, even without their equipment, and join the Fleet at sea at the earliest moment. The cruiser *Aurora* and six destroyers similarly engaged in the Clyde were ordered to Scapa. All these decisive steps were concerted with the Commander-in-Chief. In short everything available was ordered out, on the assumption—which we had by no means accepted— that a major emergency had come. At the same time the minelaying operation off Narvik, by four destroyers, was in progress, covered by the battle-cruiser *Renown*, the cruiser *Birmingham*, and eight destroyers.

When the War Cabinet met on Monday morning I reported that the minefields in the West Fiord had been laid between 4.30 and 5 a.m. I also explained in detail that all our fleets were at sea. But by now we had assurance that the main German naval force was undoubtedly making towards Narvik. On the way to lay the minefield 'Wilfred' one of our destroyers, the *Glowworm*, having lost a man overboard during the night, stopped behind to search for him and became separated from the rest of the force. At 8.30 a.m. on the 8th the *Glowworm* had reported herself engaged with an enemy destroyer about 150 miles south-west of West Fiord. Shortly afterwards she had reported seeing another destroyer ahead of her, and later that she was engaging a superior force. After 9.45 she had become silent, since when nothing had been heard from her. On this it was calculated that the German forces, unlesss intercepted, could reach Narvik about 10 p.m. that night. They would, we hoped, be engaged by the *Renown* and the *Birmingham* and their destroyers. An action might therefore take place very shortly. 'It is impossible,' I said, 'to forecast the hazards of war, but such an action should not be on terms unfavourable for us.' Moreover, the Commander-in-Chief with the whole Home Fleet would be approaching the scene from the south. He would now be about opposite Statland. He was fully informed on all points known to us, though naturally he was remaining silent. The Germans knew that the Fleet was at sea, since a U-boat near the Orkneys had been heard to transmit a long message as the Fleet left Scapa. Meanwhile the Second Cruiser Squadron, off Aberdeen, moving north, had reported that it was being shadowed by aircraft and expected to be attacked about noon. All possible measures were being taken by the Navy and the R.A.F. to bring fighters on the scene. No aircraft-carriers were available, but flying-boats were working. The weather was thick in places, but believed to be better in the north and improving.

The War Cabinet took note of my statement and invited me to pass on to the Norwegian naval authorities the information we had received about German naval movements. On the whole the opinion was that Hitler's aim was Narvik.

On April 9 Mr. Chamberlain summoned us to a War Cabinet at 8.30 a.m., when the facts, as then known to us, about the German invasion of Norway and Denmark were discussed. The War Cabinet agreed that I should authorise the Commander-in-Chief of the Home Fleet to take all possible steps to clear Bergen and Trondheim of enemy forces, and that the Chiefs of Staff should set on foot preparations for military expeditions to re-capture both those places and to occupy Narvik. These expeditions should not however move until the naval situation had been cleared up.

*   *   *

Since the war we have learned from German records what happened to the *Glowworm*. Early on the morning of Monday, the 8th, she encountered first one and then a second enemy des-troyer. A running fight ensued in a heavy sea until the cruiser *Hipper* appeared on the scene. When the *Hipper* opened fire the *Glowworm* retired behind a smoke-screen. The *Hipper*, press-ing on through the smoke, presently emerged to find the British destroyer very close and coming straight for her at full speed. There was no time for the *Hipper* to avoid the impact, and the *Glowworm* rammed her 10,000-ton adversary, tearing a hole forty metres wide in her side. She then fell away crippled and blazing. A few minutes later she blew up. The *Hipper* picked up forty survivors ; her gallant captain was being hauled to safety when he fell back exhausted from the cruiser's deck and was lost. Thus the *Glowworm*'s light was quenched, but her captain, Lieutenant-Commander Gerard Roope, was awarded the Victoria Cross posthumously, and the story will long be remembered.

When the *Glowworm*'s signals ceased abruptly we had good hopes of bringing to action the main German forces which had ventured so far. During Monday we had a superior force on either side of them. Calculations of the sea areas to be swept gave prospects of contact, and any contact meant concentration upon them. We did not then know that the *Hipper* was escorting German forces to Trondheim. She entered Trondheim that night, but the *Glowworm* had put this powerful vessel out of action for a month.

Vice-Admiral Whitworth, in the *Renown*, on receiving *Glowworm*'s signals first steered south, hoping to intercept the enemy, but on later information and Admiralty instructions he decided to cover the approaches to Narvik. Tuesday, the 9th, was a tempestuous day, with the seas running high under furious gales and snow-storms. At early dawn the *Renown* sighted two darkened ships some 50 miles to seaward of West Fiord. These were the *Scharnhorst* and *Gneisenau*, who had just completed the task of escorting their expedition to Narvik, but at the time it was believed that only one of the two was a battle-cruiser. The *Renown* opened fire first at 18,000 yards, and soon hit the *Gneisenau*, destroying her main gun-control equipment and for a time causing her to stop firing. Her consort screened her with smoke. Both ships then turned away to the north, and the action became a chase. Meanwhile the *Renown* had received two hits, but these caused little damage, and presently she scored a second and later a third hit on the *Gneisenau*. In the heavy seas the *Renown* drove forward at full speed, but soon had to reduce to 20 knots. Amid intermittent snow-squalls and German smoke-screens the fire on both sides became ineffective. Although the *Renown* strained herself to the utmost in trying to overhaul the German ships, they at last drew away out of sight to the northward.

* * *

Meanwhile on the morning of April 9 Admiral Forbes with the main fleet was abreast of Bergen. At 6.20 a.m. he asked the Admiralty for news of the German strength there, as he intended to send in a force of cruisers and destroyers under Vice-Admiral Layton to attack any German ships they might find. The Admiralty had the same idea, and at 8.20 made him the following signal:

Prepare plans for attacking German warships and transports in Bergen and for controlling the approaches to the port on the supposition that defences are still in hands of Norwegians. Similar plans as regards Trondheim should also be prepared if you have sufficient forces for both.

The Admiralty sanctioned Admiral Forbes' plan for attacking Bergen, but later warned him that he must no longer count on the defences being friendly. To avoid dispersion, the attack on Trondheim was postponed until the German battle-cruisers should be found. At about 11.30 four cruisers and seven destroyers, under the Vice-Admiral, started for Bergen, eighty miles away, making only 16 knots against a head wind and a rough sea. Presently aircraft reported two cruisers in Bergen instead of one. With only seven destroyers the prospects of success were distinctly reduced, unless our cruisers went in too. The First Sea Lord thought the risk to these vessels, both from mines and the air, excessive. He consulted me on my return from the Cabinet meeting, and after reading the signals which had passed during the morning, and a brief discussion in the War Room, I concurred in his view. We therefore cancelled the attack. Looking back on this affair, I consider that the Admiralty kept too close a control upon the Commander-in-Chief, and after learning his original intention to force the passage into Bergen we should have confined ourselves to sending him information.

That afternoon strong air attacks were made on the Fleet, chiefly against Vice-Admiral Layton's ships. The destroyer *Gurkha* was sunk, and the cruisers *Southampton* and *Glasgow* damaged by near misses. In addition the flagship *Rodney* was hit, but her strong deck-armour prevented serious damage.

When the cruiser attack on Bergen was cancelled Admiral Forbes proposed to use torpedo-carrying naval aircraft from the carrier *Furious* at dusk on April 10. The Admiralty agreed, and also arranged attacks by R.A.F. bombers on the evening of the 9th and by naval aircraft from Hatston (Orkney) on the morning of the 10th. Meanwhile our cruisers and destroyers continued to blockade the approaches. The air attacks were successful, and the cruiser *Koenigsberg* was sunk by three bombs from naval aircraft. The *Furious* was now diverted to Trondheim, where our air patrols reported two enemy cruisers and two destroyers. Eighteen aircraft attacked at dawn on the 11th, but found only two destroyers and a submarine, besides merchant ships. Unluckily the wounded *Hipper* had left during the night, no cruisers were found, and the attack on the two German destroyers failed because our torpedoes grounded in shallow water before reaching their targets.

Meanwhile our submarines were active in the Skagerrak and Kattegat. On the night of the 8th they had sighted and attacked enemy ships northward bound from the Baltic, but without success. However, on the 9th the *Truant* sank the cruiser *Karlsruhe* off Kristiansand, and the following night the *Spearfish* torpedoed the pocket-battleship *Luetzow* returning from Oslo. Besides these successes submarines accounted for at least nine enemy transport and supply ships, with heavy loss of life, during the first week of this campaign. Our own losses were severe, and three British submarines perished during April in the heavily-defended approaches to the Baltic.

* * *

On the morning of the 9th the situation at Narvik was obscure. Hoping to forestall a German seizure of the port, the Commander-in-Chief directed Captain Warburton-Lee, commanding our destroyers, to enter the fiord and prevent any landing. Meanwhile the Admiralty transmitted a Press report to him indicating that one ship had already entered the port and landed a small force. The message went on:

> Proceed to Narvik, and sink or capture enemy ship. It is at your discretion to land forces, if you think you can recapture Narvik from number of enemy present.

Accordingly Captain Warburton-Lee, with the five destroyers of his own flotilla, *Hardy, Hunter, Havock, Hotspur,* and *Hostile,* entered West Fiord. He was told by Norwegian pilots at Tranoy that six ships larger than his own and a U-boat had passed in and that the entrance to the harbour was mined. He signalled this information and added: 'Intend attacking at dawn.' Admiral Whitworth, who received the signals, considered whether he might stiffen the attacking forces from his own now augmented squadron, but the time seemed too short and he felt that intervention by him at this stage might cause delay. In fact, we in the Admiralty were not prepared to risk the *Renown*—one of our only three battle-cruisers—in such an enterprise. The last Admiralty message passed to Captain Warburton-Lee was as follows:

Norwegian coast defence ships may be in German hands: you alone can judge whether in these circumstances attack should be made. Shall support whatever decision you take.

His reply was:

Going into action.

In the mist and snowstorms of April 10 five British destroyers steamed up the fiord, and at dawn stood off Narvik. Inside the harbour were five enemy destroyers. In the first attack the *Hardy* torpedoed the ship bearing the pennant of the German Commodore, who was killed; another destroyer was sunk by two torpedoes, and the remaining three were so smothered by gunfire that they could offer no effective resistance. There were also in the harbour twenty-three merchant ships of various nations, including five British; six German were destroyed. Only three of our five destroyers had hitherto attacked. The *Hotspur* and *Hostile* had been left in reserve to guard against any shore batteries or against fresh German ships approaching. They now joined in a second attack, and the *Hotspur* sank two more merchantmen with torpedoes. Captain Warburton-Lee's ships were unscathed; the enemy's fire was apparently silenced, and after an hour's fighting no ships had come out from any of the inlets against him.

But now fortune turned. As he was coming back from a third attack Captain Warburton-Lee sighted three fresh ships approaching from Herjangs Fiord. They showed no signs of wishing to close the range, and action began at 7,000 yards. Suddenly out of the mist ahead appeared two more warships. They were not, as was at first hoped, British reinforcements, but German destroyers which had been anchored in Ballangen Fiord. Soon the heavier guns of the German ships began to tell; the bridge of the *Hardy* was shattered, Warburton-Lee mortally stricken, and all his officers and companions killed or wounded except

Lieutenant Stanning, his secretary, who took the wheel. A shell then exploded in the engine-room, and under heavy fire the destroyer was beached. The last signal from the *Hardy*'s captain to his flotilla was 'Continue to engage the enemy.'

Meanwhile the *Hunter* had been sunk, and the *Hotspur* and the *Hostile*, which were both damaged, with the *Havock*, made for the open sea. The enemy who had barred their passage was by now in no condition to stop them. Half an hour later they encountered a large ship coming in from the sea, which proved to be the *Rauenfels,* carrying the German reserve ammunition. She was fired upon by the *Havock,* and soon blew up. The survivors of the *Hardy* struggled ashore with the body of their commander, who was awarded posthumously the Victoria Cross. He and they had left their mark on the enemy and in our naval records.

*   *   *

On the 9th MM. Reynaud and Daladier, with Admiral Darlan, flew over to London, and in the afternoon a Supreme War Council meeting was held to deal with what they called 'the German action in consequence of the laying of mines within Norwegian territorial waters'. Mr. Chamberlain at once pointed out that the enemy's measures had certainly been planned in advance and quite independently of ours. Even at that date this was obvious. M. Reynaud informed us that the French War Committee, presided over by the President, had that morning decided in principle on moving forward into Belgium should the Germans attack. The addition, he said, of eighteen to twenty Belgian divisions, besides the shortening of the front, would to all intents and purposes wipe out the German preponderance in the West. The French would be prepared to connect such an operation with the laying of the fluvial mines in the Rhine. He added that his reports from Belgium and Holland indicated the imminence of a German attack on the Low Countries ; some said days, some said hours.

On the question of the military expedition to Norway, the Secretary of State for War reminded the Council that the two British divisions originally assembled for assistance to Finland had since been sent to France. There were only eleven battalions available in the United Kingdom. Two of these were sailing that night. The rest, for various reasons, would not be ready to sail for three or four days or more.

The Council agreed that strong forces should be sent where possible to ports on the Norwegian seaboard, and joint plans were made. A French Alpine division was ordered to embark within two or three days. We were able to provide two British battalions that night, a further five battalions within three days, and four more within fourteen days—eleven in all. Any additional British forces for Scandinavia would have to be withdrawn from France. Suitable measures were to be taken to occupy the Faroe Islands, and assurances of protection would be given to Iceland. Naval arrangements were concerted in the Mediterranean in the event of Italian intervention. It was also decided that urgent representations should be made to the Belgian Government to invite the Allied armies to move forward into Belgium. Finally, it was confirmed that if Germany made an attack in the West or entered Belgium 'Royal Marine' should be carried out.

* * *

I was far from content with what had happened so far in Norway. I wrote to Admiral Pound:

10.iv.40

The Germans have succeeded in occupying all the ports on the Norwegian coast, including Narvik, and large-scale operations will be required to turn them out of any of them. Norwegian neutrality and our respect for it have made it impossible to prevent this ruthless *coup*. It is now necessary to take a new view. We must put up with the disadvantage of closer air attack on our northern bases. We must seal up Bergen with a watchful minefield, and concentrate on Narvik, for which long and severe fighting will be required.

It is immediately necessary to obtain one or two fuelling bases on the Norwegian coast, and a wide choice presents itself. This is being studied by the Staff. The advantage of our having a base, even improvised, on the Norwegian coast is very great, and now that the enemy have bases there we cannot carry on without it. The Naval Staff are selecting various alternatives which are suitable anchorages capable of defence, and without communications with the interior. Unless we have this quite soon we cannot compete with the Germans in their new position.

We must also take our advantages in the Faroes.

Narvik must be fought for. Although we have been completely outwitted, there is no reason to suppose that prolonged and serious fighting in this area will not impose a greater drain on the enemy than on ourselves.

For three days we were deluged with reports and rumours from neutral countries and triumphant claims by Germany of the losses they had inflicted on the British Navy, and of their master-stroke in seizing Norway in the teeth of our superior naval power. It was obvious that Britain had been forestalled, surprised, and, as I had written to the First Sea Lord, outwitted. Anger swept the country, and the brunt fell upon the Admiralty. On Thursday, the 11th, I had to face a disturbed and indignant House of Commons. I followed the method I have always found most effective on such occasions, of giving a calm, unhurried factual narrative of events in their sequence, laying full emphasis upon ugly truths. I explained for the first time in public the disadvantage we had suffered since the beginning of the war by German's abuse of the Norwegian corridor, or 'covered way', and how we had at last overcome the scruple which 'caused us injury at the same time that it did us honour'.

It is not the slightest use blaming the Allies for not being able to give substantial help and protection to neutral countries if we are held at arm's-length until these neutrals are actually attacked on a scientifically-prepared plan by Germany. The strict observance of neutrality by Norway has been a contributory cause to the sufferings to which she is now exposed and to the limits of the aid which we can give her. I trust this fact will be meditated upon by other countries who may to-morrow, or a week hence, *or a month hence,* find themselves the victims of an equally elaborately worked out staff plan for their destruction and enslavement.

I described the recent reoccupation by our Fleet of Scapa Flow, and the instant movement we had made to intercept the German forces in the North, and how the enemy were in fact caught between two superior forces.

However, they got away. . . . You may look at the map and see flags stuck in at different points and consider that the results will be certain, but when you get out on the sea, with its vast distances, its storms and mists, and with night coming on, and all the uncertainties which exist, you cannot possibly expect that the kind of conditions which would be appropriate to the movements of armies have any application to the haphazard conditions of war at sea. . . . When we speak of the command of the seas it does not mean command of every part of the sea at the same moment, or at every moment. It only means that we can make our will prevail ultimately in any part of the seas which may be selected for operations, and thus indirectly make our will prevail in every part of the sea. Anything more foolish than to suppose that the life and strength of the Royal Navy should have been expended in ceaselessly patrolling up and down the Norwegian and Danish coasts as a target for the U-boats on the chance that Hitler would launch a blow like this cannot be imagined.

The House listened with growing acceptance to the account, of which the news had just reached me, of Tuesday's brush between the *Renown* and the enemy, of the air attack on the British fleet off Bergen, and especially of Warburton-Lee's incursion and action at Narvik. At the end I said:

Everyone must recognise the extraordinary and reckless gambling which has flung the whole German Fleet out upon the savage seas of war, as if it were a mere counter to be cast away for a particular operation. ... This very recklessness makes me feel that these costly operations may be only the prelude to far larger events which impend on land. We have probably arrived now at the first main clinch of the war.

After an hour and a half the House seemed to be very much less estranged. A little later there would have been more to tell.

* * *

By the morning of April 10 the *Warspite* had joined the Commander-in-Chief, who was proceeding towards Narvik. On learning about Captain Warburton-Lee's attack at dawn we resolved to try again. The cruiser *Penelope*, with destroyer support, was ordered to attack, 'if in the light of experience this morning you consider it a justifiable operation.' But while the signals were passing, *Penelope*, in searching for enemy transports reported off Bodo, ran ashore. The next day (12th) a dive-bombing attack on enemy ships in Narvik harbour was made from the *Furious*. The attack was pressed home in terrible weather and low visibility, and four hits on destroyers were claimed for the loss of two aircraft. This was not enough. We wanted Narvik very much, and were determined at least to clear it of the German Navy. The climax was now at hand.

The precious *Renown* was kept out of it. Admiral Whitworth shifted his flag to the *Warspite* at sea, and at noon on the 13th he entered the fiord, escorted by nine destroyers and by dive-bombers from the *Furious*. There were no minefields ; but a U-boat was driven off by the destroyers, and a second sunk by the *Warspite*'s own 'Swordfish' aircraft, which also detected a German destroyer lurking in an inlet to launch her torpedoes on the battleship from this ambush. The hostile destroyer was quickly overwhelmed. At 1.30 p.m., when our ships were through the Narrows and a dozen miles from Narvik, five enemy destroyers appeared ahead in the haze. At once a fierce fight began, with all ships on both sides firing and manœuvring rapidly. The *Warspite* found no shore batteries to attack, and intervened in deadly fashion in the destroyer fight. The thunder of her 15-inch guns reverberated among the surrounding mountains like the voice of doom. The enemy, heavily overmatched, retreated, and the action broke up into separate combats. Some of our ships went into Narvik harbour to complete the task of destruction there ; others, led by the *Eskimo*, pursued three Germans who sought refuge in the head-waters of Römbaks Fiord and annihilated them there. The bows of the *Eskimo* were blown off by a torpedo ; but in this second sea-fight off Narvik the eight enemy destroyers which had survived Warburton-Lee's attack were all sunk or wrecked without the loss of a single British ship.

When the action was over Admiral Whitworth thought of throwing a landing party of seamen and marines ashore to occupy the town, where there seemed for the moment to be no opposition. Unless the fire of the *Warspite* could dominate the scene, an inevitable counter-attack by a greatly superior number of German soldiers must be expected. With the risk from the air and from U-boats he did not feel justified in exposing this fine ship so long. His decision was endorsed when a dozen German aircraft appeared at 6 p.m. Accordingly he withdrew early next morning, after embarking the wounded from the destroyers. 'My impression,' he said, 'is that the enemy forces in Narvik were thoroughly frightened as a result of to-day's action. I recommend that the town be occupied without delay by the main landing force.' Two destroyers were left off the port to watch events, and one of these rescued the survivors of the *Hardy*, who had meanwhile maintained themselves on shore.

* * *

His Majesty, whose naval instincts were powerfully stirred by this clash of the British and German Navies in Northern waters, wrote me the following encouraging letter:

BUCKINGHAM PALACE
April 12, 1940

My dear Mr. Churchill,

I have been wanting to have a talk with you about the recent striking events in the North Sea, which, as a sailor, I have naturally followed with the keenest interest, but I have purposely refrained from taking up any of your time as I know what a great strain has been placed upon you by your increased responsibilities as Chairman of the Co-ordination Committee. I shall however ask you to come and see me as soon as there is a lull. In the meantime I would like to congratulate you on the splendid way in which, under your direction, the Navy is countering the German move against Scandinavia. I also beg of you to take care of yourself and get as much rest as you possibly can in these critical days.

Believe me,
Yours very sincerely,
GEORGE R.I.

CHAPTER 13

Narvik

Hitler's Outrage on Norway – Long-Prepared Treachery – Norwegian Resistance – Appeal to the Allies – The Position of Sweden – The Narvik Expedition – Instructions to General Mackesy – And to Lord Cork – Question of a Direct Assault – General Mackesy Adverse – My Desire to Concentrate on Narvik and to Attempt to Storm it – War Cabinet Conclusions of April 13 – The Trondheim Project Mooted – Disappointing News from Narvik – My Note to the Military Co-ordination Committee of April 17 – Our Telegram to the Naval and Military Commanders – Deadlock at Narvik.

For many generations Norway, with its homely, rugged population engaged in trade, shipping, fishing, and agriculture, had stood outside the turmoil of world politics. Far off were the days when the Vikings had sallied forth to conquer or ravage a large part of the then known world. The Hundred Years War, the Thirty Years War, the wars of William III and Marlborough, the Napoleonic convulsion, and later conflicts, had left Norway, though separated from Denmark, otherwise unmoved and unscathed. A large proportion of the people had hitherto thought of neutrality and neutrality alone. A tiny army and a population with no desires except to live peaceably in their own mountainous and semi-Arctic country now fell victims to the new German aggression.

It had been the policy of Germany for many years to profess cordial sympathy and friendship for Norway. After the previous war some thousands of German children had found food and shelter with the Norwegians. These had now grown up in Germany, and many of them were ardent Nazis. There was also the Major Quisling, who with a handful of young men had aped and reproduced in Norway on an insignificant scale the Fascist movement. For some years past Nordic meetings had been arranged in Germany to which large numbers of Norwegians had been invited. German lecturers, actors, singers, and men of science had visited Norway in the promotion of a common culture. All this had been woven into the texture of the Hitlerite military plan, and a widely-scattered internal pro-German conspiracy set on foot. In this every member of the German diplomatic or consular service, every German purchasing agency, played its part under directions from the German Legation in Oslo. The deed of infamy and treachery now performed may take its place with the Sicilian Vespers and the massacre of St. Bartholomew. The President of the Norwegian Parliament, Carl Hambro, has written:

> In the case of Poland and later in those of Holland and Belgium notes had been exchanged, ultimata had been presented. In the case of Norway the Germans under the mask of friendship tried to extinguish the nation in one dark night, silently, murderously, without any declaration of war, without any warning given. What stupefied the Norwegians more than the act of aggression itself was the national realisation that a great Power, for years professing its friendship, suddenly appeared a deadly enemy, and that men and women with whom one had had intimate business or professional relations, who had been cordially welcomed in one's home, were spies and agents of destruction. More than by the violation of treaties and every international obligation, the people of Norway were dazed to find that for years their German friends had been elaborating the most detailed plans for the invasion and subsequent enslaving of their country.*

The King, the Government, the Army, and the people, as soon as they realised what was happening, flamed into furious anger. But it was all too late. German infiltration and propaganda had hitherto clouded their vision, and now sapped their powers of resistance. Major Quisling presented himself at the radio, now in German hands, as the pro-German ruler of the conquered land. Almost all Norwegian officials refused to serve him. The Army was mobilised, and at once began, under General Ruge, to fight the invaders pressing northwards from Oslo. Patriots who could find arms took to the mountains and the forests. The King, the Ministry, and the Parliament withdrew first to Hamar, a hundred miles from Oslo. They were hotly pursued by German armoured cars, and ferocious attempts were made to exterminate them by bombing and machine-gunning from the air. They continued however to issue proclamations to the whole country urging the most strenuous resistance. The rest of the population was overpowered and terrorised by bloody examples into stupefied or sullen submission. The peninsula of Norway is

* Carl J. Hambro, *I Saw it Happen in Norway*, p. 23.

nearly a thousand miles long. It is sparsely inhabited, and roads and railways are few, especially to the northward. The rapidity with which Hitler effected the domination of the country was a remarkable feat of war and policy, and an enduring example of German thoroughness, wickedness, and brutality.

The Norwegian Government, hitherto in their fear of Germany so frigid to us, now made vehement appeals for succour. It was from the beginning obviously impossible for us to rescue southern Norway. Almost all our trained troops, and many only half trained, were in France. Our modest but growing Air Force was fully assigned to supporting the British Expeditionary Force, to Home Defence, and vigorous training. All our anti-aircraft guns were demanded ten times over for vulnerable points of the highest importance. Still, we felt bound to do our utmost to go to their aid, even at violent derangement of our own preparations and interests. Narvik, it seemed, could certainly be seized and defended with benefit to the whole Allied cause. Here the King of Norway might fly his flag unconquered. Trondheim might be fought for, at any rate as a means of delaying the northward advance of the invader until Narvik could be regained and made the base of an army. This, it seemed, could be maintained from the sea at a strength superior to anything which could be brought against it by land through five hundred miles of mountain country. The Cabinet heartily approved all possible measures for the rescue and defence of Narvik and Trondheim. The troops which had been released from the Finnish project, and a nucleus kept in hand for Narvik, could soon be ready. They lacked aircraft, anti-aircraft guns, anti-tank guns, tanks, transport, and training. The whole of Northern Norway was covered with snow to depths which none of our soldiers had ever seen, felt, or imagined. There were neither snow-shoes nor skis—still less skiers. We must do our best. Thus began this ramshackle campaign.

*   *   *

There was every reason to believe that Sweden would be the next victim of Germany or Russia, or perhaps even of both. If Sweden came to the aid of her agonised neighbour the military situation would be for the time being transformed. The Swedes had a good army. They could enter Norway easily. They could be at Trondheim in force before the Germans. We could join them there. But what would be the fate of Sweden in the months that followed? Hitler's vengeance would lay them low, and the Bear would maul them from the East. On the other hand, the Swedes could purchase neutrality by supplying the Germans with all the iron ore they wanted throughout the approaching summer. For Sweden the choice was a profitable neutrality or subjugation. She could not be blamed because she did not view the issue from the standpoint of our unready but now eager Island.

After the Cabinet on the morning of April 11 I wrote the following minute, which the sacrifices we were making for the rights of small States and the Law of Nations may justify:

Prime Minister
Foreign Secretary

I am not entirely satisfied with the result of the discussion this morning, or with my contribution to it. What we want is that Sweden should not remain neutral, but declare war on Germany. What we do not want is either to provide the three divisions which we dangled to procure the Finland project, or to keep her fully supplied with food as long as the war lasts, or to bomb Berlin, etc., if Stockholm is bombed. These stakes are more than it is worth while paying at the present time. On the other hand, we should do everything to encourage her into the war by general assurances that we will give all the help we can, that our troops will be active in the Scandinavian peninsula, that we will make common cause with her as good allies, and will not make peace without her, or till she is righted. Have we given this impulse to the Anglo-French mission? If not, there is still time to do it. Moreover, our diplomacy should be active at Stockholm.

It must be remembered that Sweden will say 'Thank you for nothing' about any offers on our part to defend the Gällivare ironfield. She can easily do this herself. Her trouble is to the south, where we can do but little. Still, it will be something to assure her that we intend to open the Narvik route to Sweden from the Atlantic by main force as soon as possible, and also that we propose to clean up the German lodgments on the Norwegian coast *seriatim*, thus opening other channels.

If the great battle opens in Flanders the Germans will not have much to spare for Scandinavia, and if, on the other hand, the Germans do not attack in the West we can afford to send troops to Scandinavia in proportion as German divisions are withdrawn from the Western Front. It seems to me we must not throw cold water on the French idea of trying to induce the Swedes to enter the war. It would be disastrous if they remained neutral and bought Germany off with ore from Gällivare, down the Gulf of Bothnia.

I must apologise for not having sufficiently gripped this issue in my mind this morning, but I only came in after the discussion had begun, and did not address myself properly to it.

There was justice in the Foreign Secretary's reply, by which I was convinced. He said that the Prime Minister and he agreed with my general view, but doubted the method I favoured of approaching Sweden.

April 11, 1940

From all the information that we have from Swedish sources that are friendly to the Allies, it appears that any representations that can be readily translated in their minds into an attempt by us to drag them into the war will be likely to have an effect opposite to that which we want. Their immediate reaction would be that we were endeavouring to get them to do what, until we have established a position in one or more of the Norwegian ports, we were unable or unwilling to do ourselves. And accordingly the result would do us more harm than good.

*   *   *

It was easy to regather at short notice the small forces for a Narvik expedition which had been dispersed a few days earlier. One British brigade and its ancillary troops began to embark immediately, and the first convoy sailed for Narvik on April 12. This was to be followed in a week or two by three battalions of Chasseurs Alpins and other French troops. There were also Norwegian forces north of Narvik which would help our landings. Major-General Mackesy had been selected on April 5 to command any expedition which might be sent to Narvik. His instructions were couched in a form appropriate to the case of a friendly neutral Power from whom some facilities are required. They contained among their appendices the following reference to bombardment:

It is clearly illegal to bombard a populated area in the hope of hitting a legitimate target which is known to be in the area but which cannot be precisely located and identified.

In the face of the German onslaught new and stiffer instructions were issued to the General on the 10th. They gave him more latitude, but did not cancel this particular injunction. Their substance was as follows:

His Majesty's Government and the Government of the French Republic have decided to send a Field Force to initiate operations against Germany in Northern Norway. The object of the force will be to eject the Germans from the Narvik area and establish control of Narvik itself. ... Your initial task will be to establish your force at Harstad, ensure the co-operation of Norwegian forces that may be there, and obtain the information necessary to enable you to plan your further operations. It is not intended that you should land in the face of opposition. You may however be faced with opposition owing to mistaken identity; you will therefore take such steps as are suitable to establish the nationality of your force before abandoning the attempt. The decision whether to land or not will be taken by the senior naval officer in consultation with you. If landing is impossible at Harstad some other suitable locality should be tried. A landing must be carried out when you have sufficient troops.

At the same time a personal letter from General Ironside, the C.I.G.S., was given to General Mackesy, which included the remark:

You may have a chance of taking advantage of naval action, and should do so if you can. Boldness is required.

This struck a somewhat different note from the formal instructions.

My contacts with Lord Cork and Orrery had become intimate in the long months during which the active discussions of Baltic strategy had proceeded. In spite of some differences of view about 'Catherine', his relations with the First Sea Lord were good. I was fully conscious from long and hard experience of the difference between pushing things audaciously on paper so as to get them explored and tested—the processes of mental reconnaissance-in-force—and actually doing them or getting them done. Admiral Pound and I were both agreed from slightly different angles that Lord Cork should command the naval forces in this amphibious adventure in the North. We both urged him not to hesitate to run risks, but to strike hard to seize Narvik. As we were all agreed and could talk things over together, we left him exceptional discretion and did not give him any written orders. He knew exactly what we wanted. In his dispatch he says, 'My impression on leaving London was quite clear that it was desired by His Majesty's Government to turn the enemy out of Narvik at the earliest possible moment, and that I was to act with all promptitude in order to attain this result.'

Our Staff work at this time had not been tempered by war experience, nor was the action of the Service departments concerted except by the meetings of the Military Co-ordination Committee, over which I had just begun to preside. Neither I, as chairman of the Committee, nor the Admiralty were made acquainted with the War Office instructions to General Mackesy, and as the Admiralty directions had been given orally to Lord Cork there was no written text to communicate to the War Office. The instructions of the two departments, although animated by the same purpose, were somewhat different in tone and emphasis ; and this may have helped to cause the divergences which presently developed between the military and naval commanders.

Lord Cork sailed from Rosyth at high speed in the *Aurora* on the night of April 12.* He had intended to meet General Mackesy at Harstad, a small port on the island of Hinnoy, in Vaags Fiord, which, although sixty miles from Narvik, had been selected as the military base. However, on the 14th he received a signal from Admiral Whitworth in the *Warspite*, who had exterminated all the German destroyers and supply ships the day before, saying, 'I am convinced that Narvik can be taken by direct assault now without fear of meeting serious opposition on landing. I consider that the main landing force need only be small. . . .' Lord Cork therefore diverted the *Aurora* to Skjel Fiord, in the Lofoten Islands, flanking the approach to Narvik, and sent a message ordering the *Southampton* to join him there. His intention was to organise a force for an immediate assault, consisting of two companies of the Scots Guards who had been embarked in the *Southampton*, and a force of seamen and marines from the *Warspite* and other ships already in Skjel Fiord. He could not however get in touch with the *Southampton* except, after some delay, through the Admiralty, whose reply contained the following sentence: 'We think it imperative that you and the General should be together and act together and that no attack should be made, except in concert.' He therefore left Skjel Fiord for Harstad, and led the convoy carrying the 24th Brigade into harbour there on the morning of the 15th. His escorting destroyers sank U.49, which was prowling near by.

* A sketch map of the Narvik operations will be found on page 229.

Lord Cork now urged General Mackesy to take advantage of the destruction of all the German naval force and to make a direct attack on Narvik as soon as possible, but the General replied that the harbour was strongly held by the enemy with machine-gun posts. He also pointed out that his transports had not been loaded for an assault, but only for an unopposed landing. He opened his headquarters at the hotel in Harstad, and his troops began to land thereabouts. The next day he stated that, on the information available, landing at Narvik was not possible, nor would naval bombardment make it so. Lord Cork considered that with the help of overwhelming gun-fire troops could be landed in Narvik with little loss ; but the General did not agree, and could find some cover in his instructions. From the Admiralty we urged an immediate assault. A deadlock arose between the military and naval chiefs.

At this time the weather greatly worsened, and dense falls of snow seemed to paralyse all movement by our troops, unequipped and untrained for such conditions. Meanwhile the Germans in Narvik held our ever-growing forces at bay with their machine-guns. Here was a serious and unexpected check.

* * *

Most of the business of our improvised campaign passed through my hands, and I prefer to record it as far as possible in my own words at the time. The Prime Minister had a strong desire, shared by the War Cabinet, to occupy Trondheim as well as Narvik. This Operation 'Maurice', as it was called, promised to be a big undertaking. According to the records of our Military Co-ordination Committee of April 13, I was

very apprehensive of any proposals which might tend to weaken our intention to seize Narvik. Nothing must be allowed to deflect us from making the capture of this place as certain as possible. Our plans against Narvik had been very carefully laid, and there seemed every chance that they would be successful if they were allowed to proceed without being tampered with. Trondheim was, on the other hand, a much more speculative affair, and I deprecated any suggestion which might lead to the diversion of the Chasseurs Alpins until we had definitely established ourselves at Narvik. Otherwise we might find ourselves committed to a number of ineffectual operations along the Norwegian coast, none of which would succeed.

At the same time consideration had already been given to

the Trondheim area, and plans were being made to secure landing-points in case a larger-scale action should be needed. A small landing of naval forces would take place at Namsos that afternoon. The Chief of the Imperial General Staff had collected a force of five battalions, two of which would be ready to land on the Norwegian coast on April 16, and three more on April 21 if desired. The actual points at which landings were to be made would be decided that night.

General Mackesy's original orders had been that, after landing at Narvik, he should push rapidly on to the Gällivare ore-field. He has now been told to go no farther than the Swedish frontier, since, if Sweden were friendly, there need be no fear for the ore-fields, and if hostile the difficulties of occupying them would be too great.

I also said that:

It might be necessary to proceed to invest the German forces in Narvik. But we should not allow the operation to degenerate into an investment except after a very determined battle. On this understanding I was willing to send a telegram to the French saying that we hoped and thought that we should be successful in seizing Narvik by a *coup-de-main*. We should explain that this had been made easier by a change in the orders, which did not now require the expedition to go beyond the Swedish frontier.

It was decided by the War Cabinet to attempt both the Narvik and Trondheim operations. The Secretary of State for War, with foresight, warned us that reinforcements for Norway might soon be required from our Army in France, and suggested that we should address the French on the point at a very early date. I agreed with this, but thought it premature to approach the French for a day or two. This was accepted. The War Cabinet approved a proposal to inform the Swedish and Norwegian Governments that we intended to recapture both Trondheim and Narvik; that we recognised the supreme importance of Trondheim as a strategic centre, but that it was important to secure Narvik as a naval base. We added that we had no intention that our forces should proceed over the Swedish frontier. We were at the same time to invite the French Government to give us liberty to use the Chasseurs Alpins for operations elsewhere than at Narvik, telling them what we were saying to the Swedish and Norwegian Governments. Neither I nor Mr. Stanley liked the dispersion of our forces. We were still inclined to concentrate all on Narvik, except for diversions elsewhere.

But we deferred to the general view, for which there was no lack of good reasons.

* * *

On the night of the 16th–17th disappointing news arrived from Narvik. General Mackesy had, it appeared, no intention of trying to seize the town by an immediate assault protected by the close-range bombardment of the Fleet, and Lord Cork could not move him. I stated the position to my Committee as it then appeared.

April 17

1. Lord Cork's telegram shows that General Mackesy proposes to take two unoccupied positions on the approaches to Narvik and to hold on there until the snow melts, perhaps at the end of the month. The General expects that the first demi-brigade of Chasseurs Alpins will be sent to him, which it certainly will not be. This policy means that we shall be held up in front of Narvik for several weeks. Meanwhile the Germans will proclaim that we are brought to a standstill and that Narvik is still in their possession. The effects of this will be damaging both upon Norwegians and neutrals. Moreover, the German fortification of Narvik will continue, requiring a greater effort when the time comes. This information is at once unexpected and disagreeable. One of the best Regular brigades in the Army will be wasting away, losing men by sickness, and playing no part. It is for consideration whether a telegram on the following lines should not be sent to Lord Cork and General Mackesy:

'Your proposals involve damaging deadlock at Narvik and the neutralisation of one of our best brigades. We cannot send you the Chasseurs Alpins. The *Warspite* will be needed elsewhere in two or three days. Full consideration should therefore be given by you to an assault upon Narvik, covered by the *Warspite* and the destroyers, which might also operate at Römbaks Fiord. The capture of the port and town would be an important success. We should like to receive from you the reasons why this is not possible, and your estimate of the degree of resistance to be expected on the waterfront. Matter most urgent.'

2. The second point which requires decision is whether the Chasseurs Alpins shall go straight on to join General Carton de Wiart at or beyond Namsos, or whether, as is easy, they should be held back at Scapa and used for the Trondheim operation on the 22nd or 23rd, together with other troops available for this main attack.

3. Two battalions of the 146th Brigade will, it is hoped, have been landed before dawn to-day at Namsos and Bandsund. The 3rd Battalion, in the *Chrobry*, will make a dangerous voyage to-morrow to Namsos, arriving, if all is well, about dusk, and landing. The anchorage of Lillejonas was bombed all the afternoon without the two transports being hit, and the large 18,000-tonner is now returning empty to Scapa Flow. If the leading Chasseurs Alpins are to be used at Namsos they must go there direct instead of making rendezvous at Lillejonas.

4. The question of whether the forces now available for the main attack on Trondheim are adequate must also be decided to-day. The two Guards battalions that were to be mobilised, i.e., equipped, cannot be ready in time. The two French Foreign Legion battalions cannot arrive in time. A Regular brigade from France can however be ready to sail from Rosyth on the 20th. The first and second demi-brigades of the Chasseurs Alpins can also be in time. A thousand Canadians have been made available. There is also a brigade of Territorials. Is this enough to prevail over the Germans in Trondheim? The dangers of delay are very great and need not be restated.

5. Admiral Holland leaves to-night to meet the Commander-in-Chief Home Fleet on his return to Scapa on the 18th, and he must carry with him full and clear decisions. It may be taken as certain that the Navy will cheerfully undertake to carry troops to Trondheim.

6. It is probable that fighting will take place to-night and to-morrow morning for the possession of Andalsnes. We hope to have landed an advance party from the cruiser *Calcutta*, and are moving sufficient cruisers to meet a possible attack by five enemy destroyers at dawn.

7. The naval bombardments of Stavanger aerodrome will begin at dawn [to-day].

The Committee agreed to the telegram, which was accordingly sent. It produced no effect. It must remain a matter of opinion whether such an assault would have succeeded. It involved no marches through the snow, but, on the other hand, landings from open boats both in Narvik harbour and in Römbaks Fiord, under machine-gun fire. I counted upon the effect of close-range bombardment by the tremendous ship's batteries, which would blast the waterfronts and cover with smoke and clouds of snow and earth the whole of the German machine-gun posts. Suitable high-explosive shells had been provided by the Admiralty both for the battleship and the destroyers. Certainly

Lord Cork, on the spot and able to measure the character of the bombardment, was strongly in favour of making the attempt. We had over four thousand of our best Regular troops, including the Guards Brigade and Marines, who, once they set foot on shore, would become intermingled at close quarters with the German defenders, whose regular troops, apart from the crews rescued from the sunken destroyers, we estimated, correctly as we now know, at no more than half their number. This would have been considered a fair proposition on the Western Front in the previous war, and no new factors were at work here. Later on in this war scores of such assaults were made and often succeeded. Moreover, the orders sent to the commanders were of such a clear and imperative character, and so evidently contemplated heavy losses, that they should have been obeyed. The responsibility for a bloody repulse would fall exclusively on the home authorities, and very directly upon me. I was content that this should be so; but nothing I or my colleagues or Cork could do or say produced the slightest effect on the General. He was resolved to wait till the snow melted. As for the bombardment, he could point to the paragraph in his instructions against endangering the civil population. When we contrast this spirit with the absolutely reckless gambling in lives and ships and the almost frenzied vigour, based upon long and profound calculations, which had gained the Germans their brilliant success, the disadvantages under which we lay in waging this campaign are obvious.

CHAPTER 14

Trondheim

*A Key Objective – The Obvious Plan – Operation 'Hammer'
– Attitude of the Commander-in-Chief Home Fleet – Choice of
Generals – A Chapter of Accidents – Situation on April 14
– Situation on April 17 – Second Thoughts of the Staffs – Power
of Unopposed Air Force – The Change of Plan – Sir Roger
Keyes' Desires and Credentials – My Report to the Co-ordina-
tion Committee of April 19 – The War Cabinet Accept the Aban-
donment of 'Hammer' – Urgency of Narvik, April 20 – General
Ismay's Summary.*

Trondheim, if it were within our strength, was of course the
key to any considerable operations in Central Norway. To gain
it meant a safe harbour with quays and docks upon which an
army of 50,000 men or more could be built up and based.
Near by was an air-field from which several fighter squadrons
could work. The possession of Trondheim would open direct
railway contact with Sweden, and greatly improve the chances
of Swedish intervention or the degree of mutual aid possible
if Sweden were herself attacked. From Trondheim alone the
northward advance of the German invasion from Oslo could be
securely barred. On the broadest grounds of policy and strategy
it would be good for the Allies to fight Hitler on the largest
possible scale in Central Norway, if that was where he wanted
to go. Narvik, far away to the north, could be stormed or reduced at leisure and would all the while be protected. We had
the effective command of the sea. As to the air, if we could
establish ourselves firmly on Norwegian airfields we should not
hesitate to fight the German Air Force there to any extent which
the severely limiting conditions allowed to either side.

All these reasons had simultaneously convinced the French
War Council, the British War Cabinet, and most of their advisers. The British and French Prime Ministers were at one.
General Gamelin was willing to withdraw French or release
British divisions from France for Norway to the same extent
that the Germans diverted their forces thither. He evidently
welcomed a prolonged battle on a large scale south of Trond-

heim, where the ground was almost everywhere favourable to defence. It seemed that we could certainly bring forces and supplies to the scene across the open sea and through Trondheim far quicker than the Germans could fight their way up the single road and railway-line from Oslo, both of which might be cut behind them by bombs or parties dropped from the air. The only question was, could we take Trondheim in time? Could we get there before the main enemy army arrived from the south? and for this purpose could we obtain even a passing relief from their present unchallenged air domination?

There was a surge of opinion in favour of Trondheim which extended far beyond Cabinet circles. The advantages were so obvious that all could see them. The public, the clubs, the newspapers and their military correspondents had for some days past been discussing such a policy freely. My great friend Admiral of the Fleet Sir Roger Keyes, champion of forcing the Dardanelles, hero and victor of Zeebrugge, passionately longed to lead the Fleet or any portion of it past the batteries into the Trondheim Fiord and storm the town by landings from the sea. The appointment of Lord Cork, also an Admiral of the Fleet, to command the naval operations at Narvik although he was senior to the Commander-in-Chief, Admiral Forbes, himself, seemed to remove the difficulties of rank. Admirals of the Fleet are always on the active list, and Keyes had many contacts at the Admiralty. He spoke and wrote to me repeatedly with vehemence, reminding me of the Dardanelles and how easily the straits could have been forced if we had not been stopped by timid obstructionists. I also pondered a good deal upon the lessons of the Dardanelles. Certainly the Trondheim batteries and any minefields that might have been laid were trivial compared with those we had then had to face. On the other hand, there was the aeroplane, capable of dropping its bombs on the unprotected decks of the very few great ships which now constituted the naval power of Britain on the oceans.

At the Admiralty the First Sea Lord and the Naval Staff generally did not shrink from the venture. On April 13 the Admiralty had officially informed the Commander-in-Chief of the Supreme Council's decision to allot troops for the capture of Trondheim, and had raised with him in a positive manner the question whether the Home Fleet should not force the passage.

Do you consider [the message ran] that the shore batteries could be either destroyed or dominated to such an extent as to permit transports to enter? If so, how many ships and what type would you propose?

On this Admiral Forbes asked for details about the Trondheim defences. He agreed that the shore batteries might be destroyed or dominated in daylight by battleships, if provided with suitable ammunition. None was carried at that moment in Home Fleet ships. The first and most important task, he said, was to protect troopships from heavy air attack over the thirty-miles approach through narrow waters, and the next to carry out an opposed landing of which ample warning had been given. In the circumstances he did not consider the operation feasible.

The Naval Staff persisted in their view, and the Admiralty, with my earnest agreement, replied on April 15 as follows:

We still think that the operation described should be further studied. It could not take place for seven days, which would be devoted to careful preparation. Danger from air not appreciably less wherever these large troopships are brought into the danger zone. Our idea would be that in addition to R.A.F. bombing of Stavanger aerodrome *Suffolk* should bombard with high explosive at dawn, hoping thereby to put the aerodrome out of business. The aerodrome at Trondheim could be dealt with by Fleet Air Arm bombers and subsequently by bombardment. High-explosive shells for 15-inch guns have been ordered to Rosyth. *Furious* and First Cruiser Squadron would be required for this operation. Pray therefore consider this important project further.

Admiral Forbes, although not fully convinced of its soundness, therefore addressed himself to the project in an increasingly favourable mood. In a further reply he said that he did not anticipate great difficulties from the naval side, except that he could not provide air defence for the transports while carrying out the landing. The naval force required would be the *Valiant* and *Renown* to give air defence to the *Glorious*, the *Warspite* to bombard, at least four ack-ack cruisers, and about twenty destroyers.

* * *

While plans for the frontal attack on Trondheim from the sea were being advanced with all speed, two subsidiary landings were already in progress designed to develop the town from the landward side. Of these the first was a hundred miles to the north, at Namsos, where Major-General Carton de Wiart, V.C., had been chosen to command the troops, with orders 'to secure the Trondheim area'. He was informed that the Navy were making a preliminary lodgment with a party about three hundred strong in order to take and hold points for his disembarkation. The idea was that two infantry brigades and a light division of Chasseurs Alpins should land hereabouts in conjunction with the main attack by the Navy upon Trondheim, Operation 'Hammer'. For this purpose the 146th Brigade and the Chasseurs Alpins were being diverted from Narvik. Carton de Wiart started forthwith in a flying-boat, and reached Namsos under heavy air attack on the evening of the 15th. His staff officer was wounded, but he took effective charge on the spot. The second landing was at Andalsnes, about a hundred and fifty miles by road to the south-west of Trondheim. Here also the Navy had made a lodgment, and on April 18 Brigadier Morgan with a military force arrived and took command. Lieutenant-General Massy was appointed Commander-in-Chief of all the forces operating in Central Norway. This officer had to exercise his command from the War Office because there was as yet no place for his headquarters on the other side.

*　　*　　*

On the 15th I reported that all these plans were being developed, but the difficulties were serious. Namsos was under four feet of snow and offered no concealment from the air. The enemy enjoyed complete air mastery, and we had neither anti-aircraft guns nor any airfield from which protecting squadrons might operate. Admiral Forbes had not, I said, at first been very keen on forcing his way into Trondheim because of the risk of air attack. It was of course of first importance that the Royal Air Force should continue to harass the Stavanger airfield, by which the enemy aeroplanes were passing northwards. The *Suffolk* would bombard the Stavanger airfield with her 8-inch guns on April 17. This was approved and the bombardment took place as planned. Some damage was done to the airfield, but during her withdrawal the *Suffolk* was continuously bombed for seven hours. She was heavily hit, and reached Scapa Flow the following day with her quarterdeck awash.

*　　*　　*

The Secretary of State for War had now to nominate a Military Commander. The auspices were unfavourable. Colonel Stanley's first choice fell upon Major-General Hotblack, who was highly reputed, and on April 17 he was briefed for his task at a meeting of the Chiefs of Staff held in the Admiralty. That night at 12.30 a.m. he had a fit on the Duke of York's Steps, and was picked up unconscious some time later. He had luckily left all his papers with his staff, who were working on them. The next morning Brigadier Berney-Ficklin was appointed to succeed Hotblack. He too was briefed, and started by train for Edinburgh. On April 19 he and his staff left by air for Scapa. They crashed on the airfield at Kirkwall, and the pilot was seriously injured. Every day counted.

On April 17 I explained in outline to the Supreme War Council the plan which the staffs were making for the landing at Trondheim. The forces immediately available were one Regular brigade from France (2,500 strong), 1,000 Canadians, and about 1,000 of a Territorial brigade as a reserve. The Military Co-ordination Committee had been advised that the forces available were adequate and that the risks, although very considerable, were justified. The operation would be supported by the full strength of the Fleet, and two carriers would be available, with a total of about 100 aircraft, including 45 fighters. The provisional date for the landing was April 22. The second demi-brigade of Chasseurs Alpins would not reach Trondheim until April 25, when it was hoped they would be able to disembark at the quays at Trondheim.

Asked whether the Chiefs of Staff were in agreement with the plans as outlined, the Chief of the Air Staff said on their behalf and in their presence that they were. The operation was of course attended by considerable risks, but these were worth running. The Prime Minister agreed with this view, and emphasised the importance of air co-operation. The War Cabinet gave cordial approval to the enterprise. I did my best to have it carried out.

Up to this point all the staffs and their chiefs had seemed resolved upon the central thrust at Trondheim. Admiral Forbes was actively preparing to strike, and there seemed no reason why the date of the 22nd should not be kept. Although Narvik was my pet, I threw myself with increasing confidence into this daring adventure, and was willing that the Fleet should risk the petty batteries at the entrance to the fiord, the possible minefields, and, most serious, the air. The ships carried what was in those days very powerful anti-aircraft armament. A group of ships had a combined overhead fire-power which few aircraft would care to encounter at a distance where bombing would be accurate. I must here explain that the power of an air force is terrific when there is nothing to oppose it. The pilots can fly as low as they please, and are often safer fifty feet off the ground than high up. They can cast their bombs with precision and use their machine-guns on troops with no more risk than that of a lucky rifle-bullet. These hard conditions had to be faced by our small expeditions at Namsos and Andalsnes, but the Fleet, with its A.A. batteries and a hundred seaborne aeroplanes, might well be superior during the actual operation to any air-power the enemy could bring. If Trondheim were taken, the neighbouring airfield of Vaernes would be in our hands, and in a few days we could have not only a considerable garrison in the town but also several fighter squadrons of the R.A.F. in action. Left to myself, I would have stuck to my first love, Narvik ; but, serving as I did a loyal chief and friendly Cabinet, I now looked forward to this exciting enterprise to which so many staid and cautious Ministers had given their strong adherence, and which seemed to find much favour with the Naval Staff and indeed among all our experts. Such was the position on the 17th.

Meanwhile I felt that we should do our utmost to keep the King of Norway and his advisers informed of our plans by sending him an officer who understood the Norwegian scene and could speak with authority. Admiral Sir Edward Evans was well suited to this task, and was sent to Norway by air through Stockholm to make contact with the King at his headquarters. There he was to do everything possible to aid the Norwegian Government in their resistance and explain the measures which the British Government were taking to assist them. From April 22 he was for some days in consultation with the King and the principal Norwegian authorities, helping them to understand both our plans and our difficulties.

*   *   *

During the 18th a vehement and decisive change in the opinions of the Chiefs of Staff and of the Admiralty occurred. This change was brought about first by increasing realisation of the magnitude of the naval stake in hazarding so many of our finest capital ships, and also by War Office arguments that even if the Fleet got in and got out again the opposed landing of the troops in the face of the German air-power would be perilous. On the other hand, the landings which were already being successfully carried out both north and south of Trondheim seemed to all these authorities to offer a far less dangerous solution. The Chiefs of Staff drew up a long paper opposing Operation 'Hammer'.

This began with a reminder that a combined operation involving an opposed landing was one of the most difficult and hazardous operations of war. The Chiefs of Staff had always realised that this particular operation would involve very serious risks ; for, owing to the urgency of the situation, there had not been time for the detailed and meticulous preparation which should have been given to an operation of this character, and as there had been no reconnaissance or air photographs the plan had been worked out from maps and charts. The plan had the further disadvantage that it would involve concentrating almost the whole of the Home Fleet in an area where it could be subjected to heavy attack from the air. There were also new factors in the situation which should be taken into account. We had seized the landing places at Namsos and Andalsnes and established forces ashore there ; there were reliable reports that the Germans were improving the defences at Trondheim, and reports of our intentions to make a direct landing at Trondheim, had appeared in the Press. On reconsidering the original project in the light of these new factors the Chiefs of Staff unanimously recommended a change of plan.

They still thought it essential that we should seize Trondheim and use it as a base for subsequent operations in Scandinavia ; but they urged that, instead of the direct frontal assault, we should take advantage of our unexpected success in landing forces at Namsos and Andalsnes and develop a pincers movement on Trondheim from north and south. By this means, they declared, we could turn a venture which was attended by grave hazards into an operation which could achieve the same results with much less risk. By this change of plan the Press reports of our intentions could also be turned to our advantage ; for by judicious leakages we could hope to leave the enemy under the impression that we still intended to persist in our original plan. The Chiefs of Staff therefore recommended that we should push in the maximum forces possible at Namsos and Andalsnes, seize control of the road and rail communications running through Dombas, and envelop Trondheim from the north and south. Shortly before the main landings at Namsos and Andalsnes the outer forts at Trondheim should be bombarded from the sea with a view to leading the enemy to suppose that a direct assault was due to take place. We should thus invest Trondheim by land and blockade it by sea ; and although its capture would take longer than originally contemplated, our main forces might be put ashore at a slightly earlier date. Finally, the Chiefs of Staff pointed out that such an enveloping operation, as opposed to a direct assault, would release a large number of valuable units of the Fleet for operations in other areas, e.g., at Narvik. These powerful recommendations were put forward with the authority not only of the three Chiefs of Staff, but of their three able deputies, including Admiral Tom Phillips and Sir John Dill, newly appointed.

No more decisive stopper on a positive amphibious plan can be imagined, nor have I seen a Government or Minister who would have overridden it. Under the prevailing arrangement the Chiefs of Staff worked as a separate and largely independent body, without guidance or direction from the Prime Minister or any effective representative of the supreme executive power. Moreover, the leaders of the three Services had not yet got the conception of the war as a whole, and were influenced unduly by the departmental outlook of their own Services. They met together, after talking things over with their respective Ministers, and issued *aide-mémoires* or memoranda which carried enormous weight. Here was the fatal weakness of our system of conducting war at this time.

When I became aware of this right-about-turn I was indignant, and questioned searchingly the officers concerned. It was soon plain to me that all professional opinion was now adverse to the operation which only a few days before it had spontaneously espoused. Of course there was at hand, in passionate ardour for action and glory, Sir Roger Keyes. He was scornful of these belated fears and second thoughts. He volunteered to lead a handful of older ships with the necessary transports into Trondheim Fiord, land the troops, and storm the place, before the Germans got any stronger. Roger Keyes had formidable credentials of achievement. In him there burned a flame. It was suggested in the May debates that 'the iron of the Dardanelles had entered into my soul', meaning that on account of my downfall on that occasion I had no longer the capacity to dare ; but this was really not true. The difficulties of acting from a subordinate position in the violent manner required are of the first magnitude.

Moreover, the personal relations of the high naval figures involved were peculiar. Roger Keyes, like Lord Cork, was senior to the Commander-in-Chief and the First Sea Lord. Admiral Pound had been for two years Keyes' Staff Officer in the Mediterranean. For me to take Roger Keyes' advice against his would have entailed his resignation, and Admiral Forbes might well have asked to be relieved of his command. It was certainly not my duty in the position I held to confront the Prime Minister and my War Cabinet colleagues with these personal dramas at such a time, and upon an operation which, for all its attractiveness and interest, was essentially minor even in relation to the Norwegian campaign, to say nothing of the general war. I therefore had no doubt that we must accept the Staff view in spite of their change of mind and the obvious objections that could be raised against their mutilated plan.

I accordingly submitted to the abandonment of 'Hammer'. I reported the facts to the Prime Minister on the afternoon of the 18th, and though bitterly disappointed he, like me, had no choice but to accept the new position. In war, as in life, it is often necessary, when some cherished scheme has failed, to take up the best alternative open, and if so it is folly not to work for it with all your might. I therefore turned my guns round too. I reported in writing to the Co-ordinating Committee on April 19 as follows:

1. The considerable advance made by Carton de Wiart, the very easy landings we have had at Andalsnes and other ports in this southern fiord, the indiscretions of the Press, pointing to a storm of Trondheim, and the very heavy naval forces required for this operation called 'Hammer', with the undoubted major risk of keeping so many valuable ships so many hours under close air attack, have led the Chiefs of Staff and their deputies to advise that there should be a complete alteration of the emphasis between the two pincers attacks and the centre attack ; in the following sense: that the main weight should be thrown into the northern and southern pincers, and that the central attack on Trondheim should be reduced to a demonstration.

2. Owing to the rapidity with which events and opinions have moved, it became necessary to take a decision, of which the Prime Minister had approved, as set out above, and orders are being issued accordingly.

3. It is proposed to encourage the idea that a central attack upon Trondheim is afoot, and to emphasise this by a bombardment by battleships of the outer forts at the suitable moment.

4. Every effort will be made to strengthen Carton de Wiart with artillery, without which his force is not well composed.

5. All the troops we have now under orders for 'Hammer' will be shoved in as quickly as possible, mostly in warships, at the various ports of the Romsdal Fiord, to press on to Dombas, and then, some delaying force being sent southward to the Norwegian main front, the bulk will turn north towards Trondheim. There is already one brigade (Morgan's) ashore beyond Andalsnes, with the 600 Marines. The brigade from France and the supporting Territorial brigade will all be thrown in here as quickly as possible. This should enable Dombas to be secured, and the control to be extended to the more easterly of the two Norwegian railways running from Oslo to Trondheim, Storen being a particularly advantageous point. The destination of the second demi-brigade of Chasseurs Alpins, the two battalions of the French Foreign Legion, and the thousand Canadians can for to-day or to-morrow be left open.

6. The position of the Namsos force must be regarded as somewhat hazardous, but its commander is used to taking risks. On the other hand, it is not seen why we cannot bring decisive superiority to bear along the Andalsnes–Dombas railway, and operate as occasion serves beyond that most important point, the object being the isolation of Trondheim and its capture.

7. Although this change of emphasis is to be deprecated on account of its being a change, it must be recognised that we move from a more hazardous to a less hazardous operation, and greatly reduce the strain upon the Navy involved in 'Hammer'. It would seem that our results would be equally achieved by the safer plan, and it does not follow that they will be delayed. We can certainly get more men sooner on to Norwegian soil by this method than the other.

8. It is not possible to deprive Narvik of its battleship at the moment when we have urged strenuous action. *Warspite* has therefore been ordered to return [there]. Some further reinforcement will be required for Narvik, which must be studied at once. The Canadians should be considered.

9. At the same time the sweep of the Skagerrak will now become possible, to clear away the enemy anti-submarine craft and aid our submarines.

The next day I explained to the War Cabinet the

circumstances in which it had been decided to call off the direct assault on Trondheim, and stated that the new plan which the Prime Minister had approved was broadly to send the whole of the 1st Light Division of Chasseurs Alpins to General Carton de Wiart for his attack on the Trondheim area from the north, and to send the regular brigades from France to reinforce Brigadier Morgan, who had landed at Andalsnes and had pushed on troops to hold Dombas. Another Territorial brigade might be put in on the southern line. It might be possible to push part of this southern force right forward to reinforce the Norwegians on the Oslo front. We had been fortunate in getting all our troops ashore without loss so far (except of the ship carrying all Brigadier Morgan's vehicles), and the present plans provided for the disembarkation of some 25,000 men by the end of the first week in May. The French had offered two more light divisions. The chief limiting factor was the provision of the necessary bases and lines of communication on which the forces were to be maintained. These would be liable to heavy air attack.

The Secretary of State for War then said that the new plan was little less hazardous than the direct attack on Trondheim. Until we had secured the Trondheim aerodrome little could be done to offset the heavy scale of enemy air attack. Nor was it altogether correct to describe the new plan as a 'pincers movement' against Trondheim, since while the northern force would bring pressure to bear in the near future, the first task of the southern force must be to secure themselves against a German attack from the south. It might well be a month before any serious move could be made against Trondheim from this direction. This was a sound criticism. General Ironside however strongly supported the new movement, expressing the hope that General Carton de Wiart, who when reinforced by the French would have, he said, quite a large force at his disposal, a large part of which would be highly mobile, might get astride the railway from Trondheim to Sweden. The troops already at Dombas had no guns or transport. They should however be able to hold a defensive position. I then added that the direct assault on Trondheim had been deemed to involve undue risk both to the Fleet and to our landing-parties. If in the course of a successful assault the Fleet were to lose a capital ship by enemy air action this loss would have to be set against the success of the operation. Again, it was obvious that the landing parties might suffer heavy casualties, and General Massy took the view that the stake was out of proportion to the results desired, particularly as these could be obtained by other methods. The Secretary of State for War, having justly pointed out that these other methods offered no sure or satisfactory solution, was content they should be tried. It was evident to us all that we had in fact only a choice of unpleasant courses before us, and also a compulsion to act. The War Cabinet endorsed the transformation of the plan against Trondheim.

I now reverted to Narvik, which seemed at once more important and more feasible since the attack on Trondheim was abandoned, and addressed a note to my Committee as follows:

> The importance and urgency of reaching a decision at Narvik can hardly be overrated. If the operations become static the situation will deteriorate for us. When the ice melts in the Gulf of Bothnia, at the latest in a month from now, the Germans may demand of the Swedes free passage for their troops through the ore-field in order to reinforce their people in Narvik, and may also demand control of the ore-field. They might promise Sweden that if she agreed to this in the far North she would be let entirely alone in the rest of the country. Anyhow, we ought to take it for granted that the Germans will try to enter the ore-field and carry succour to the Narvik garrison by force or favour. We have therefore at the outside only a month to spare.
>
> 2. In this month we have not only to reduce and capture the town and the landed Germans, but to get up the railway to the Swedish frontier and to secure an effective, well-defended seaplane base on some lake, in order, if we cannot obtain control of the ore-field, to prevent its being worked under German control. It would seem necessary that at least 3,000 [more] good troops should be directed upon Narvik forthwith, and should reach there by the end of the first week in May at latest. The orders for this should be given now, as nothing will be easier than to divert the troops if in the meanwhile the situation is cleared up. It would be a great administrative advantage if these troops were British, but if this cannot be managed for any reason, could not the leading brigade of the Second French Light Division be directed upon Narvik? There ought to be no undue danger in bringing a big ship into Skjel Fiord or thereabouts.
>
> 3. I should be very glad if the Deputy Chief of Naval Staff could consult with an officer of equal standing in the War Office upon how this need can be met, together with ships and times. Failure to take Narvik will be a major disaster, and will carry with it the control by Germany of the ore-field.

The general position as it was viewed at this moment cannot be better stated than in a paper written by General Ismay on April 21.

The object of operations at Narvik is to capture the town and obtain possession of the railway to the Swedish frontier. We should then be in a position to put a force, if necessary, into the Gällivare ore-fields, the possession of which is the main objective of the whole of the operations in Scandinavia.

As soon as the ice melts in Luleå, in about a month's time, we must expect that the Germans will obtain, by threats or force, a passage for their troops, in order that they themselves may secure Gällivare and perhaps go forward and reinforce their troops at Narvik. It is therefore essential that Narvik should be liquidated in about a month.

The object of operations in the Trondheim area is to capture Trondheim, and thereby obtain a base for further operations in Central Norway, and Sweden if necessary. Landings have been made at Namsos on the north of Trondheim and Andalsnes on the south. The intention is that the Namsos force will establish itself astride the railway running eastward from Trondheim, thus encircling the Germans there on the east and north-east. The force landed at Andalsnes has as its first *rôle* the occupation of a defensive position, in co-operation with the Norwegians at Lillehammer, to block any reinforcement of Trondheim from the main German landing at Oslo. The roads and railways between Oslo and Trondheim have both to be covered. When this has been achieved some troops will work northward and bring pressure to bear on Trondheim from the south.

At the present moment our main attention is directed to the Trondheim area. It is essential to support the Norwegians and ensure that Trondheim is not reinforced. The capture of Narvik is not at the present moment so urgent, but it will become increasingly so as the thaw in the Gulf of Bothnia approaches. If Sweden enters the war Narvik becomes the vital spot.

The operations in Central Norway which are now being undertaken are of an extremely hazardous nature, and we are confronted with serious difficulties. Among these the chief are, first, that the urgent need of coming to the assistance of the Norwegians without delay has forced us to throw ashore hastily-improvised forces—making use of whatever was readily available ; secondly, that our entry into Norway is perforce through bases which are inadequate for the maintenance of big formations. The only recognised base in the area is Trondheim, which is in the hands of the enemy. We are making use of Namsos and Andalsnes, which are only minor ports, possessing few, if any, facilities for unloading military stores, and served by poor communications with the interior. Consequently, the landing of mechanical transport, artillery, supplies, and petrol (nothing is obtainable locally) is a matter which, even if we were not hampered in other ways, would present considerable difficulty. Thus, until we succeed in capturing Trondheim the size of the forces which we can maintain in Norway is strictly limited.

Of course it may be said that all Norwegian enterprises, however locally successful, to which we might have committed ourselves would have been swept away by the results of the fearful battle in France which was now so near. Within a month the main Allied armies were to be shattered or driven into the sea. Everything we had would be drawn into the struggle for life. It was therefore lucky for us that we were not able to build up a substantial army and air force round Trondheim. The veils of the future are lifted one by one, and mortals must act from day to day. On the knowledge we had in the middle of April, I remain of the opinion that, having gone so far, we ought to have persisted in carrying out Operation 'Hammer' and the threefold attack on Trondheim, on which all had been agreed; but I accept my full share of responsibility for not enforcing this upon our expert advisers when they became so decidedly adverse to it and presented us with serious objections. In that case however it would have been better to abandon the whole enterprise against Trondheim and concentrate all upon Narvik. But for this it was now too late. Many of the troops were ashore, and the Norwegians crying for help.

CHAPTER 15

Frustration in Norway

*Lord Cork Appointed to the Supreme Command at Narvik –
His Letter to Me – General Mackesy's Protest against Bombard-
ment – The Cabinet's Reply – The Eighth Meeting of the Supreme
War Council, April 22 – German and Allied Strength on Land
and in the Air – The Scandinavian Tangle – Decisions upon
Trondheim and Narvik – A Further Change in Control –
Directive of May 1 – The Trondheim Operation – The Namsos
Failure – Paget in the Andalsnes Excursion – Decision of the
War Cabinet to Evacuate Central Norway – The Mosjoen
Fiasco – My Report of May 4 – Gubbins' Force – The German
Northward Advance – German Superiority in Method and
Quality.*

On April 20 I had procured agreement to the appointment of
Lord Cork as sole commander of the naval, military, and air
forces in the Narvik areas, thus bringing General Mackesy
directly under his authority. There was never any doubt of
Lord Cork's vigorously offensive spirit. He realised acutely the
danger of delay ; but the physical and administrative difficulties
were far greater on the spot than we could measure at home.
Moreover, naval officers, even when granted the fullest authority, are chary of giving orders to the Army about purely military
matters. This would be even more true if the positions were
reversed. We had hoped that by relieving General Mackesy
from direct major responsibility we should make him feel
more free to adopt bold tactics. The result was contrary to this
expectation. He continued to use every argument, and there
was no lack of them, to prevent drastic action. Things had
changed to our detriment in the week that had passed since the
idea of an improvised assault upon Narvik Town had been rejected. The 2,000 German soldiers were no doubt working
night and day at their defences, and these and the town all lay
hidden under a pall of snow. The enemy had no doubt by now
also organised two or three thousand sailors who had escaped
from the sunken destroyers. Their arrangements for bringing
air-power to bear improved every day, and both our ships and

landed troops endured increasing bombardment. On the 21st Lord Cork wrote to me as follows:

I write to thank you for the trust you have reposed in me. I shall certainly do my best to justify it. The inertia is difficult to overcome, and of course the obstacles to the movement of troops are considerable, particularly the snow, which on northern slopes of hills is still many feet deep. I myself have tested that, and as it has been snowing on and off for two days the position has not improved. The initial error was that the original force started on the assumption they would meet with no resistance, a mistake we often make—*e.g.*, Tanga.* As it is, the soldiers have not yet got their reserves of small arms ammunition, or water, but tons of stuff and personnel they do not want....

What is really our one pressing need is fighters; we are so overmatched in the air. There is a daily inspection of this place, and they come when there are transports or steamers to bomb. Sooner or later they must get a hit. I flew over Narvik yesterday, but it was very difficult to see much. The rocky cliff is covered with snow, except for rock outcrops, round which the drifts must be deep. It is snow down to the water's edge, which makes it impossible to see the nature of the foreshore.

While waiting for the conditions necessary for an attack we are isolating the town from the world by breaking down the railway culverts, etc., and the large ferry steamer has been shelled and burnt. ... It is exasperating not being able to get on, and I quite understand your wondering why we do not, but I assure you that it is not from want of desire to do so.

Lord Cork decided upon a reconnaissance in force, under cover of a naval bombardment, but here General Mackesy interposed. He stated that before the proposed action against Narvik began he felt it his duty to represent that there was no officer or man in his command who would not feel ashamed for himself and his country if thousands of Norwegian men, women and children in Narvik were subjected to the proposed bombardment. Lord Cork contented himself with forwarding this statement without comment. Neither the Prime Minister nor I could be present at the Defence Committee meeting on April 22, as we had to attend the Supreme War Council in Paris on that day. Before leaving I had drafted a reply which was approved by our colleagues:

* The landing at Tanga, near Zanzibar, in 1914.

I presume that Lord Cork has read the Bombardment Instructions issued at the outbreak of war. If he finds it necessary to go beyond these instructions on account of the
enemy using the shelter of buildings to maintain himself in
Narvik, he may deem it wise to give six hours' warning by
every means at his disposal, including, if possible, leaflets, and
to inform the German commander that all civilians must leave
the town, and that he would be held responsible if he
obstructed their departure. He might also offer to leave the
railway line unmolested for a period of six hours to enable
civilians to make good their escape by that route.

The Defence Committee endorsed this policy, strongly
expressing the view that 'it would be impossible to allow the
Germans to convert Norwegian towns into forts by keeping the
civilians in the towns to prevent us from attacking'.

*   *   *

We arrived in Paris with our minds oppressed by the anxieties
and confusion of the campaign in Norway, for the conduct of
which the British were responsible. But M. Reynaud, having
welcomed us, opened with a statement on the general military
position which by its gravity dwarfed our joint Scandinavian
excursions. Geography, he said, gave Germany the permanent
advantage of interior lines. She had 190 divisions, of which 150
could be used on the Western Front. Against these the Allies
had 100, of which 10 were British. In the previous war, Germany, with a population of 65 millions, had raised 248 divisions,
of which 207 fought on the Western Front. France on her part
had raised 118 divisions, of which 110 had been on the Western
Front, and Great Britain 89 divisions, of which 63 had been on
the Western Front, giving a total of 173 Allied against 207
German divisions in the West. Equality had been attained only
when the Americans arrived with their 34 divisions. How much
worse was the position today! The German population was
now 80 millions, from which she could conceivably raise 300
divisions. France could hardly expect that there would be 20
British divisions in the West by the end of the year. We must
therefore face a large and increasing numerical superiority,
which was already three to two and would presently rise to two
to one. As for equipment, Germany had the advantage both in
aviation and aircraft equipment and also in artillery and stocks
of ammunition. Thus Reynaud.

To this point then had we come from the days of the Rhineland occupation in 1936, when a mere operation of police would have sufficed; or since Munich, when Germany, occupied with Czechoslovakia, could spare but thirteen divisions for the Western Front; or even since September 1939, when, while the Polish resistance lasted, there were but forty-two German divisions in the West. All this terrible superiority had grown up because at no moment had the once victorious Allies dared to take any effective step, even when they were all-powerful, to resist repeated aggressions by Hitler and breaches of the treaties.

* * *

After this sombre overture, of the gravity of which we were all conscious, we turned to the Scandinavian tangle. The Prime Minister explained the position with clarity. We had landed 13,000 men at Namsos and Andalsnes without loss. Our forces had pushed forward farther than had been expected. On finding that the direct attack on Trondheim would demand a disproportionate amount of naval force, it had been decided to make a pincers movement from the north and south instead. But in the last two days these new plans had been rudely interrupted by a heavy air attack on Namsos. As there had been no anti-aircraft fire to oppose them the Germans had bombed at will. Meanwhile all German warships at Narvik had been destroyed. But the German troops there were strongly fortified, so that it had not yet been possible to attack them by land. If our first attempt did not succeed it would be renewed.

About Central Norway Mr. Chamberlain said that the British command were anxious to reinforce the troops who had gone there, to protect them against the German advance from the south, and to co-operate subsequently in the capture of Trondheim. It was already certain that reinforcements would be required. 5,000 British, 7,000 French, 3,000 Poles, three British mechanised battalions, one British light tank battalion, three French light divisions, and one British Territorial division were to be available in the near future. The limitation would not be the number of troops provided, but the number that could be landed and maintained in the country. M. Reynaud said that four French light divisions would be sent.

I now spoke for the first time at any length in these conferences, pointing out to the French the difficulties of landing troops and stores in the face of enemy aircraft and U-boats.

Every single ship had to be convoyed by destroyers, every land-ing port continuously guarded by cruisers or destroyers, not only during the landing, but till A.A. guns could be mounted ashore. So far the Allied ships had been extraordinarily lucky and had sustained very few hits. The tremendous difficulties of the operation would be understood. Although 13,000 men had now been safely landed, the Allies had as yet no established bases, and were operating inland with weak and slender lines of communication, practically unprovided with artillery or sup-porting aircraft. Such was the position in Central Norway. At Narvik the Germans were less strong, the port far less exposed to air attack, and once the harbour had been secured it would be possible to land at a very much faster rate. Any forces which could not be landed at ports farther south should go to Narvik. Among the troops assigned to the Narvik operation, or indeed in Great Britain, there were none able to move across country in heavy snow. The task at Narvik would be not only to free the harbour and the town, nor even to clear the whole district of Germans, but to advance up the railway to the Swedish frontier in strength commensurate with any further German designs. It was the considered view of the British command that this could be done without slowing down the rate of landing at other ports beyond the point to which it was already restricted by the diffi-culties described.

We were all in full agreement on the unpleasantness of our plight and the little we could do at the moment to better it. The Supreme War Council agreed that the immediate military ob-jectives should be

    (*a*) the capture of Trondheim, and
    (*b*) the capture of Narvik, and the concentration of an ade-quate Allied force on the Swedish frontier.

The next day we talked about the dangers to the Dutch and Belgians and their refusal to take any common measures with us. We were very conscious that Italy might declare war upon us at any time, and various naval measures were to be concerted in the Mediterranean between Admiral Pound and Admiral Darlan. To our meeting General Sikorski, the head of the Polish Government, also was invited. He declared his ability to con-stitute a force of a hundred thousand men within a few months. Active steps were also being taken to recruit a Polish division in the United States.

At this meeting it was agreed also that if Germany invaded Holland the Allied armies should at once advance into Belgium without further approaches to the Belgian Government; and that the R.A.F. could bomb the German marshalling yards and the oil refineries in the Ruhr.

* * *

When we got back from the conference I was so much concerned at the complete failure not only of our efforts against the enemy, but of our method of conducting the war, that I wrote as follows to the Prime Minister:

> Being anxious to sustain you to the best of my ability, I must warn you that you are approaching a head-on smash in Norway.
> I am very grateful to you for having at my request taken over the day-to-day management of the Military Co-ordination [Committee], etc. I think I ought however to let you know that I shall not be willing to receive that task back from you without the necessary powers. At present no one has the power. There are six Chiefs [and Deputy Chiefs] of the Staff, three Ministers, and General Ismay, who all have a voice in Norwegian operations (apart from Narvik). But no one is responsible for the creation and direction of military policy except yourself. If you feel able to bear this burden, you may count upon my unswerving loyalty as First Lord of the Admiralty. If you do not feel you can bear it, with all your other duties, you will have to delegate your powers to a deputy who can concert and direct the general movement of our war action, and who will enjoy your support and that of the War Cabinet unless very good reason is shown to the contrary.

Before I could send it off I received a message from the Prime Minister saying that he had been considering the position in Scandinavia and felt it to be unsatisfactory. He asked me to call on him that evening at Downing Street after dinner to discuss the whole situation in private.

I have no record of what passed at our conversation, which was of a most friendly character. I am sure I put the points in my unsent letter, and that the Prime Minister agreed with their force and justice. He had every wish to give me the powers of direction for which I asked, and there was no kind of personal difficulty between us. He had however to consult and persuade a number of important personages, and it was not till May 1 that he was able to issue the following Note to the Cabinet and those concerned.

May 1, 1940

I have been examining, in consultation with the Ministers in charge of the Service departments, the existing arrangements for the consideration and decision of Defence questions, and I circulate for the information of my colleagues a Memorandum describing certain modifications which it has been decided to make in these arrangements forthwith. The modifications have been agreed to by the three Service Ministers. With the approval of the First Lord of the Admiralty, Major-General H. L. Ismay, C.B., D.S.O., has been appointed to the post of Senior Staff Officer in charge of the Central Staff which, as indicated in the Memorandum, is to be placed at the disposal of the First Lord. Major-General Ismay has been nominated, while serving in this capacity, an additional member of the Chiefs of Staff Committee.   N.C.

DEFENCE ORGANISATION

In order to obtain a greater concentration of the direction of the war, the following modifications of present arrangements will take effect:

The First Lord of the Admiralty will continue to take the chair at all meetings of the Military Co-ordination Committee at which the Prime Minister does not preside himself, and in the absence of the Prime Minister will act as his deputy at such meetings on all matters delegated to the Committee by the War Cabinet.

He will be responsible on behalf of the Committee for giving guidance and direction to the Chiefs of Staff Committee, and for this purpose it will be open to him to summon that Committee for personal consultation at any time when he considers it necessary.

The Chiefs of Staff will retain their responsibility for giving their collective views to the Government, and, with their respective staffs, will prepare plans to achieve any objectives indicated to them by the First Lord on behalf of the Military Co-ordination Committee, and will accompany their plans by such comments as they consider appropriate.

The Chiefs of Staff, who will in their individual capacity remain responsible to their respective Ministers, will at all times keep their Ministers informed of their conclusions.

Where time permits, the plans of the Chiefs of Staff, with their comments and any comments by the First Lord, will be circulated for approval to the Military Co-ordination Committee, and, unless the Military Co-ordination Committee is authorised by the War Cabinet to take final decision, or in the case of disagreement on the Military Co-ordination Committee, circulated to the War Cabinet.

In urgent cases it may be necessary to omit the submission of plans to a formal meeting of the Committee, but in such cases the First Lord will no doubt find means of consulting the Service Ministers informally, and in the case of dissent the decision will be referred to the Prime Minister.

In order to facilitate the general plan outlined above and to afford a convenient means of maintaining a close liaison between the First Lord and the Chiefs of Staff, the First Lord will be assisted by a suitable Central Staff (distinct from the Admiralty Staff), under a Senior Staff Officer, who will be an additional member of the Chiefs of Staff Committee.

I accepted this arrangement, which seemed an improvement. I could now convene and preside over the meetings of the Chiefs of Staff Committee, without whom nothing could be done, and I was made responsible formally 'for giving guidance and direction' to them. General Ismay, the Senior Staff Officer in charge of the Central Staff, was placed at my disposal *as my Staff Officer and representative,* and in this capacity was made a full member of the Chiefs of Staff Committee. I had known Ismay for many years, but now for the first time we became hand-in-glove, and much more. Thus the Chiefs of Staff were to large extent made responsible to me in their collective capacity, and as a deputy of the Prime Minister I could nominally influence with authority their decisions and policies. On the other hand, it was only natural that their primary loyalties should be to their own Service Ministers, who would have been less than human if they had not felt some resentment at the delegation of a part of their authority to one of their colleagues. Moreover, it was expressly laid down in the Memorandum that my responsibilities were to be discharged *on behalf of* the Military Co-ordination Committee. I was thus to have immense responsibilities, without effective power in my own hands to discharge them. Nevertheless I had a feeling that I might be able to make the new organisation work. It was destined to last only a week. But my personal and official connection with General Ismay and his relation to the Chiefs of Staff Committee was preserved unbroken and unweakened from May 1, 1940, to July 27, 1945, when I laid down my charge.

*   *   *

It is now necessary to recount the actual course of the fighting for Trondheim. Our northern force, from Namsos, was 80 miles from the town, and our southern force, from Andalsnes, was 150 miles away. The central attack through the fiord ('Hammer') had been abandoned, partly through fear of its cost and partly through hopes of the flanking movements. Both these movements now failed utterly. The Namsos force, commanded by Carton de Wiart, hastened forward in accordance with his instructions against the Norwegian snow and the German air. A brigade reached Verdal, fifty miles from Trondheim, at the head of the fiord, on the 19th. It was evident to me, and I warned the staffs, that the Germans could send in a single night a stronger force by water from Trondheim to chop them. This occurred two days later. Our troops were forced to withdraw some miles to where they could hold the enemy. The intolerable snow conditions, now sometimes in thaw, and the fact that the Germans who had come across the inner fiord were, like us, destitute of wheeled transport, prevented any serious fighting on the ground ; and the small number of scattered troops plodding along the road offered little target to the unresisted airpower. Had Carton de Wiart known how limited were the forces he would have, or that the central attack on Trondheim had been abandoned—a vital point of which our staff machinery did not inform him—he would no doubt have made a more methodical advance. He acted in relation to the main objective as it had been imparted to him.

In the end nearly everybody got back exhausted, chilled, and resentful to Namsos, where the French Chasseur Brigade had remained ; and Carton de Wiart, whose opinion on such issues commanded respect, declared that there was nothing for it but evacuation. Preparations for this were at once made by the Admiralty. On April 28 the evacuation of Namsos was ordered. The French contingent would re-embark before the British, leaving some of their ski troops to work with our rearguard. The probable dates for leaving were the nights of the 1st and 2nd of May. Eventually the withdrawal was achieved in a single night. All the troops were re-embarked on the night of the 3rd, and were well out to sea when they were sighted by the German air reconnaissance at dawn. From eight o'clock in the morning to three in the afternoon wave after wave of enemy bombers attacked the warships and the transports. As no British air forces were available to protect the convoy we were lucky that no transport was hit. The French destroyer *Bison* and H.M.S. *Afridi,* which carried our rearguard, were 'sunk fighting to the end'.

* * *

A different series of misfortunes befell the troops landed at Andalsnes ; but here at least we took our toll of the enemy. In response to urgent appeals from General Ruge, the Norwegian Commander-in-Chief, Brigadier Morgan's 148th Infantry Brigade had hastened forward as far as Lillehammer. Here it joined the tired-out, battered Norwegian forces whom the Germans, in the overwhelming strength of three fully-equipped divisions, were driving before them along the road and railway from Oslo towards Dombas and Trondheim. Severe fighting began. The ship carrying Brigadier Morgan's vehicles, including all artillery and mortars, had been sunk, but his young Territorials fought well with their rifles and machine-guns against the German vanguards, who were armed not only with 5·9 howitzers, but many heavy mortars and some tanks. On April 24 the leading battalion of the 15th Brigade, arriving from France, reached the crumbling front. General Paget, who commanded these Regular troops, learned from General Ruge that the Norwegian forces were exhausted and could fight no more until they had been thoroughly rested and re-equipped. He therefore assumed control, brought the rest of this brigade into action as fast as they arrived, and faced the Germans with determination in a series of spirited engagements. By adroit use of the railway, which fortunately remained unbroken, Paget extricated his own troops, Morgan's brigade, which had lost 700 men, and some Norwegian units. For one whole day the bulk of the British force hid in a long railway tunnel, fed by their precious supply train, and were thus completely lost to the enemy and his all-seeing air. After fighting five rearguard actions, in several of which the Germans were heavily mauled, and having covered over a hundred miles, he reached the sea again at Andalsnes. This small place, like Namsos, had been flattened out by bombing ; but by the night of May 1 the 15th Brigade, with what remained of Morgan's 148th Brigade, had been taken on board British cruisers and destroyers, and reached home without further trouble. General Paget's skill and resolution during these days opened his path to high command as the war developed.

A forlorn, gallant effort to give support from the air should be recorded. The only landing 'ground' was the frozen lake of

Lesjeskogen, forty miles from Andalsnes. There a squadron of Gladiators, flown from the *Glorious*, arrived on April 24. They were at once heavily attacked. The Fleet Air Arm did their best to help them ; but the task of fighting for existence, of covering the operations of two expeditions 200 miles apart, and of protecting their bases was too much for a single squadron. By April 26 it could fly no more. Long-range efforts by British bombers, working from England, were also unavailing.

* * *

Our withdrawal enforced by local events had conformed to the decision already taken by the War Cabinet on the advice of the Military Co-ordination Committee, with the Prime Minister presiding. We had all come to the conclusion that it was beyond our power to seize and hold Trondheim. Both claws of the feeble pincers were broken. Mr. Chamberlain announced to the Cabinet that plans must be made for evacuating our forces both from Namsos and Andalsnes, though we should in the meanwhile continue to resist the German advance. The Cabinet was distressed at these proposals, which were however inevitable.

* * *

In order to delay to the utmost the northward advance of the enemy towards Narvik, we were now sending special companies raised in what was afterwards called 'Commando' style, under an enterprising officer, Colonel Gubbins, to Mosjoen, 120 miles farther up the coast. I was most anxious that a small part of the Namsos force should make their way in whatever vehicles were available along the road to Grong. Even a couple of hundred would have sufficed to fight small rearguard actions. From Grong they would have to find their way on foot to Mosjoen. I hoped by this means to gain the time for Gubbins to establish himself so that a stand could be made against the very small numbers which the enemy could as yet send there. I was repeatedly assured that the road was impassable. General Massy from London sent insistent requests. It was replied that even a small party of French Chasseurs, with their skis, could not traverse this route. 'It seemed evident,' wrote General Massy a few days later in his dispatch, 'that if the French Chasseurs could not retire along this route the Germans could not advance along it. . . . This was an error, as the Germans have since made full use of it and have advanced so rapidly along it that our troops in Mosjoen have not had time to get properly established, and it is more than likely that we shall not be able to hold the place.' This proved true. The destroyer *Janus* took a hundred Chasseurs Alpins and two light A.A. guns round by sea, but they left again before the Germans came.

* * *

We have now pursued the Norwegian campaign to the point where it was overwhelmed by gigantic events. The superiority of the Germans in design, management, and energy was plain. They put into ruthless execution a carefully-prepared plan of action. They comprehended perfectly the use of the air arm on a great scale in all its aspects. Moreover, their individual ascendancy was marked, especially in small parties. At Narvik a mixed and improvised German force barely six thousand strong held at bay for six weeks some twenty thousand Allied troops, and, though driven out of the town, lived to see them depart. The Narvik attack, so brilliantly opened by the Navy, was paralysed by the refusal of the military commander to run what was admittedly a desperate risk. The division of our resources between Narvik and Trondheim was injurious to both our plans. The abandonment of the central thrust on Trondheim wears an aspect of vacillation in the British High Command for which not only the experts but the political chiefs who yielded too easily to their advice must bear a burden. At Namsos there was a muddy waddle forward and back. Only in the Andalsnes expedition did we bite. The Germans traversed in seven days the road from Namsos to Mosjoen, which the British and French had declared impassable. At Bodo and Mo during the retreat of Gubbins' force to the north we were each time just too late, and the enemy, although they had to overcome hundreds of miles of rugged, snow-clogged country, drove us back in spite of gallant episodes. We, who had the command of the sea and could pounce anywhere on an undefended coast, were outpaced by the enemy moving by land across very large distances in the face of every obstacle. In this Norwegian encounter some of our finest troops, the Scots and Irish Guards, were baffled by the vigour, enterprise and training of Hitler's young men.

We tried hard at the call of duty to entangle and imbed ourselves in Norway. We thought fortune had been cruelly against us. We can now see that we were well out of it. Meanwhile we had to comfort ourselves as best we might by a series of successful evacuations. Failure at Trondheim! Stalemate at Narvik! Such in the first week of May were the only results we could show to the British nation, to our Allies, and to the neutral world, friendly or hostile. Considering the prominent part I played in these events and the impossibility of explaining the difficulties by which we had been overcome, or the defects of our staff and governmental organisation and our methods of conducting war, it was a marvel that I survived and maintained my position in public esteem and Parliamentary confidence. This was due to the fact that for six or seven years I had predicted with truth the course of events, and had given ceaseless warnings, then unheeded but now remembered.

* * *

Twilight War ended with Hitler's assault on Norway. It broke into the glare of the most fearful military explosion so far known to man. I have described the trance in which for eight months France and Britain had been held while all the world wondered. This phase proved most harmful to the Allies. From the moment when Stalin made terms with Hitler the Communists in France took their cue from Moscow and denounced the war as 'an imperialist and capitalist crime against democracy'. They did what they could to undermine morale in the Army and impede production in the workshops. The morale of France, both of her soldiers and her people, was now in May markedly lower than at the outbreak of war.

Nothing like this happened in Britain, where Soviet-directed Communism, though busy, was weak. Nevertheless we were still a party Government, under a Prime Minister from whom the Opposition was bitterly estranged, and without the ardent and positive help of the trade union movement. The sedate, sincere, but routine character of the Administration did not evoke that intense effort, either in the governing circles or in the munitions factories, which was vital. The stroke of catastrophe and the spur of peril were needed to call forth the dormant might of the British nation. The tocsin was about to sound.

NORWAY
1940

Tromsö

Vaags Fjord

Harstad
Allies land, 14·4·40.
withdrawal, 8·6·40.

Narvik

Skjel Fjord
Allied mines
laid, 8·4·40.

Vest Fjord

LOFOTEN

Allies land, 29·4·40,
withdrawal, 29·5·40.

Allies land, 4·5·40.
withdrawal, 18·5·40.

Germans land,
9·4·40.
1st. Naval action
10·4·40
2nd. Naval action
13·4·40.

Allies land, 2·5·40,
withdrawal, 10·5·40.

Mo

Mosjoen

Captured by
Allies, 28·5·40.
Allies with-
draw, 8·6·40.

Allies land, 14·4·40
withdrawal, 3·5·40.

Mandsos
Aabörg
Sterkfoord
Vaersal

German landing on
flank of Allies, 21·4·40.

British base formed, 18·4·40.
King and Govt. of Norway
embarked in H.M.S. Glasgow
for Tromso, 29·4·40.

Trondheim

Germans land, 9·4·40.

Allies land, 18·4·40
withdrawal, 1·5·40.

Molde
Alesund

Andalsnes

Lesjaskog
Dombaas

Allies land, 17·4·40
withdrawal, 2·5·40.

FAROE IS.
British Forces
land, 13·4·40.
(Approx. 220 miles
from Scapa)

Stadtlandet

Lillehammer

SWEDEN

SHETLAND

Bergen

Germans
land 9·4·40

Oslo

Germans land,
9·4·40

Shetland Is. to Bergen 200 miles

ORKNEY IS.

SCAPA

Stavanger
Germans land, 9·4·40.
Airfield bombarded
17·4·40.

Kristiansand

SKAGERRAK

0°   5°   15°

R.C.

CHAPTER 16

Norway: The Final Phase

Immediate Assault on Narvik Abandoned – The Landings in May – General Auchinleck Appointed to the Chief Military Command – The Capture of the Town, May 28 – The Battle in France Dominates All – Evacuation – The Homeward Convoys – Apparition of the German Battle-Cruisers – The Loss of the 'Glorious' and 'Ardent' – The Story of the 'Acasta' – Air Attack on German Ships at Trondheim – One Solid Result – The German Fleet Ruined.

In defiance of chronology, it is well to set forth here the end of the Norwegian episode.

After April 16 Lord Cork was compelled to abandon the idea of an immediate assault on Narvik. A three hours' bombardment on April 24, carried out by the battleship *Warspite* and three cruisers, was not effective in dislodging the garrison. I had asked the First Sea Lord to arrange for the replacement of the *Warspite* by the less valuable *Resolution*, which was equally useful for bombarding purposes. Meanwhile the arrival of French and Polish troops, and still more the thaw, encouraged Lord Cork to press his attack on the town. The new plan was to land at the head of the fiord beyond Narvik, and thereafter to attack Narvik across Römbaks Fiord. The 24th Guards Brigade had been drawn off to stem the German advance from Trondheim; but by the beginning of May three battalions of Chasseurs Alpins, two battalions of the French Foreign Legion, four Polish battalions, and a Norwegian force of about 3,500 men were available. The enemy had for their part been reinforced by portions of the 3rd Mountain Division, which had either been brought by air from Southern Norway or smuggled in by rail from Sweden.

The first landing, under General Béthouart, the commander of the French contingent, took place on the night of May 12–13 at Bjerkvik, with very little loss. General Auchinleck, whom I had sent to command all the troops in Northern Norway, was present and took charge the next day. His instructions were to cut off the iron ore supplies and to defend a foothold in Norway for the King and his Government. The new British commander naturally asked for very large additions to bring his force up to seventeen battalions, two hundred heavy and light anti-aircraft guns, and four squadrons of aeroplanes. It was only possible to promise about half these requirements.

But now tremendous events became dominant. On May 24, in the crisis of shattering defeat, it was decided, with almost universal agreement, that we must concentrate all we had in France and at home. The capture of Narvik had however to be achieved, both to ensure the destruction of the port and to cover our withdrawal. The main attack across Römbaks Fiord was begun on May 27 by two battalions of the Foreign Legion and one Norwegian battalion under the able leadership of General Béthouart. It was entirely successful. The landing was effected with practically no loss and the counter-attack beaten off. Narvik was taken on May 28. The Germans, who had so long resisted forces four times their strength, retreated into the mountains, leaving four hundred prisoners in our hands.

We now had to relinquish all that we had won after such painful exertions. The withdrawal was in itself a considerable operation, imposing a heavy burden on the Fleet, already fully extended by the fighting both in Norway and in the Narrow Seas. Dunkirk was upon us, and all available light forces were drawn to the south. The Battle Fleet must itself be held in readiness to resist invasion. Many of the cruisers and destroyers had already been sent south for anti-invasion duties. The Commander-in-Chief had at his disposal at Scapa the capital ships *Rodney, Valiant, Renown,* and *Repulse.* These had to cover all contingencies.

Good progress in evacuation was made at Narvik, and by June 8 all the troops, French, British, and Polish amounting to 24,000 men together with large quantities of stores and equipment, were embarked and sailed in four convoys without hindrance from the enemy, who indeed now amounted on shore to no more than a few thousand scattered, disorganised but victorious individuals. During these last days valuable protection was afforded against the German Air Force not only by naval aircraft, but by a shore-based squadron of Hurricanes. This squadron had been ordered to keep in action till the end, destroying their aircraft if necessary. However, by their skill and daring these pilots performed the unprecedented feat—their last—of flying their Hurricanes on board the carrier *Glorious,* which sailed with the *Ark Royal* and the main body.

To cover all these operations Lord Cork had at his disposal, in addition to the carriers, the cruisers *Southampton* and *Coventry* and sixteen destroyers, besides smaller vessels. The cruiser *Devonshire* was meanwhile embarking the King of Norway and his staff from Tromsö, and was therefore moving independently. Lord Cork informed the Commander-in-Chief of his convoy arrangements, and asked for protection against possible attack by heavy ships. Admiral Forbes dispatched the *Valiant* on June 6 to meet the first convoy of troopships and escort it north of the Shetlands and then return to meet the second. Despite all other preoccupations, he had intended to use his battle-cruisers to protect the troopships, but on June 5 reports had reached him of two unknown ships apparently making for Iceland, and later of an enemy landing there. He therefore felt compelled to send his battle-cruisers to investigate these reports, which proved to be false. Thus on this unlucky day our available forces in the north were widely dispersed. The movement of the Narvik convoys and their protection followed closely the method pursued without mishap during the past six weeks. It had been customary to send transports and warships, including aircraft-carriers, over this route with no more than anti-submarine escort. No activity by German heavy ships had hitherto been detected. Now, having repaired the damage they had suffered in the earlier encounters, they suddenly appeared off the Norwegian coast.

The battle-cruisers *Scharnhorst* and *Gneisenau*, with the cruiser *Hipper* and four destroyers, left Kiel on June 4, with the object of attacking shipping and bases in the Narvik area and thus providing relief for what was left of their landed forces. No hint of our intended withdrawal reached them till June 7. On the news that British convoys were at sea the German admiral decided to attack them. Early the following morning, the 8th, he caught a tanker with a trawler escort, an empty troopship *Orama*, and the hospital ship *Atlantis*. He respected the immunity of the *Atlantis*. All the rest were sunk. That afternoon the *Hipper* and the destroyers returned to Trondheim, but the battle-cruisers, continuing their search for prey, were rewarded when at 4 p.m. they sighted the smoke of the aircraft-carrier *Glorious*, with her two escorting destroyers, the *Acasta* and *Ardent*. The *Glorious* had been detached early that morning to proceed home independently owing to shortage of fuel, and by now was nearly two hundred miles ahead of the main convoy.

This explanation is not convincing. The *Glorious* presumably had enough fuel to steam at the speed of the convoy. All should have kept together.

The action began about 4.30 p.m. at over 27,000 yards. At this range the *Glorious*, with her 4-inch guns, was helpless. Efforts were made to get her torpedo-bombers into the air, but before this could be done she was hit in the forward hangar, and a fire began which destroyed the Hurricanes and prevented torpedoes being got up from below for the bombers. In the next half-hour she received staggering blows which deprived her of all chance of escape. By 5.20 she was listing heavily, and the order was given to abandon ship. She sank about twenty minutes later.

Meanwhile her two destroyers behaved nobly. Both made smoke in an endeavour to screen the *Glorious*, and both fired their torpedoes at the enemy before being overwhelmed. The *Ardent* was soon sunk. The story of the *Acasta,* commanded by Commander C. E. Glasfurd, R.N., now left alone at hopeless odds, has been told by the sole survivor, Leading-Seaman C. Carter.

On board our ship, what a deathly calm, hardly a word spoken, the ship was now steaming full speed away from the enemy, then came a host of orders, prepare all smoke floats, hose-pipes connected up, various other jobs were prepared, we were still stealing away from the enemy, and making smoke, and all our smoke floats had been set going. The Captain then had this message passed to all positions: 'You may think we are running away from the enemy, we are not, our chummy ship [*Ardent*] has sunk, the *Glorious* is sinking, the least we can do is make a show, good luck to you all.' We then altered course into our own smoke-screen. I had the order to stand by to fire tubes 6 and 7, we then came out of the smoke-screen, altered course to starboard firing our torpedoes from port side. It was then I had my first glimpse of the enemy, to be honest it appeared to me to be a large one [ship] and a small one, and we were very close. I fired my two torpedoes from my tubes [aft], the foremost tubes fired theirs, we were all watching results. I'll never forget that cheer that went up ; on the port bow of one of the ships a yellow flash and a great column of smoke and water shot up from her. We knew we had hit, personally I could not see how we could have missed so close as we were. The enemy never fired a shot at us, I feel they must have been very surprised. After we had fired our torpedoes we went back into our own smoke-screen, altered course again to starboard. 'Stand by to fire remaining torpedoes'; and this time as soon as we poked our nose out of the smoke-screen, the enemy let us have it. A shell hit the engine-room, killed my tubes' crew, I was blown to the after end of the tubes, I must have been knocked out for a while, because when I came to, my arm hurt me; the ship had stopped with a list to port. Here is something believe it or believe it not, I climbed back into the control seat, I see those two ships, I fired the remaining torpedoes, no one told me to, I guess I was raving mad. God alone knows why I fired them, but I did. The *Acasta's* guns were firing the whole time, even firing with a list on the ship. The enemy then hit us several times, but one big explosion took place right aft, I have often wondered whether the enemy hit us with a torpedo, in any case it seemed to lift the ship out of the water. At last the Captain gave orders to abandon ship. I will always remember the Surgeon Lt.,* his first ship, his first action. Before I jumped over the side, I saw him still attending to the wounded, a hopeless task, and when I was in the water I saw the Captain leaning over the bridge, take a cigarette from a case and light it. We shouted to him to come on our raft, he waved 'Good-bye and good luck'—the end of a gallant man.

Thus perished 1,474 officers and men of the Royal Navy and forty-one of the Royal Air Force. Despite prolonged search, only thirty-nine were rescued and brought in later by a Norwegian ship. In addition six men were picked up by the enemy and taken to Germany. The *Scharnhorst*, heavily damaged by the *Acasta's* torpedo, made her way to Trondheim.

While this action was going on the cruiser *Devonshire*, with the King of Norway and his Ministers, was about a hundred miles to the westward. The *Valiant*, coming north to meet the convoy, was still a long way off. The only message received from the *Glorious* was corrupt and barely intelligible, which suggests that her main wireless equipment was destroyed from an early stage. The *Devonshire* alone received this message, but as its importance was not apparent she did not break wireless silence to pass it on, as to do so would have involved serious risk of revealing her position, which in the circumstances was highly undesirable. Not until the following morning were suspicions aroused. Then the *Valiant* met the hospital ship *Atlantis*, who informed her of the loss of the *Orama* and that enemy capital ships were at sea. The *Valiant* signalled the information and pressed on to join Lord Cork's convoy. The Commander-in-

* Temporary Surgeon-Lieutenant H. J. Stammers, R.N.V.R.

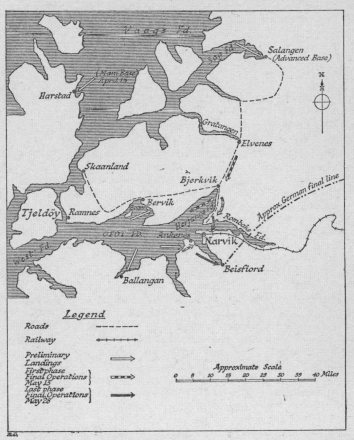

Sketch Map: Narvik Operations

Chief, Admiral Forbes, at once proceeded to sea with the only ships he had, the *Rodney*, the *Renown*, and six destroyers.

The damage inflicted on the *Scharnhorst* by the heroic *Acasta* had important results. The two enemy battle-cruisers abandoned further operations and returned at once to Trondheim. The German High Command were dissatisfied with the action of their admiral in departing from the objective which had been given him. They sent the *Hipper* out again ; but it was then too late.

On the 10th Admiral Forbes ordered the *Ark Royal* to join him. Reports showed that enemy ships were in Trondheim, and he hoped to make an air attack. This was delivered by R.A.F. bombers on the 11th without effect. On the following morning fifteen Skuas from the *Ark Royal* made a dive-bombing attack. Enemy reconnaissance gave warning of their approach, and no fewer than eight were lost. To add one last misfortune to our tale, it is now known that one bomb from a Skua struck the *Scharnhorst* but failed to explode.

Whilst these tragedies were in progress the Narvik convoys passed on safely to their destination, and the British campaign in Norway came to an end.

*   *   *

From all this wreckage and confusion there emerged one fact of major importance potentially affecting the future of the war. In their desperate grapple with the British Navy the Germans ruined their own, such as it was, for the impending climax. The Allied losses in all this sea-fighting off Norway amounted to one aircraft-carrier, two cruisers, one sloop, and nine destroyers. Six cruisers, two sloops, and eight destroyers were disabled, but could be repaired within our margin of sea-power. On the other hand, at the end of June 1940, a momentous date, the effective German Fleet consisted of no more than *one 8-inch-gun cruiser, two light cruisers, and four destroyers*. Although many of their damaged ships, like ours, could be repaired, the German Navy was no factor in the supreme issue of the invasion of Britain.

CHAPTER 17

The Fall of the Government

Debate of May 7 – A Vote of Censure Supervenes – Lloyd George's Last Parliamentary Stroke – I Do My Best with the House – My Advice to the Prime Minister – Conferences of May 9 – The German Onslaught – A Conversation with the Prime Minister, May 10 – The Dutch Agony – Mr. Chamberlain Resigns – The King Asks Me to Form a Government – Accession of the Labour and Liberal Parties – Facts and Dreams.

The many disappointments and disasters of the brief campaign in Norway caused profound perturbation at home, and the currents of passion mounted even in the breasts of some of those who had been most slothful and purblind in the years before the war. The Opposition asked for a debate on the war situation, and this was arranged for May 7. The House was filled with Members in a high state of irritation and distress. Mr. Chamberlain's opening statement did not stem the hostile tide. He was mockingly interrupted, and reminded of his speech of April 4, when in quite another connection he had incautiously said, 'Hitler missed the bus.' He defined my new position and my relationship with the Chiefs of Staff, and in reply to Mr. Herbert Morrison made it clear that I had not held those powers during the Norwegian operations. One speaker after another from both sides of the House attacked the Government, and especially its chief, with unusual bitterness and vehemence, and found themselves sustained by growing applause from all quarters. Sir Roger Keyes, burning for distinction in the new war, sharply criticised the Naval Staff for their failure to attempt the capture of Trondheim. 'When I saw,' he said, 'how badly things were going I never ceased importuning the Admiralty and War Cabinet to let me take all responsibility and lead the attack.' Wearing his uniform as Admiral of the Fleet, he supported the complaints of the Opposition with technical details and his own professional authority in a manner very agreeable to the mood of the House. From the benches behind the Government Mr. Amery quoted, amid ringing cheers, Cromwell's imperious words to the Long Parliament: 'You have sat too long here for any good you have been doing. Depart, I say, and let us have done with you. In the name of God, go!' These were terrible words, coming from a friend and colleague of many years, a fellow Birmingham Member, and a Privy Counsellor of distinction and experience.

On the second day, May 8, the debate, although continuing upon an Adjournment Motion, assumed the character of a Vote of Censure, and Mr. Herbert Morrison, in the name of the Opposition, declared their intention to have a vote. The Prime Minister rose again, accepted the challenge, and in an unfortunate passage appealed to his friends to stand by him. He had a right to do this, as these friends had sustained his action, or inaction, and thus shared his responsibility in 'the years which the locusts had eaten' before the war. But to-day they sat abashed and silenced, and some of them had joined the hostile demonstrations. This day saw the last decisive intervention of Lloyd George in the House of Commons. In a speech of not more than twenty minutes he struck a deeply-wounding blow at the head of the Government. He endeavoured to exculpate me: 'I do not think that the First Lord was entirely responsible for all the things which happened in Norway.' I immediately interposed, 'I take complete responsibility for everything that has been done by the Admiralty, and I take my full share of the burden.' After warning me not to allow myself to be converted into an air-raid shelter to keep the splinters from hitting my colleagues, Mr. Lloyd George turned upon Mr. Chamberlain. 'It is not a question of who are the Prime Minister's friends. It is a far bigger issue. He has appealed for sacrifice. The nation is prepared for every sacrifice so long as it has leadership, so long as the Government show clearly what they are aiming at, and so long as the nation is confident that those who are leading it are doing their best.' He ended, 'I say solemnly that the Prime Minister should give an example of sacrifice, because there is nothing which can contribute more to victory in this war than that he should sacrifice the seals of office.'

As Ministers we all stood together. The Secretaries of State for War and Air had already spoken. I had volunteered to wind up the debate, which was no more than my duty, not only in loyalty to the chief under whom I served, but also because of the exceptionally prominent part I had played in the use of our inadequate forces during our forlorn attempt to succour Norway. I did my very best to regain control of the House for the

Government in the teeth of continuous interruption, coming chiefly from the Labour Opposition benches. I did this with good heart when I thought of their mistakes and dangerous pacifism in former years, and how only four months before the outbreak of the war they had voted solidly against conscription. I felt that I, and a few friends who had acted with me, had the right to inflict these censures, but they had not. When they broke in upon me I retorted upon them and defied them, and several times the clamour was such that I could not make myself heard. Yet all the time it was clear that their anger was not directed against me, but at the Prime Minister, whom I was defending to the utmost of my ability and without regard for any other considerations. When I sat down at eleven o'clock the House divided. The Government had a majority of 81, but over 30 Conservatives voted with the Labour and Liberal Oppositions, and a further 60 abstained. There was no doubt that in effect, though not in form, both the debate and the division were a violent manifestation of want of confidence in Mr. Chamberlain and his Administration.

After the debate was over he asked me to go to his room, and I saw at once that he took the most serious view of the sentiment of the House towards himself. He felt he could not go on. There ought to be a National Government. One party alone could not carry the burden. Someone must form a Government in which all parties would serve, or we could not get through. Aroused by the antagonisms of the debate, and being sure of my own past record on the issues at stake, I was strongly disposed to fight on. 'This has been a damaging debate, but you have a good majority. Do not take the matter grievously to heart. We have a better case about Norway than it has been possible to convey to the House. Strengthen your Government from every quarter, and let us go on until our majority deserts us.' To this effect I spoke. But Chamberlain was neither convinced nor comforted, and I left him about midnight with the feeling that he would persist in his resolve to sacrifice himself if there was no other way, rather than attempt to carry the war further with a one-party Government.

I do not remember exactly how things happened during the morning of May 9, but the following occurred. Sir Kingsley Wood was very close to the Prime Minister as a colleague and a friend. They had long worked together in complete confidence. From him I learned that Mr. Chamberlain was resolved upon the formation of a National Government, and if he could not be the head he would give way to anyone commanding his confidence who could. Thus by the afternoon I became aware that I might well be called upon to take the lead. The prospect neither excited nor alarmed me. I thought it would be by far the best plan. I was content to let events unfold. In the afternoon the Prime Minister summoned me to Downing Street, where I found Lord Halifax, and after a talk about the situation in general we were told that Mr. Attlee and Mr. Greenwood would visit us in a few minutes for a consultation.

When they arrived we three Ministers sat on one side of the table and the Opposition Leaders on the other. Mr. Chamberlain declared the paramount need of a National Government, and sought to ascertain whether the Labour Party would serve under him. The Conference of their party was in session at Bournemouth. The conversation was most polite, but it was clear that the Labour leaders would not commit themselves without consulting their people, and they hinted, not obscurely, that they thought the response would be unfavourable. They then withdrew. It was a bright, sunny afternoon, and Lord Halifax and I sat for a while on a seat in the garden of Number 10 and talked about nothing in particular. I then returned to the Admiralty, and was occupied during the evening and a large part of the night in heavy business.

*   *   *

The morning of the 10th of May dawned, and with it came tremendous news. Boxes with telegrams poured in from the Admiralty, the War Office, and the Foreign Office. The Germans had struck their long-awaited blow. Holland and Belgium were both invaded. Their frontiers had been crossed at numerous points. The whole movement of the German Army upon the invasion of the Low Countries and of France had begun.

At about ten o'clock Sir Kingsley Wood came to see me, having just been with the Prime Minister. He told me that Mr. Chamberlain was inclined to feel that the great battle which had broken upon us made it necessary for him to remain at his post. Kingsley Wood had told him that, on the contrary, the new crisis made it all the more necessary to have a National Government, which alone could confront it, and he added that Mr. Chamberlain had accepted this view. At eleven o'clock I was again summoned to Downing Street by the Prime Minister.

There once more I found Lord Halifax. We took our seats at the table opposite Mr. Chamberlain. He told us that he was satisfied that it was beyond his power to form a National Government. The response he had received from the Labour leaders left him in no doubt of this. The question therefore was whom he should advise the King to send for after his own resignation had been accepted. His demeanour was cool, unruffled, and seemingly quite detached from the personal aspect of the affair. He looked at us both across the table.

I have had many important interviews in my public life, and this was certainly the most important. Usually I talk a great deal, but on this occasion I was silent. Mr. Chamberlain evidently had in his mind the stormy scene in the House of Commons two nights before, when I had seemed to be in such heated controversy with the Labour Party. Although this had been in his support and defence, he nevertheless felt that it might be an obstacle to my obtaining their adherence at this juncture. I do not recall the actual words he used, but this was the implication. His biographer, Mr. Feiling, states definitely that he preferred Lord Halifax. As I remained silent a very long pause ensued. It certainly seemed longer than the two minutes which one observes in the commemorations of Armistice Day. Then at length Halifax spoke. He said that he felt that his position as a Peer, out of the House of Commons, would make it very difficult for him to discharge the duties of Prime Minister in a war like this. He would be held responsible for everything, but would not have the power to guide the assembly upon whose confidence the life of every Government depended. He spoke for some minutes in this sense, and by the time he had finished it was clear that the duty would fall upon me—had in fact fallen upon me. Then for the first time I spoke. I said I would have no communication with either of the Opposition parties until I had the King's Commission to form a Government. On this the momentous conversation came to an end, and we reverted to our ordinary easy and familiar manners of men who had worked for years together and whose lives in and out of office had been spent in all the friendliness of British politics. I then went back to the Admiralty, where, as may well be imagined, much awaited me.

The Dutch Ministers were in my room. Haggard and worn, with horror in their eyes, they had just flown over from Amsterdam. Their country had been attacked without the slightest pretext or warning. The avalanche of fire and steel had rolled across the frontiers, and when resistance broke out and the Dutch frontier guards fired an overwhelming onslaught was made from the air. The whole country was in a state of wild confusion. The long-prepared defence scheme had been put into operation; the dykes were opened, the waters spread far and wide. But the Germans had already crossed the outer lines, and were now streaming down the banks of the Rhine and through the inner Gravelines defences. They threatened the causeway which encloses the Zuyder Zee. Could we do anything to prevent this? Luckily, we had a flotilla not far away, and this was immediately ordered to sweep the causeway with fire and take the heaviest toll possible of the swarming invaders. The Queen was still in Holland, but it did not seem she could remain there long.

As a consequence of these discussions, a large number of orders were dispatched by the Admiralty to all our ships in the neighbourhood and close relations were established with the Royal Dutch Navy. Even with the recent overrunning of Norway and Denmark in their minds, the Dutch Ministers seemed unable to understand how the great German nation, which up to the night before had professed nothing but friendship, should suddenly have made this frightful and brutal onslaught. Upon these proceedings and other affairs an hour or two passed. A spate of telegrams pressed in from all the frontiers affected by the forward heave of the German armies. It seemed that the old Schlieffen plan, brought up to date with its Dutch extension, was already in full operation. In 1914 the swinging right arm of the German invasion had swept through Belgium but had stopped short of Holland. It was well known then that had that war been delayed for three or four years the extra army group would have been ready and the railway terminals and communications adapted for a movement through Holland. Now the famous movement had been launched with all these facilities and with every circumstance of surprise and treachery. But other developments lay ahead. The decisive stroke of the enemy was not to be a turning movement on the flank, but a break through the main front. This none of us or the French, who were in responsible command, foresaw. Earlier in the year I had, in a published interview, warned these neutral countries of the fate which was impending upon them, and which was evident from the troop dispositions and road and rail development, as well as from the captured German plans. My words had been resented.

In the splintering crash of this vast battle the quiet conversations we had had in Downing Street faded or fell back in one's mind. However, I remember being told that Mr. Chamberlain had gone, or was going, to see the King, and this was naturally to be expected. Presently a message arrived summoning me to the Palace at six o'clock. It only takes two minutes to drive there from the Admiralty along the Mall. Although I suppose the evening newspapers must have been full of the terrific news from the Continent, nothing had been mentioned about the Cabinet crisis. The public had not had time to take in what was happening either abroad or at home, and there was no crowd about the Palace gates.

I was taken immediately to the King. His Majesty received me most graciously and bade me sit down. He looked at me searchingly and quizzically for some moments, and then said, 'I suppose you don't know why I have sent for you?' Adopting his mood, I replied, 'Sir, I simply couldn't imagine why.' He laughed and said, 'I want to ask you to form a Government.' I said I would certainly do so.

The King had made no stipulation about the Government being National in character, and I felt that my commission was in no formal way dependent upon this point. But in view of what had happened, and the conditions which had led to Mr. Chamberlain's resignation, a Government of National character was obviously inherent in the situation. If I found it impossible to come to terms with the Opposition parties, I should not have been constitutionally debarred from trying to form the strongest Government possible of all who would stand by the country in the hour of peril, provided that such a Government could command a majority in the House of Commons. I told the King that I would immediately send for the leaders of the Labour and Liberal Parties, that I proposed to form a War Cabinet of five or six Ministers, and that I hoped to let him have at least five names before midnight. On this I took my leave and returned to the Admiralty.

Between seven and eight, at my request, Mr. Attlee called upon me. He brought with him Mr. Greenwood. I told him of the authority I had to form a Government, and asked if the Labour Party would join. He said they would. I proposed that they should take rather more than a third of the places, having two seats in the War Cabinet of five, or it might be six, and I asked Mr. Attlee to let me have a list of men so that we could discuss particular offices. I mentioned Mr. Bevin, Mr. Alexander, Mr. Morrison, and Mr. Dalton as men whose services in high office were immediately required. I had, of course, known both Attlee and Greenwood for a long time in the House of Commons. During the ten years before the outbreak of war I had in my more or less independent position come far more often into collision with the Conservative and National Governments than with the Labour and Liberal Oppositions. We had a pleasant talk for a little while, and they went off to report by telephone to their friends and followers at Bournemouth, with whom of course they had been in the closest contact during the previous forty-eight hours.

I invited Mr. Chamberlain to lead the House of Commons as Lord President of the Council, and he replied by telephone that he accepted, and had arranged to broadcast at nine that night, stating that he had resigned, and urging everyone to support and aid his successor. This he did in magnanimous terms. I asked Lord Halifax to join the War Cabinet while remaining Foreign Secretary. At about ten I sent the King a list of the five names, as I had promised. The appointment of the three Service Ministers was vitally urgent. I had already made up my mind who they should be. Mr. Eden should go to the War Office, Mr. Alexander should come to the Admiralty, and Sir Archibald Sinclair, Leader of the Liberal Party, should take the Air Ministry. At the same time I assumed the office of Minister of Defence, without however attempting to define its scope and powers.

Thus, then, on the night of the 10th of May, at the outset of this mighty battle, I acquired the chief power in the State, which henceforth I wielded in ever-growing measure for five years and three months of world war, at the end of which time, all our enemies having surrendered unconditionally or being about to do so, I was immediately dismissed by the British electorate from all further conduct of their affairs.

During these last crowded days of the political crisis my pulse had not quickened at any moment. I took it all as it came. But I cannot conceal from the reader of this truthful account that as I went to bed at about 3 a.m. I was conscious of a profound sense of relief. At last I had the authority to give directions over the whole scene. I felt as if I were walking with destiny, and that all my past life had been but a preparation for this hour and for this trial. Ten years in the political wilderness had freed me from ordinary party antagonisms. My warnings over the last six years had been so numerous, so detailed, and were now so terribly vindicated, that no one could gainsay me. I could not be reproached either for making the war or with want of preparation for it. I thought I knew a good deal about it all, and I was sure I should not fail. Therefore, although impatient for the morning, I slept soundly and had no need for cheering dreams. Facts are better than dreams.